Noble Powell and the
Episcopal Establishment in the Twentieth Century

Studies in Anglican History

Series Editor
Peter W. Williams, Miami University

A list of books in the series appears at the end of this book.

Sponsored by the Historical Society of the Episcopal Church

Noble Powell and the
Episcopal Establishment
in the Twentieth Century

DAVID HEIN

UNIVERSITY OF ILLINOIS PRESS
URBANA AND CHICAGO

© 2001 by the Board of Trustees of the University of Illinois
All rights reserved
Manufactured in the United States of America
⊗ This book is printed on acid-free paper.

Library of Congress Cataloging-in-Publication Data
Hein, David.
Noble Powell and the Episcopal establishment in the twentieth century / David Hein.
p.   cm. — (Studies in Anglican history)
Includes bibliographical references and index.
ISBN 0-252-02643-8
1. Powell, Noble C. (Noble Cilley), 1891–1968.
2. Episcopal Church—Clergy—Biography.
I. Title.
II. Series.
BX5995.P69H45   2001
283'.092—dc21   00-010903

C 5 4 3 2 1

To my parents, Charles and Ruth Hein,
and to my brother, Stephen D. Hein

Series Editor's Preface

PETER W. WILLIAMS

Studies in Anglican History is a series of scholarly monographs sponsored by the Historical Society of the Episcopal Church and published by the University of Illinois Press. It is intended to bring the best of contemporary international scholarship on the history of the entire Anglican Communion, including the Church of England and the Episcopal church in the United States, to a broader readership.

In this volume David Hein, who teaches at Hood College in Maryland, tells the story of Noble Powell, the Episcopal bishop of Maryland during the middle years of the twentieth century. Powell's life, though in many ways an ecclesiastical success story, has dimensions bordering on the tragic as well. For many years he represented the "establishment" at its best; through his personal connections, which were in large part those that accrued to his episcopal incumbency, he counted as his friends many of the most influential civil and political figures of his city and state, and he could quietly bring about many good things through discreet personal interventions. Here was the very model of a benign, moderately progressive churchman who was very much in tune with his culture. When that culture came under more radical challenge from the civil rights movement, however, Powell found himself bordering on irrelevance, since the new advocates of justice were not respecters of the old ways of moderate adjustments within the system—a system that ultimately conspired in the maintenance of the color line. Powell's life is thus instructively exemplary of an era of ecclesiastical gentility that, perhaps sadly, had to yield to more compelling forces of the inexorable zeitgeist that had to prevail if the Christian community's ultimate goals were to be realized. Hein's work is thus a valuable addition both to our understanding of the history of the Episcopal church and, more broadly, to the stories of the roles that organized religion played in major social change, as well as to the dynamics that led to the undermining of the Protestant "mainline" as a compelling force in American social and religious life.

Contents

Acknowledgments

Looking back in gratitude is the lightest and happiest of the duties remaining to an author after he has finished a manuscript. The present study would not be nearly as complete as it is without the generous assistance furnished by members of the Powell family in Maryland and Alabama and by scores of individuals—University of Virginia alumni, Episcopal clergy and laypersons, and representatives of other denominations—who submitted to my questions or wrote to me with their recollections of Noble Powell or of his successor, Harry Lee Doll. Among the friends and associates of Bishop Powell, Dorothy McIlvain Scott, sometime president of the Woman's Auxiliary in the diocese of Maryland, was an especially gracious and enthusiastic supporter of this work.

I am also grateful to Hood College for research grants awarded by its board of associates and for assistance provided by the staff of the Beneficial-Hodson Library. In addition, I appreciate not only the summer stipend awarded by the Louisville Institute but also the delightful opportunity for the collegial exchange of ideas and insights which that institution hosted one snowy weekend in the winter of 1998.

Among those who have supported me in this enterprise, the following deserve special thanks for their advice and encouragement: Jim Boston, Madeline Duntley, Marie Finn, David Baily Harned, David L. Holmes, F. Garner Ranney, Tom Samet, Mark Sandona, Gardiner H. Shattuck Jr., Charlie and Lee Tidball, and Amy Day Zielinski. In addition, the series editor, Peter W. Williams, and the anonymous readers for the University of Illinois Press offered many useful suggestions for revision. But even the good counsel of these friends and colleagues could not eliminate all faults, the responsibility for which is of course mine alone.

The greatest help as well as the greatest hindrance arose, however, as the result of my own personal history. In relation to the Episcopal church, I am in some ways an insider, with all the occasions for insight and partiality which that vantage affords. As a boy I not only experienced the benefits and burdens peculiar to being a child of the rectory but also was raised by parents who knew Noble Powell quite well from the 1940s until his death in 1968. Thus I grew up hearing stories about him, accounts that often bordered on the hagiographic. Now, as a biographer, I realize that I have reaped biases as well as blessings that were planted in my past.

But I have an outsider's perspective, too, which I hope has also given me something of value. I am neither in orders nor in any lay office of distinction, and I have nothing to do with local or national church hierarchies. An ambivalent Episcopalian, I have had little trouble keeping in mind potential readers whose first choice for a biographical subject might not be a noncontroversial, orthodox, dead-white-male Episcopal bishop. In any event, I have set out here to sketch a portrait that I hope Episcopalians as well as those outside the Anglican Communion, both nonacademics and scholars, will find of interest.

Noble Powell and the
Episcopal Establishment in the Twentieth Century

Introduction

Fifteen years ago, when I knew comparatively little about the history of the Episcopal church, I supposed, rightly or wrongly, that the figure most likely to be identified as a leading churchman of the fifties and early sixties was the dean and bishop James Albert Pike (1913–69). At the Cathedral of St. John the Divine and later in California, Pike attracted considerable attention, not only through the media of sermons, books, and television but also through his increasingly radical theological pronouncements. His own physical and spiritual wanderings came to stand for those of many other Americans in the 1960s.[1] After Pike's death in the Judean desert, a writer for *America* noted that the former Episcopal bishop's "dying was . . . like his living: he was very much in the news but his precise whereabouts was unknown."[2]

Assuming that Pike was among the most familiar churchmen of his day, is he representative—let alone representative of the best—of the Episcopal church in the postwar decades? In 1986, when I mentioned to the eminent historian Anne Firor Scott my irritation at the way historical writing seemed to be slightly skewed in favor of those who were prone to self-promotion and away from more modest but nonetheless influential men and women, she responded that of course that was true and assured me that, indeed, "history is a crapshoot."

I had Pike and Powell in mind when I asked Professor Scott about this business of history. In fact, I do not take Powell to have been a more significant historical actor than Pike and therefore more worthy of consideration, but I do think that Powell is more representative of his era, including some of its finest characteristics, and a remarkable person in his own right.

The biographical treatment of a figure such as Noble Powell affords us the opportunity to look at the history of the Episcopal church at closer range than a chronicle of the entire denomination allows, while requiring us to keep the larger social and ecclesiastical context continually in view. And it makes possible a broader examination of the church's past than the history of an individual parish or diocese would permit. It has, in addition, the intrinsic appeal of following the life and career of one man, in this case an individual of unusual charisma who thrived during a period that has been somewhat neglected by historians of the Episcopal church.

One reason for Powell's appeal as bishop was that he enjoyed a certain cachet that derived from his origins in another time and place. His pince-nez, perched on the aristocratic nose of this scion of southern planters, betokened not merely distinction but a patrician assurance born of a bygone era. Before the 1960s it did mainline religion no good to be seen as "new and improved." A bishop was supposed to provide continuity with the past, not the latest fashions in management or even theology. Thus, to Episcopalians who knew him, Powell seemed wise, well grounded, and, later, venerable— but not anachronistic; people thought him, in Hemingway's phrase, the "true gen."

His father was an impoverished planter, and Noble was raised a Baptist rather than an Episcopalian, but otherwise his background fit the conception of his personal history held by most who knew him. The first Powells came to Alabama in 1818, one year before the territory became a state, and established themselves as prosperous cotton planters and county leaders. Around the nadir of the Deep South's fortunes, in 1911, young Noble left home, first for Auburn and later for the University of Virginia and a career in the Episcopal church. Before he left he absorbed essential elements of his native culture, including not only features of the South's intertwined religious faiths—evangelical Christianity and southern civic piety—but also some of his region's deepest values and habits of the heart.

The theologian Julian N. Hartt, who was always aware of the effect that growing up on the American prairie had on his own development, observed that we not only "have histories"; "we are creatures defined by historicality."[3] Chapter one of this book discusses the formative influences in Noble Powell's life, delineating the factors that appear to have shaped his later thinking and acting. This chapter suggests a trajectory that runs throughout the rest of his life.

One way of thinking about the source of this trajectory—and of Powell's attraction—is to see his existence as grounded in what he took to be timeless principles. Powell was not only "the last bishop of the old church," as some have styled him, and therefore emblematic of an entire era of Episcopal church history; he was also consciously committed to what his contemporary William Faulkner extolled as "the old verities and truths of the heart, the old universal truths . . . love and honor and pity and pride and compassion and sacrifice."[4]

We can also perceive upon closer inspection that Powell's life was particularly rooted in a belief in the perduring value of the cardinal virtues of the Victorian South. In the postbellum evangelical culture in which he was raised, Powell came to appreciate the importance of diligence and self-mastery, of control over the natural impulses. Believing in a cosmos governed by eternal laws and superintended by a benevolent deity, he accepted his culture's stress on the humanizing advantages of education, refinement, religion, and family love. As a child of the local aristocracy, he learned how a gentleman should use his stature and personality to help civilize others, bringing order and hope to lives in disarray.[5]

We gain a sharper awareness of this mentality if we compare it with the outlook of those who rose to challenge it at the very time that young Noble was leaving his home in the Black Belt and striking out on his own. Modernist playwrights, novelists, musicians, architects, and painters, who were developing their ideas in the years before and after World War I, held views that were almost diametrically opposed to the mindset that Noble Powell embodied.

For the modernists, the opacity of the universe was a condition to be accepted, even welcomed; moral or epistemological certainty was impossible. The world was more strange and chaotic than rational and stable; the human psyche contained dark subterranean forces whose savage, uncivilized nature should be recognized and explored. Rebelling against what they viewed as the Victorians' unnatural repression of vitality, the modernists repudiated fusty ideals of bourgeois harmony in favor of a tentative integration that admitted unpredictability and contrarieties. Seeking liberation from Victorian culture's imposed innocence, modernists embraced criticism and conflict. Fresh artistic forms—free verse, atonal music, abstract painting, and stream-of-consciousness writing—expressed the artists' rejection of outmoded structures and their desire to affirm subjectivity. After the First World War, this same intellectual and artistic sensibility incorporated a powerful current of disillusionment and melancholy, symbolic of ruined civilizations and shattered perspectives.[6]

The modern artist and the traditional cleric had dissimilar ambitions growing out of different vocations. A half-century would pass before anything resembling the modernist temper would enter the Episcopal church in force. Not until the 1960s, when the denomination was compelled to respond to a variety of challenges from within and outside its walls, would the church be dramatically unsettled by the major dislocations of the twentieth century. Bishop James Pike would have his day, as would other, more thoughtful and less mercurial instigators of change. At this time the church would confront not only a mess of problems but also a host of opportunities, joining in the effort to break down old barriers.[7] In retrospect we can interpret Noble Powell as standing for the church as it existed before its epochal displacement. His years as bishop occurred during what one might call an Indian summer for the Episcopal church—and the rest of the Protestant establishment—in America.

The idea of the priest instantiating the old truths and virtues in his own person is present in the image of the minister as parson, a theme that is introduced explicitly in chapter two. Teaching more by example than precept, the parson conveyed truth as much through his personality and character as through liturgy and preaching.[8] This approach to ministry is part of a characteristically Anglican understanding of the duties of a priest, one that emphasizes personal engagement, pastoral care, and prayer: the ordained person as a distinctive kind of mediator and exemplar.

Self-possessed, approachable, and respected, Powell prospered as chaplain to the University of Virginia in a setting that partook of an older romanticism and a place that remained committed to proper form, convention, and order. As parson, Powell guided students within a subculture still mildly redolent of Victorian innocence.[9]

In this second chapter, we see Powell functioning in a position of influence at a time when the Episcopal church and other old-line denominations began to commit their resources to college work and to the domestic missionary enterprise. Powell's efforts in Charlottesville won him national recognition in the Episcopal church, and he served in the archdeaconry of the Blue Ridge under a man who had already achieved a notable record in the mission field: Frederick W. Neve, the tireless champion of the mountain people. This chapter provides a window onto a significant phase of the church's history as well as glimpses of a lost world.

Somewhat isolated in Charlottesville, Powell moved to the heart of the Episcopal establishment in the 1930s when he became rector of one of the most prominent parishes on the East Coast and then dean of the Washington National Cathedral and warden of the College of Preachers. Surrounded if not overborne by the grand institutions of the church, Powell in this chapter lies partially hidden from our gaze. But even at the National Cathedral—America's Westminster Abbey—and at the College of Preachers Powell made his humane presence felt, converting administration into a project that served the ends of ecumenism and evangelism. By the time he left Washington he was one of the best-known leaders in the Episcopal church, admired by clergy and laypeople throughout the United States and by many in the Church of England as well.

Chapters four and five develop the theme of the coalescence of episcopal authority and community validation. In a manner analogous to the way in which ancient heroic societies—unlike ours—maintained a moral and social framework conducive to the flourishing of heroes, postwar American society enabled mainline Protestant leaders to succeed, albeit, one could argue, largely on its own terms.[10]

Episcopal bishops such as Noble Powell not only launched the first building campaigns in many years, established new diocesan programs and institutions, and oversaw the revitalization of liturgy and Christian education; they also reached beyond their denomination's boundaries to foster ties with other civil and religious leaders and to play prominent roles in their communities. The dominant culture embraced the mainline churches, and Powell thrived in the pastoral office of bishop. His authority, grounded in all three of the ways—legal, traditional, and charismatic—in which leaders gain and exercise legitimate authority, was widely acknowledged. At the end of his career, however, we see Powell being challenged by new methods in the struggle for civil rights.

Noble Powell is a representative figure, then, but finally uninteresting if only a type. A supporting social environment and an ecclesiastical era that placed more emphasis than later generations on the authority of one man are not enough to make a bishop a compelling figure. The key in Powell's case is an amalgam of character traits—spiritual depth, self-discipline, a sense of humor, confidence, and effortless magnetism, among others—that worked together in the service of a practical theology of Christian friendship. The result was an authentic brand of spiritual availability (*disponibilité*), a goodly supply of pastoral wisdom generously applied, and a gentle strength that drew people in and affirmed their best selves.

The book ends with an attempt to provide something in the nature of a dénouement, depicting Powell's own decline and the declension, for good or ill, of the church he stood for. After a consideration of Powell's legacy which focuses on themes that suffused his episcopate comes an effort to place Powell within H. Richard Niebuhr's familiar typology of "Christ and culture." The chapter then sketches how fresh demands and a posttraditional society emerged, bringing about a shift in our views of leadership and cultural legitimation. Referring to the role of exemplary figures within Anglicanism, the book's conclusion offers an assessment of Powell's career and a comment on the nature of his influence.

Formation, 1891–1920

Many years ago I found a little Baptist boy in one of our country missions. At an early age his mind turned to Confirmation. His parents . . . objected. I taught him to bide his time. Even before his Confirmation, his mind turned to the Ministry. I gave him books to read and nursed the thought. Later he was Confirmed, and then came the question of his education. Many leaders were cast to the wind of which he knew nothing. Presently he was given a work at Auburn under one of the Professors, and this opened the chance at the school. He took advantage of all that was presented, and carried with him his Church training, and allowed that influence to be felt among the boys. When under age, I licensed him a Layreader. . . . Further efforts upon the part of those, whose interest was in the boy, resulted in an opening at the University of Virginia.

—Charles M. Beckwith, Episcopal Bishop of Alabama

Noble Powell's Family and Community

If outsiders remember the county of Noble Powell's birth today, they remember it as "Bloody Lowndes," the rural region just west of Montgomery that became famous during the civil rights era as the scene of triumph and tragedy. In 1965 Martin Luther King Jr. and his followers marched through Lowndes County on their way from Selma to the state capital. And in Lowndes County the civil rights workers Viola Liuzzo, a white homemaker, and Jon Daniels, a white Episcopal seminary student, were shot to death, victims of the same species of racist attack that had long bedevilled the county's black citizens.[1]

For many decades this region's dark soil had nurtured cotton, corn, and cattle, violence and virtue. By the time of the civil rights movement almost a century and a half had passed since the first member of the Powell family established a home in this part of Alabama. Born in Virginia, Seymour Powell Jr. (1792–1834) moved with his family to Georgia as a child, married at twenty-one, acquired some slaves, and joined thousands of other former residents of Virginia, the Carolinas, and Georgia who, hungry for fresh opportunities, ventured into the Mississippi and Alabama territories in the years following the War of 1812. The supreme attraction, of course, was fertile land, particularly that narrow crescent of gently rolling grasslands known as the Black Belt. Its African-American slaves and rich clay soils gave this region its name, and its moderate rainfall and long growing season—253 days—confirmed its value for growing cotton.[2]

In 1818—one year before Alabama was admitted as a state—Seymour Powell brought his wife, Martha, their two children, and his bondservants to the Black Belt, to a piece of ground near the Alabama River in Montgomery County (Lowndes County was not a separate jurisdiction until 1830), about four miles north of present-day Lowndesboro. Over the next sixteen years, before his death at age forty-two, Powell acquired over three thousand acres from the United States government, most of it purchased at the land office in Cahaba, the old state capital deep within the Black Belt, in forty- and eighty-acre lots. He prospered, aided greatly by the labor of his score of slaves, and joined the ranks of the planter minority that would control local politics for generations to come. In 1819 he was appointed Justice of the Montgomery County Court, and in 1830 he became the first clerk of the Circuit Court of Lowndes County.[3]

After moving to Alabama from Georgia, Martha and Seymour Powell had eight more children. In 1852 their second child, Seymour Herb Powell (1817–1902), born in Oglethorpe County, Georgia, married Josephine Judson Rice (1833–1909), a native of Hayneville and the daughter of the Reverend William Rice, a well-known minister in the early days of Alabama's pioneer history. Under Powell's supervision the plantation continued to be a highly successful enterprise. The 1855 state census lists him as the owner of twenty-six slaves.[4] He and his wife lived long enough for their grandson, Noble Cilley Powell, who was born in Lowndesboro on 27 October 1891, to have known them quite well in his boyhood.[5]

The village where the Powells lived was originally called McGills Hill, after the large number of McGills who had migrated from South Carolina in 1815. A scattered pioneer community for many years, the settlement of houses on a bend of the Alabama River began to grow after about 1830. By 1833 it had a new name, Lowndesborough, honoring the South Carolina planter-politician William Lowndes (1782–1822). Over the years more people arrived, from Virginia, South Carolina, Georgia, and Tennessee, attracted by Lowndesborough's location and opportunities. Planters built fine homes in town for themselves and their families so that they could enjoy the society of their peers; they travelled to their fields each day or left much of the routine supervision to hired overseers. A community with a disproportionate share of mansions in the Greek Revival style, Lowndesborough became what one historian of the state has termed "the jewel of Alabama's planter villages."[6]

Not nearly as isolated as the residents of some towns in the Black Belt, Lowndesborough citizens benefited from, among other things, quality merchandise carried up the river from Mobile. But just when the small town was thriving as never before, with private boys' and girls' academies and a flourishing business district, secession and war shattered familiar routines and ushered in years of poverty and frustration. Lowndesboro—the name was shortened in the 1860s—never regained its prewar vigor. In 1927 a fire destroyed the town's business section, and it was never rebuilt.

The region's decline is reflected in the population figures for Lowndes County. By the time Noble Powell left home in 1911, the white population of the county had been decreasing since the onset of the Civil War. From an 1860 high of 8,362 it had fallen to 3,769 by 1910, when the black population also started to drop, as African Americans began their migration out of the Deep South and away from the harsh limitations imposed by sharecropping and Jim Crow.[7]

Noble's father, Benjamin Shelley (Shell) Powell (1859–1928), was a cotton planter, devoted to the soil that his father and grandfather had worked.[8] He was also, with much less conviction, a member of the Methodist Episcopal church, South. When Shell was fourteen, the Sunday school he attended presented him with an edition of the poems of William Wordsworth. This gift was not sufficient inducement, however, to sustain his commitment to Methodism.[9] His middle child, Louise Howard Powell (1896–1993), recalled that in the strict Methodist home her father had known as a boy, "almost everything was deemed wrong [to do on Sunday] except eating and sleeping. . . . I think because he was reared in such a way he turned away [from formal religion]. His family was such rabid Methodists [that] they made Sunday a nightmare to him. They were God-fearing people, surely more fearing than loving." Consequently, her father was "not religiously inclined." Although he was "not a churchman, he was plenty good."[10]

Roberta Meadows McGavock, a Lowndesboro resident and a relative of the Powells, remembered Shell as a tall man who "had a rough side. He was a plain, outspoken man who would tell you what he thought. He had a good heart. [But] Noble got his sweetness from his mother."[11] In the end, Louise found her father "an enigma, very austere; he had a hard shell to crack. [He performed] many kind deeds, often unsung. His heart was his land."[12]

Shell Powell was dedicated to sustaining the family plantation, but during Noble's childhood, cotton production, which until the early 1900s provided almost all of Alabama's agricultural wealth, was proving less and less profitable. Overproduction of cotton in the American South, including the vast fields of Texas, occurred at the same time that countries on the other side of the world were increasing their production.[13] The average market price for cotton had been falling since the late 1870s, and within another ten years it dropped to between five and six cents a pound, earning planters less than it had cost to produce the crop.[14] Prices rose in the late 1890s and early 1900s, but by the 1910s soil depletion and boll weevils were causing planters to experience severe failures of their cotton crop. "We were poor," Louise said; "the cotton was eaten up by the boll weevil. I think that's what killed my father. He would have hung himself rather than watch the land go."[15] But he did watch the land go, and by 1920, like many others, he had lost it all. In debt, he hired himself out as an overseer.[16]

Shell's wife was Mary Irving Whitman Powell (1857–1942); they were married in the Lowndesboro Baptist Church on 18 December 1890. In 1898 Noble and Louise were joined by a sister, Josephine Seymour Powell (d. 1980). Their mother, known as "Mamie," was the thirteenth child of the Alabama planter and merchant James Kast Whitman (1813–80), a native of Virginia, and Mary Brown McCall (1818–74). Several of Mamie's brothers fought for the Confederate army; two of them died from wounds received in battle.

Mamie Powell lived her life in a highly traditional manner, focusing her attention on the private sphere of family and church. She would have defined herself as a child of God, a wife, and a mother, and she spent her time raising children, managing servants, running the household, and maintaining community ties and bonds of affection through visiting, conversation, and letter writing. The journeys she made outside her community were rare. Her husband handled affairs in the public realm, including political, legal, and financial matters. In important respects, Mamie's life did not differ appreciably from that of her antebellum counterpart.[17]

His mother was the most important person in Noble Powell's life. Gracious and gentle, she appears to have been loved by everyone who knew her, black and white alike. "Noble adored our mother; she had the most beautiful character I've ever known," her daughter Louise said years later.[18] A longtime resident of the community remembered Mamie as "the most beloved person in Lowndesboro. She was kind [to black people] and could always give them time."[19] Mamie lived long enough to travel to Baltimore in 1941 to attend her son's consecration as bishop. When she died the following year, Noble conducted the funeral service in Lowndesboro, assisted by the local Methodist pastor. Louise recalled that "when the ashes-to-ashes part came, [Noble couldn't go on]; he turned to the other minister, handed him the prayer book, and bowed his head. The evening sun cast a beautiful glow that seemed to let her go, while Noble lingered there to say to her words of goodbye."[20]

"Noble's love of his mother," Louise said, "was beautiful to see. She was the inspiration of his life. . . . My brother said her influence and love was why he chose his career. She was the cause of his decision [to go into the ministry]."[21] Mamie's personal witness may indeed have been a leading factor in her son's choice of career, but we should not overlook the possibility that the example of his father's negative experience also affected him deeply. Seeing his father slowly fall victim to the mischief of the market and the weevil could have influenced not only Noble's decision to choose a less vulnerable way of life but also his determination to strive unremittingly in his work and to establish himself securely in his position.

Besides his parents there was one other Lowndesboro resident who played a crucial role in young Noble's life: a physician, Philip Noble Cilley (1821–1912), whom Noble and his sisters called "Bappa." Not only was Noble named after him, in 1930 Noble named his first son Philip Noble Powell after Dr. Cilley. His first wife having died, Dr. Cilley married Sarah (Sallie) Kast Whitman in 1859, when Sallie's sister Mamie was only two. Dr. Cilley and his wife helped to raise Mamie.

The son of Seth Noble Cilley, a soldier in the War of 1812, and Sarah Cavis Cilley, Philip Noble Cilley at the age of sixteen began to earn a livelihood as a schoolteacher in New Hampshire, his native state. Suffering from asthma, he moved when he was twenty-three to Union District, South Carolina, where he taught school for a year before settling in Macon County, Alabama, east of Montgomery. There he not only continued to teach but also undertook the study of medicine, reading in the office of a local physician. Five years later he moved further west to Lowndes County, where he would pursue the general practice of medicine for sixty years.

Dr. Cilley and his family lived in a handsome two-story house across from the Powells' home. He also had a large plantation outside of town.[22] In 1886–87 he represented his district—as well as the Baptists and the Sons of Temperance—in the Alabama legislature. As a member of the Committee on Temperance he drafted and shepherded to final passage a law prohibiting the sale of intoxicants in Lowndes County.[23]

Dr. Cilley, whose only son had died as a young child in 1857, served as Noble Powell's mentor. "Noble got help," a family friend remarked, "by meeting someone so cultured."[24] In an era in which planters' sons were becoming lawyers and physicians, it is not surprising that Noble developed a keen interest in following in his uncle's professional footsteps.[25] Lowndes County provided plenty of opportunity for a country doctor to be of service: regular outbreaks of malaria, smallpox, typhoid, and hookworm continued to occur well into the twentieth century.[26] Dr. Cilley gave his nephew gold coins to help pay for his education in medicine; he looked forward to the day when his namesake would take over his large practice.[27]

It undoubtedly never occurred to him that Noble would one day want to become an Episcopal priest. Dr. Cilley was an ardent Baptist, the superintendent of the Sunday school, and a deacon; his daughter, Rosa Bibb Cilley, had married a prominent Baptist minister, Robert M. Hunter. Mamie and her children were all Baptists. As Roberta Meadows McGavock, a longtime member of the Lowndesboro Baptist Church, remarked, "Dr. Cilley had him [Noble] a Baptist."[28]

As a boy growing up in Lowndesboro, Noble Powell received not only the support of his parents and Dr. Cilley but also the affection and admiration of other children. His young companions even supported his early training in homiletics. "His preaching began," his sister Louise recalled, "when he asked his Methodist grandmother Powell to make him a long preacher's gown with a cross [sewn on the front]." Properly fitted out, "he'd round up neighborhood children and speak from a soap box under our old oak tree in the garden at Mockingbird Place [the family home]." Others who knew him in those days remembered this early testing of his vocation. "There was plenty of meat in his sermon even at a tender age. He would tolerate no levity. If a child misbehaved, he would hold up his hand and address the Negro monitor, 'Mammy, remove this child.'"[29] Usually Noble's little sister Jo or one of their cousins was the offender. In fact, it was the latter who for a time took to calling him "Monk" in recognition of his religious inclinations.[30]

Relatives and neighbors recalled a good-natured boy, full of fun, who "could do anything a country boy could do."[31] He could cook on camping trips, tend a garden, tell amusing stories, mend clothes, repair broken equipment, and make toys for his sisters and their friends: a merry-go-round and sleds for a steep pine-needle hill. The other boys looked up to him and enjoyed his companionship. The girls simply wanted him: "they realized he was someone of importance";[32] "Noble was a hero to us children."[33] For a time he was in love with a girl up in Prattville, but "there was nobody too serious until Mary [his future wife] came along."[34]

As a child her brother was "a wonderful-looking little gentleman," Louise remembered; they lived in a house that "was almost papered with the likeness of him."[35] Town elders, however, kept him from becoming too high on himself. One day—in all likelihood "one of those still, hot days" of the kind that the poet and planter William Alexander Percy recollected, "when earth things lie tranced at the bottom of a deep sea of summer sun"—Noble and another lad were sitting on a bench in Lowndesboro discussing the opposite sex. "If there's one thing I know about, it's women," Noble declared. An older gentleman leaned over them and said, "Noble, if there's one thing you *don't* know about, it's women!" The bishop of Maryland relished telling that story about himself half a century later.[36]

His most distinctive trait as a boy stayed with him his entire life: he had a way, as his sister Louise put it, of "easing the heart, of comforting people." This faculty went beyond his being "good at calming a difficult situation," though that ability was an important manifestation of his gifts.[37] His particular strength was rooted in an unusually attractive and benevolent nature that called forth and affirmed the best in others. Louise engaged in no sisterly hyperbole when she stated that "There was that about him that drew people to him."[38]

Playing ball, growing watermelons in the yard, and tramping the dirt streets of Lowndesboro—an idyllic existence in many ways but one surrounded by a society that was making life much less bearable for the greater portion of its members.[39] The famous case of *Plessy v. Ferguson* was decided in 1896, when Noble was five years old. The United States Supreme Court put its stamp of approval on segregation, effectively legitimating the racial caste system in the South.[40] Agricultural poverty and the failure of the Populist challenge intensified the frustration and anger of poor whites in the South. Their racism and rage were converted by leaders of the political establishment into increased power for themselves. The South was entering the worst period of race relations in its postslavery history.[41]

During Noble Powell's boyhood, blacks were almost completely disfranchised. A rewriting of the voting provisions of the Alabama constitution in 1901 virtually excluded blacks from the polls. In 1900, a hundred thousand black men could exercise the franchise in Alabama; ten years later only 3,752 were registered to vote. In Lowndes County there were 5,500 black registrants in 1900; after the first registration period under the new constitution only forty-four African Americans were eligible to cast ballots in an election. In 1964 not a single black person was registered to vote in Lowndes County.[42]

African Americans not only lost the franchise; many also lost their lives. Lynching, which had earlier been used mainly against whites, was now used mostly against blacks. By the time Noble was ten years old, two blacks a week were being lynched in the South. In Alabama between 1889 and 1918, 271 men and women were lynched, 237 of whom were African Americans. In the Black Belt during the depression period between 1892 and 1897, thirty-three lynchings occurred. Only five of the Black Belt's sixty-eight recorded lynchings were of white men.[43]

Of the lynchings that were carried out in Lowndes County, the one that occurred in 1914 must have been known to Noble Powell. An unmasked mob hanged a black man named Will Jones from a telegraph pole in broad daylight. A coroner's jury ruled that he had died at the hands of a "party or parties unknown," and a special grand jury declined to return any indictments in the case.[44]

Of course public lynchings did not constitute the only threat to African Americans' physical well-being. Besides the thrashings that white farmers might give their tenants to keep them in line, many quiet murders were carried out. An authority on the history of Lowndes County has pointed out that "whites probably killed countless blacks in . . . fields, forests, and swamps." Sometimes a planter would force a black man to ride off with him in his car, and the passenger would never be heard from again.[45] The Alabama native Silas Emmett Lucas Jr. (1931–94), an Episcopal priest and local historian who served churches in Lowndesboro and Montgomery in the 1960s, spoke of one planter he had known in Lowndes County who was reputed to have killed "six or eight black men" but "never served a day in prison." A black man, however, would be killed "for stealing a bird dog." "How many [black people]," Lucas wondered, "disappeared in the Big Swamp?" Lowndes County in his view had even worse race relations than Dallas County (wherein lies the city of Selma). Dallas County, he said, contained "more of a Charleston aristocracy"; people in Lowndes "were more apt to vent their anger in physical ways."[46]

The effort to hold African Americans in an inferior position had the support not only of the poor masses of uneducated whites in the South but also of the region's leading businessmen, clergy, lawyers, physicians, and educators. The pillars of the community and the trustees of the commonweal overwhelmingly backed white supremacy. As long as white superiority and black subservience were recognized, "good" and "industrious" blacks were treated with a kindly paternalism. If blacks were deemed insolent or violent they received severe punishment. All men were not equal in the Alabama Black Belt. A clear sense of place, of ordered arrangement, obtained there for all classes of society. Everyone was expected to follow the proper forms and rituals in social relations.[47]

The Religion of the Churches

Noble Powell grew up in a community in which the religious bodies focused on individual salvation rather than large-scale social change. White churches in the South were generally more concerned with preserving than transforming cultural institutions. In the North, exponents of the social gospel were presenting a theologically informed critique of the wrongs of industrial society and championing the interests of working men, women, and children. But in the South evangelical religion since the antebellum period had embraced a personalistic gospel whose concept of "community" was largely restricted to the local congregation.

White southern clergy—particularly the vast majority of ministers who did not hold big-city pastorates—tended to view advocates of the social gospel as Yankees tainted by liberalism and rationalism. Rural isolation, the absence of widespread social upheaval occasioned by immigration and industrialization, and the natural resistance of ordinary folk to sophisticated new theological notions also helped prevent the social gospel from taking hold in the South. The common understanding among southern Protestants was that society would improve as individuals experienced redemption and underwent personal reformation.[48]

White churches in the Deep South were not, of course, completely apolitical. Not only had their clergy labored to defend slavery and secession; in Noble Powell's time they supported legislation to control gambling, alcohol, prostitution, political corruption, and Sabbath-breaking. Although white Protestant ministers focused for the most part on issues of public policy that affected the moral conduct of individuals, they sometimes sought more extensive reformation as well. In the 1880s and 1890s many Baptist farmer-preachers in Alabama set themselves against the Redeemer Democratic status quo and committed themselves to the proposals for agrarian reform backed by the Farmers' Alliance and Populist movements.[49]

During the years of Noble Powell's youth, from 1900 to the First World War, white southern Protestant leaders began to address problems brought about by nascent industrialization and the rise of commercial centers. For example, the temperance and social service commission of the Southern Baptist Convention condemned sweatshops, corporate greed, and political graft, and Baptist leaders in Alabama spoke out against the worst excesses of corporate monopolies and in favor of a minimum living wage and better working conditions. Southern Methodists joined Baptists in advocating the regulation of child labor, and Methodist bishops expressed concern for the residents of crowded tenements. This interest in issues of social justice, however, was represented almost entirely in the public proclamations of the ecclesiastical leadership, in the pronouncements of pastors of big-steeple churches, in the resolutions of regional conferences, and in the editorials of denominational newspapers. Individual congregations in small towns and rural communities continued to focus on the gospel of personal redemption.[50]

Although liberal theology and the social gospel found few adherents among white southern Protestants, many did embrace a form of "social Christianity," which prompted them to protest against the inhumane treatment of prisoners and mental patients and to build institutions to care for orphans, mountain children, the elderly, and the sick. Some clergy in urban centers began institutional churches with significant social ministries. The Methodists sponsored settlement houses in several Alabama cities, and the Presbyterians undertook similar efforts on behalf of steelworkers in Birmingham. In the 1920s Baptists and Methodists raised large amounts of money for the construction of hospitals.[51]

Rather than trying to bring about radical changes in the structures of society, white Protestant ministers typically sought instead to ameliorate the conditions of the unfortunate and in selected cases to use political means to promote moral reform.[52] At its best, Christianity in the South, which influenced attitudes toward everything from childhood to marriage to death, stimulated church members to care for the poor, to assist the exploited, and to recognize a common humanity, even a form of equality, among all believers, black and white.[53]

At their worst white southern churches were so closely tied to the mores of the surrounding culture that they had trouble gaining perspective on and offering a critical analysis of the problems at their doorsteps. They failed to furnish their members with the vision and the will to confront their society's deepest wrongs. Deeds of kindness and generosity on the part of the dominant race toward those deemed inferior were morally impaired substitutes for a Christian love that celebrated and enacted the full humanity of every person. The white churches had difficulty seeing that friendliness between black and white was a poor stand-in for real equality. And so they rarely attempted to improve the social or economic standing of African Americans.[54]

One of the clergymen in the South whom historians associate with the social gospel was an Episcopal priest: the Arkansas native Edgar Gardner Murphy (1869–1913).[55] Rector of St. John's Church in Montgomery for a brief period (1898–1901), Murphy was a conservative reformer who achieved partial success in improving conditions for child workers in the Alabama textile mills.[56] While he might have been known to Noble Powell, it is more likely that Powell did not encounter him at this time but only heard of him later.

St. John's, the congregation Murphy served as rector, was the leading Episcopal church in Alabama and the home parish of some of the state's largest planters and richest merchants. The oldest church structure in downtown Montgomery, the parish typically counted among its members the state's governors and senators. The Confederate president Jefferson Davis, for example, attended St. John's regularly when he was in Montgomery. Comprising only 1.1 percent of the total white church population in 1900, the Episcopal church in Alabama enrolled as members the wealthier and better-educated classes and thus enjoyed substantial representation within the political and cultural leadership of the state.[57]

At the same time it is important to note that in Mississippi and Alabama Episcopalians not only had a smaller market share and less influence than they had in Virginia and South Carolina but were probably also more affected by their religious environment. Evangelical religion, whose values and language permeated the culture, stressed emotion more than reason and the personal over the social. Emphasizing the "feminine" virtues of harmony, peace, and piety, evangelicals enjoined standards of behavior that fostered gentleness of character and sweetness of temperament. Evangelical principles stood in opposition to the violence and disorder and the drinking, swearing, fighting, and gambling that were all too prevalent in the male world of town and farm. Nineteenth- and early-twentieth-century evangelicals sought to respond to the grace they had received in their conversions by remaking themselves through the liberating disciplines of self-control and personal improvement.[58] These powerful religiocultural currents undoubtedly shaped the attitudes and actions of Alabama Episcopalians. Elements of the evangelical outlook and way of life are evident in the story of Noble Powell's development as a Christian.[59]

Within this common evangelical culture it was not unusual for white southerners in small towns to follow a practical ecumenism according to which worshipers attended whichever (white) Protestant church in their community was holding services on a particular Sunday. Each church preached a similar message on the essentials of God and good conduct. In addition, members of the community seem to have appreciated the opportunity for fellowship across denominational lines and to have enjoyed the knowledge that they were all part of a larger Christian community.[60]

In Lowndesboro, Noble Powell and his relatives attended a Baptist church on the first Sunday of each month (morning and evening services), and Methodist, Episcopal, and Presbyterian churches on the following Sundays. For some years, the four churches shared one interdenominational choir.[61] A longtime resident of the town said, "Most people in Lowndesboro are Baptists, but they [the churches] all take different turns. We go to each other's churches. We are not narrow-minded."[62]

Noble's home town clearly reflected the way in which religion dominated the landscape of the South; its six churches made the tiny community "a mile-long line of steeples and open doors."[63] The Powell home was situated across the street from the Lowndesboro Baptist Church and next door to the Methodist church.

St. Paul's, the Episcopal church in Lowndesboro, began in 1845; its building was erected in 1857, and for years afterward black and white Episcopalians worshiped together there. Its minister-in-charge, Valentine George Lowery, a native of New York City, was only nine years older than Noble Powell. Ordained in 1910, Lowery served both St. Paul's and St. Andrew's Church, in Hayneville, from 1910 to 1924. At the centennial celebration of St. Paul's in 1957, Noble Powell said that Lowery had "'shaped my life from a shy, young, gangling lad and changed the whole course of it.'"[64]

Although Episcopalians were frowned upon and avoided in many parts of the South for their "popish" ceremony and mannered ways, they apparently provoked no ill will in Lowndesboro. Throughout Alabama, their extremely low churchmanship (mode of liturgical expression) made them appear acceptably Protestant to their neighbors. Evangelical, ecumenical, and fairly puritanical, for the most part Alabama Episcopalians blended into the religious mainstream.[65]

The bishop of Alabama throughout most of Noble Powell's childhood was Richard Hooker Wilmer (1816–1900), who had been diocesan since the first year of the Civil War. By the 1890s, owing to his physical infirmities, he was spending most of each year at his home in Spring Hill, outside Mobile, where he wrote tracts and pamphlets.[66] The Alabama bishop who made a significant impact on Noble Powell's life was Charles M. Beckwith (1851–1928), who was fiercely Low Church and extremely intolerant of anything suggesting High Churchmanship, including vested choirs. Growing more rigid with age, he tried toward the end of his episcopate to remove a rector in Montgomery for using acolytes in the service.[67]

Dominating the state of Alabama at the beginning of the twentieth century were the Baptists and the Methodists. The Lowndesboro Baptist Church, of which Dr. Cilley was a chief founder, began in 1852 with a congregation composed of black and white members. After the Civil War, most of the white members, not wanting to worship with freedmen, left the church, joining a nearby Baptist congregation or attending one of the other churches in Lowndesboro. In 1868 the black members of Lowndesboro Baptist, who now outnumbered whites in the congregation 137 to 5, voted to start a separate church, which they were soon able to accomplish. Occupying their new building, the membership of the Lowndesboro Baptist Church swelled to 327 by 1870. Dr. Cilley, the sole remaining white member, continued with the congregation for eighteen years as the church clerk, assisting in the effort to establish the church on a sure footing.[68]

In 1886 white Baptists founded a new church in Lowndesboro; its four-teen members included Mamie Powell and Dr. Cilley. Over the next couple of years the two Baptist churches in town worked out what each would be called. The black congregation took the name "First Baptist Church," while the resuscitated white congregation reclaimed "Lowndesboro Baptist Church."[69]

In the latter church, during a protracted meeting in July 1909, Louise Powell became a candidate for baptism. Three years later, again during the revival month of July, her younger sister, Josephine, formally joined the church. But their older brother, Noble, seems never to have undergone the requisite experience of conversion and become a full member of the Baptist church.[70]

The Civic Piety of the South

Alongside of and overlapping with the religion of the churches was the religion of the South itself. Noble Powell was deeply influenced not only by the beliefs and practices of southern Episcopalians, Methodists, and Baptists but also by the very fact of being a southerner. He was shaped by the distinctive ethos of the South, by the body of stories, symbols, and rituals in which every southern white boy of his era was immersed. The South had its own holy places and sacred memories, its own saints and martyrs, its own morals and folkways.[71] No extended area of the United States had a more profound effect on the ways in which its inhabitants understood themselves. And in no part of the country was the past a more powerful constituent of the present.[72]

W. J. Cash stretched the truth a bit when he wrote in 1941 that "Southerners in 1900 [saw] the world in much the same terms in which their fathers had seen it in 1830."[73] In the case of Noble Powell too much had changed during those years for him to be able to regard his place in the world in the same way his ancestors had. In the end he turned his back on the Deep South and travelled north to answer his calling.

But if Cash exaggerated the reality, he nonetheless reminded readers of the extreme rootedness of southerners of Noble Powell's background. When he was forty-four years of age and rector of a large Baltimore parish, Powell wrote to his family in Lowndesboro words that pointed—beneath the conventional sentiment expressed—to the connection he always felt to kin and community: "My heart is there," he said, "even if I am here."[74]

Although cotton was no longer king and Lowndesboro's glory days were largely confined to the antebellum period, young Noble's world was in striking continuity with the world of his forebears. When he was born the state of Alabama was still 90 percent rural and only 10 percent urban.[75] What Noble experienced as a small child was literally the microcosm his fathers—and their slaves—had made: Mockingbird Place, the ancestral home, built in 1838 by Seymour Herb Powell from timber grown on the land during the period that large landowners were moving off the plantations and erecting "townlets" for purely social reasons.[76]

The house that Noble's grandfather built was a simple, typical, but nonetheless charming antebellum box: a raised cottage with four rooms on the main floor, bisected by a hallway.[77] In Noble Powell's day there hung on one wall the family coat of arms, with the motto *Una anima in amicis* (one feeling among friends). Against another wall, in the front part of the hall, was a large, heavy, slave-built bookcase of dark wood, containing the required reading of the antebellum South: the historical novels of Sir Walter Scott, which provided planters with models of courtly conduct. After the war, particularly during the years of Noble's youth, Scott's depictions of the chivalric ideal took on new life, as southerners looked back upon their Confederate heroes through the mists of romanticized history, seeing their fighting men as valiant knights defending virtue and honor.[78]

While living in Lowndesboro, Noble wrote his name in his own copies of Scott's *Ivanhoe* and *Lady of the Lake,* in James Fenimore Cooper's *The Spy* and *The Pioneers,* and in Washington Irving's *The Sketch Book of Geoffrey Crayon, Gentn.,* a gift from Dr. Cilley to Mamie, who passed it on to her son. As a boy Noble also studied Shakespeare, Dickens, Browning, the Romantic poets, and other classics of English literature.

In this house were other books as well, including one that its ten-year-old owner undoubtedly read with particular interest: *The Life of General Robert E. Lee, for Children, in Easy Words, Illustrated,* by Mary L. Williamson, published in Richmond, Virginia, in 1895, for use in the public schools.[79] The faint, pencilled inscription on its flyleaf can still be made out: "Noble Powell, Lowndesboro, Ala., Sept. 15, 1902." The frontispiece depicts an important event in the history of the religion of the South: the unveiling of the Lee Monument in Richmond in 1890.[80] In her preface, the author urged teachers to encourage their pupils to study "the names and deeds of our great men." "In looking over the lives of our American heroes," she wrote, "we find not one which presents such a picture of moral grandeur as that of Lee."

This biography, produced during the romantic age of southern history writing, provides an instructive reminder of popular attitudes at this time.[81] The picture of slavery sketched in the book not surprisingly portrays white southerners in a favorable light, especially relative to the greedy northerners. Williamson depicts Lee not merely as a preeminent leader but as "noble" and "Christ-like," a person who returned "good for evil." Moral purists would have approved of her mentioning that the South's chief warrior was a man who "never touched tobacco, brandy or whiskey."[82]

Robert E. Lee—who was not only the archetypal Christian gentleman but also a Low Church Episcopalian—was Noble Powell's lifelong hero. After stepping down as diocesan in 1963, the retired bishop of Maryland often spent a portion of his days reading Douglas Southall Freeman's magisterial, four-volume biography of Lee, which elevated its subject to saintly status.[83]

At Mockingbird Place young Noble lived and played in the company of the black servants whose families had been linked with his for generations. Like the white children of the antebellum plantations, he had a black mammy, whom he called "Mammy Lucy"; an elderly black "uncle," "Uncle George," who undoubtedly kept him amused with ancient stories; and black playmates, who, as we have seen, assumed small roles in the development of Noble's vocation.[84]

These servants were members of the McCall family, which traced its lineage back to the scores of slaves who belonged to the Lowndes County planter Hugh B. McCall, Mamie Powell's grandfather. Noble's upbringing required that he observe the social rules that reinforced the old hierarchical distinctions between the races. This code of racial etiquette included the requirement that he be kind to all blacks who were elderly or considered worthy. Maintaining relations of courtesy and affection with them was understood to be a sign of good character among this class of white southerner.[85]

Foundation for Life

His years in Lowndesboro, rich in human and social capital, provided Noble Powell with a foundation whose core consisted of the love of his family and neighbors. These associations helped to establish in him an abiding sense of confidence in himself and a basic trust in the meaningfulness of existence, as well as a lifelong appreciation for the natural ties of blood and community. His family, like all southerners, had known defeat and disappointment, but Powell encountered few obstacles in his own life and none—until he reached his seventies—that he could not overcome. Believing that although evil abounds life is essentially good and Being is gracious, his was a consistently positive outlook. Bright, energetic, and cheerful, he invariably viewed existence, according to the Virginia Seminary theologian Clifford Stanley, with "a plus sign" in front of it.[86]

Inevitably Powell was influenced by the principles and traditions of the southern planter class, by a code of personal honor and noblesse oblige that had changed little since the days of his antebellum ancestors.[87] This heritage not only reinforced his sense of his own right and responsibility to lead others but also undergirded his desire and capacity to do so in a manner consistent with the character of a Robert E. Lee. Powell esteemed the virtues of the Old South: integrity, courtesy, dignity, self-control, generosity, faith, humility, patience, fortitude, loyalty, and, not least, amiability. An outstanding raconteur, he was the gifted product of a region famous for, as the student of rhetoric Richard M. Weaver remarked, its "reverence for the word," its "cultivation of legend and anecdote."[88] Patrician in appearance, Noble Powell was always and easily a democrat in accepting and engaging everyone with whom he came in contact.

Powell's heritage also shaped his attitude toward modernity. Tradition-minded and relatively uncomplicated, as an adult he was habitually suspicious—and often disdainful—of bureaucracy (civil and ecclesiastical), technology, big government, selfish individualism, and pretentiousness in any form. He loved the natural world and endured cities; he favored the local over the national.[89] Conservative without succumbing to reaction, Powell attempted in church and society to be the ally of authentic—and orderly—progress.[90] Powell's sanguine temperament, his certain trust in a beneficent Providence, and his somewhat less certain faith in his fellow citizens led him to face the future with hope.

His views on politics and society were such that Noble Powell would have felt comfortable at the table of Edmund Burke and Samuel Johnson—that is, if the accidents of his birth were radically rearranged, making him not only 170 years older and an inhabitant of the British Isles but also of a decidedly more intellectual bent. An intelligent, hard-working student, Powell was never deeply engaged by scholarly questions or pursuits. No doubt he left the rural South partly because his mind required a more expansive environment than his region's inhibiting distrust of intellectual activity allowed. And his decision to join the Episcopal church might have been related to that denomination's avoidance of the ugly battles over Darwin and biblical inerrancy that were plaguing Baptists and other communions during Noble's youth. But he retained the southerner's tendency to place religious experience—and the life of virtue that flowed from it—at the heart of the Christian enterprise, with theology and ritual as important adjuncts to that central endeavor.[91]

"Noble was born to the land," his sister Louise said, "and his heart would love it always. Yet it did not satisfy [his] ambition."[92] Clearly young Powell wanted to make something of himself—and his family and community fully expected that he would. To him and to others who participated in the venerable American tradition of self-improvement, realizing one's potential did not mean anything quite so crass as simply gaining a higher social status or power or wealth or fame. It certainly did not mean arriving at a place in life where one could do whatever one pleased. "Making something of oneself" meant self-mastery, not self-indulgence: developing the higher faculties of conscience and reason while controlling the passions. Then one could freely and productively exercise one's true talents and put them in the service of the common good.[93]

Auburn, 1911–15

Powell's journey to ordination in the Episcopal church was somewhat circuitous, partly no doubt because so much was expected of him by others. After completing high school at the Lowndesboro public school (1906–10), Noble spent about a year reading medicine under the guidance of Dr. Cilley.[94] Upon realizing that he was not called to the life and work of a country doctor, he left home in 1911 and journeyed to Auburn—less than sixty miles east of Lowndesboro—and took up a post as secretary to Dr. W. E. Hinds, professor of entomology at Alabama Polytechnic Institute (renamed Auburn University in 1960).[95] During his four years at API, Noble attended various classes, although he was not a regular student there and never earned a college degree.[96]

Several months after his arrival, he wrote to Bappa (Dr. Cilley). His words evince not only his devotion to his uncle but also his growing commitment to Christian ministry—to the exclusion, for the time being at least, of other pursuits. "Wish I was going to run in on you this afternoon for several hours. . . . I am getting along very well indeed with my Bible class work and like it better each week. If I just had you to help me along I think I would like it better than I do now." Like other beginning teachers, he was learning how to handle difficult questions from students: "Some of the boys ask awful hard questions sometimes and I have to think fast but I usually assume a very learned air and that helps a whole lot with them." He has heard that "Cupid is busy in the old town [of Lowndesboro]," but "I had best stay away for the present . . . for I might get in the notion and I am not that now by a good deal. This is the first place I ever was that I didn't get me a new girl. Give my love to all the folks and keep a big, big share for your own dear self. As ever, devotedly, Noble."[97]

A year later, Noble turned twenty-one, a milestone that evoked his sense of duty and responsibility. He wrote to his aunt and uncle, the Cilleys: "In closing, I wish to say, that, as I have tried in my boyhood to give my life a service for Christ to Mankind, so may I be granted strength to do manyfold more for him in my manhood." Three weeks later Bappa was dead.[98]

Noble Powell's work in Auburn ran along two separate tracks. One important field of endeavor was his employment as a budding scientist. He helped to carry out research for the Bureau of Entomology of the United States Department of Agriculture, studying the spread of the boll weevil and investigating the germ resistance of seed to various insecticides.[99]

The second field of activity was his mission work among young people. This undertaking was connected to an event that took place rather quietly a few months before Noble left for Auburn. On 11 June 1911, at the age of nineteen and a half, he was confirmed by Bishop Beckwith in the Church of the Ascension in Montgomery. Understandably, Noble kept this information from Bappa, a stalwart Baptist as well as his mentor and benefactor.[100] Dr. Cilley's son-in-law, Robert M. Hunter, did not hear until the fall of 1912 that Noble had joined the Episcopal church. When he did learn of it, he sent Noble a scorching letter rebuking him not only for affiliating with the wrong church but also for failing to discuss any of this with Bappa.

A Baptist preacher since 1883 and an ardent prohibitionist, Hunter was not Noble's most cherished relative. Louise Powell, who invariably tried to avoid saying anything unpleasant about anyone, recalled that "Robert Hunter was a generous man, but very few of the kinsmen liked him." She indicated his loyalty and his choleric temperament by remarking that "he would have cut off the ear of the soldier [at Jesus's arrest in the garden of Gethsemane]."[101]

Hunter's letter to Noble is no longer extant, but, like the arguments of the opponents of Catholic Christianity during the patristic age, the lineaments of the antagonist's position are revealed in the response. "I must confess that I was greatly surprised at the contents of your letter," Noble began his five-page answer, and "[I] shall try to the best of my ability to reply as clearly and intelligently as I can and shall try to keep in mind your motive in writing as you have." Noble's letter was respectful without being too deferential, forceful without becoming shrill. He patiently laid out his case for the action he had taken.

Hunter had told him he was "mortified" when he heard that Noble was "thinking of deserting the Baptist church" and could hardly sleep the night he received the news. "Now, I too, was mortified," Noble replied, "when I first read your letter to know that you, a standard bearer of the Christ, should harbor such ill will toward the Episcopal Church." Hunter's words, he said, fail to manifest love and charity; they show he does not understand that "men are led much more easily than driven." Hunter's "harsh words" are not the way to "deter anyone from such a course." "Then too, uncle Robert, you are wrong in some things that I can prove historically, but I shall refer to those later."

First Noble pointed out that he could not have told Bappa of his intention to join the Episcopal church. There was no time during the three years prior to Dr. Cilley's death "when he was fully able to discuss a thing like that." Noble mentioned that "for several years I thought I would follow the profession which was ennobled by having as its follower one whose life was as high, noble and pure as my dear Bappa, but when I got away from our quiet little town and out into the world and saw its rough side, I realized I was needed more in the task of curing men's souls than their bodies." The ministry has a greater need of men than the medical profession. If "I had had the privilege of talking this matter over fully from every view point with dear Bappa while he was in condition to talk with me, [then] one of his broad intellect and great charity would have given me his blessing and God speed." Noble pointed out that Dr. Cilley "loved a Christian brotherhood. He was a Baptist and believed the teachings of that faith but with all that he loved a man who would stand out in the front ranks of any denomination as a worker for Christ and not as a worker for his personal aggrandizement."

Noble responded to Hunter's comment that Dr. Cilley would find out one day in heaven what his nephew had done and "the delusion under which he died will be dispelled." Noble said that Bappa, resting in Paradise, "already knows better" and can see and understand what prompted him to take this step. "My choice of a life work is in reality merely a culmination of the teachings of my loved ones, some of whom have already passed into the great beyond."

Apparently Hunter raised a question about how Mamie had responded to her son's decision. "Now I claim," Noble wrote, "to be very well acquainted with my Mother, who is, as you say, my best friend on earth. That I have long since realized. But I must say in her behalf that she is too charitable, too broad minded and too sincere to look with disapproval upon the step which I have taken." His mother, he said, was not opposed to his becoming an Episcopalian. "She wishes me to be where my work for our Lord can be most effective. Her Christianity is not circumscribed by any four walls on God's green earth."

Noble then launched into an interesting but lengthy review of the history of the Episcopal church, correcting Hunter's misapprehensions about the "founding" of the Church of England by Henry VIII. In marshalling the facts for his case, Noble demonstrated familiarity with personages ranging from Gregory the Great to Phillips Brooks, picking up Stephen Langton, John Colet, Hugh Latimer, and Nicholas Ridley along the way. After arguing against Hunter's point concerning the established church's responsibility for numerous instances of torture, Noble pointed out that the world had advanced over the past 250 years, the stake and the rack had been replaced by "love, charity and good will," and the Episcopal church in the United States was, after all, "foremost with [America's] heroes in our war for freedom and independence. I name only one—George Washington."[102]

Noble also defended the use of vestments and declared that it was not true that "there is nothing in the Episcopal Church that savors of the New Testament." In response to Hunter's claim that the Baptist church is the oldest church in existence and the Roman Catholic church the next oldest, Noble offered a more accurate historical recounting, locating the origins of the Baptist church in the sixteenth and seventeenth centuries.

Finally, Noble provided some news regarding his recent activities in Auburn. "When I came to Auburn I found the Episcopal Church here [Holy Innocents] without a rector. I immediately investigated conditions and was licensed Layreader by the Bishop." He had carried out his responsibilities as layreader since the first Sunday of 1912. He told Uncle Robert that the following October, on his birthday, his parents visited him and went to the Episcopal church "to hear me conduct services. They both spoke very sweetly and appreciatingly to me of the stand I have taken here in Auburn and I know that neither of them would have me anything that I could not conscientiously be." "What we need in this world," Noble wrote, "is not the man who is constantly trying to pick a flaw in another man's religion but a man who is constantly trying to pick a flaw in the workings of the devil." He concluded by declaring, "I am trying to have my labors count for something for the Master and shall continue in the work in which I am now engaged if all goes well."[103]

Noble Powell's labors for the Master would focus on young people for fully twenty years. The first phase of this activity, his work in Auburn, was encouraged by Bishop Beckwith, who was endeavoring at this time to find able young men like Noble Powell who could undertake effective ministries to college and university students.[104]

After Noble returned from a state conference of college YMCAs in Tuscaloosa in November 1912, he confessed to his mother that he had gone to a football game with some of the students. Mamie was undoubtedly one of those traditional southerners who still viewed football as a violent, time-wasting, body-exalting activity associated with hooliganism, drinking, gambling, and Yankeedom. Since the 1890s the sport had been regularly assailed by conservative Baptist and Methodist clergy in the South.[105] Noble was hopeful, however, that his mother would understand his need to be present at these athletic events: "[I] know that you would not have me do anything that will in the least curtail my influence with the boys here at Auburn with whom I work. These little things are the ones that they notice. . . . [If] we take no interest in what they do, [then] they will do likewise. Often we have to go against our own feelings to maintain what little influence we may have."[106]

It did not take many such outings for Powell to overcome whatever qualms he might at first have had about joining students and professors at these contests. By the early decades of the twentieth century, the football craze, having quickly outstripped the appeal of the old literary and debating societies, was well established on college campuses in the North and South. By the 1920s even most southern evangelicals had grown to at least tolerate the game, deciding that football was perhaps not at odds with building moral character after all. Certainly Noble Powell believed that anyone concerned with the religious lives of undergraduates would do well to observe the students' devotion to the pagan ritual taking place on the gridiron and in the stands. In addition, he clearly came to derive a large measure of enjoyment from attending these games and from getting to know the players.[107]

The years at API were important for Powell because it was in Auburn that he settled upon his vocation. On 16 April 1913 he wrote to Bishop Beckwith asking to be admitted as a postulant for holy orders.[108] At about this time, he informed his father of his decision. Louise remembered Shell's reaction: "When Noble told his father—born to the land he was—that he could not follow the land, that his leanings were to become a minister, his father said, 'That is fine by me, son, but please don't be a *jackleg* preacher.'"[109]

Noble chose the Episcopal church, Louise said, because "from his tender years he had warmly felt the Episcopal way; he loved the mode of service, the tenets and vestments."[110] Particularly in its early-twentieth-century, Deep South, small-town form, "the Episcopal way" that Noble followed was a species of Anglican evangelicalism that stressed an unembellished approach to faith and practice. Certainly at this stage of his life he would have been reluctant to adopt any other variety of Episcopalianism. With conviction and confidence he responded to the Anglican ethos, to its reserve and its simple beauty, to its call for love of God and the created order.[111] Moreover, the Episcopal church answered his ambition, perhaps appearing to him to have fewer "jackleg" preachers than the other denominations.

During the summer before his final year at API, Noble travelled to Black Mountain, North Carolina, to attend the Southern Student Conference, a gathering of four hundred student delegates from eighty-seven colleges. Under the auspices of the International Committee of the Young Men's Christian Association, the conference had a number of purposes: to "build enthusiasm for Christian fellowship," to "study the best methods of Christian work employed by college men," and to "learn the vision of the Christian life among students." Organizers instructed each delegate to bring with him his college flag, pennants, songs, and school spirit: "you will feel lost without them."[112] Among the featured speakers at this conference was, not surprisingly, the peripatetic Methodist John R. Mott, an internationally prominent champion of missions, young people, and ecumenism.[113]

Just before Powell left Auburn, he met a man who, during a conversation on a baggage truck at the local train depot, inspired him to alter his design for further education: "I had planned," Powell told a newspaper reporter in 1937, "to go to Sewanee to attend the University of the South and continue my academic education. Then one day Bishop [Beverley Dandridge] Tucker [of Southern Virginia] . . . came to preach the commencement sermon at [API]." The president of the institute, Dr. Charles Thach, had asked Noble to conduct the service in the college chapel, a request that he answered "with fear and trembling." There he met Bishop Tucker "and fell completely in love with him. I attended the dinner in his honor and my admiration . . . has increased ever since."

The next morning, when the bishop left to take the train back to Virginia, "I accompanied him to the station to say Goodbye. The train was late and the Bishop's host was unable to remain. . . . I availed myself of the opportunity for further conversation with the Bishop and there, at the station, as we sat on a baggage truck, Bishop Tucker convinced me I should go to his old Seminary at Alexandria, Virginia." Noble recalled that Tucker's "deep love for Virginia Seminary was so obvious and compelling that the next year I changed my plans, entered the University of Virginia for my academic work and then went on to the Virginia Theological Seminary."[114]

The University of Virginia, 1915–17

Wishing to shore up his foundation in the liberal arts before proceeding to seminary, Noble Powell, a robust six feet, three inches and 170 pounds, left Alabama in 1915 to begin two years of study at the University of Virginia.[115] He was admitted as a "special student," which required that he be at least twenty years of age (he was almost twenty-four), give evidence of seriousness of purpose, and demonstrate adequate prior training. Special students were not eligible for degrees.[116]

The adequacy of his prior training was attested to by S. M. Dinkins, who had taught him in high school in Lowndesboro.[117] Dinkins described his former pupil as "a young man far above the average," who had completed not only the standard courses in English, history, math, and science but Latin (Caesar and Cicero) as well. He concluded his recommendation with a personal testimonial: "Though it has not been called for, I wish to make a statement as to who Mr. Powell is. He was born and reared here, and he is regarded by all here as the very best type of young man. He is of a good family. He has energy and ability. His character is of the highest order. Any service rendered him or favor shown him would be highly appreciated by his hosts of friends in Alabama."[118]

Once admitted, Noble still faced the problem of paying for his tuition, room, and board. The story was passed down within his family that he did so by "putting down on the table at the University the gold he had collected since childhood" from Dr. Cilley and perhaps other relatives as well.[119] But it is clear that this source of funding, if used at all, did not suffice. In July 1915 Powell told James M. Page, the dean of the university, "I am exceedingly anxious to begin my college work and very much doubt my ability to do so without such aid as the [Skinner] scholarship will give."[120] Page was soon able to inform him that, having heard from President Alderman and the chairman of the executive committee of the board of trustees, he could safely predict that Powell would indeed be awarded a Skinner scholarship in the fall.[121]

The personal attention Noble received was owing in part to the small size of the university at this time. It comprised a little over a thousand students; about half of them were non-Virginians, and most of these came from other southern states.[122] Throughout this period the Episcopal church claimed the allegiance of the largest proportion of matriculants of the University of Virginia, and hundreds of students participated in the events of the university branch of the YMCA.[123] Thus Noble Powell soon had ample cause to fall in love with the place.

During these two years in Charlottesville he took courses in history, English, philosophy, Greek, and the Bible. He performed particularly well in the history courses (earning an A- average), but he had to struggle with the unfamiliar Greek language (achieving an average of D+). One of the books he studied with care was *The Working Principles of Rhetoric* (1900), by John Franklin Genung.[124] Powell was a good but not outstanding student.[125]

His extracurricular activities revolved around his religious interests. He came to know the Reverend Beverley Dandridge Tucker Jr., the rector of St. Paul's Memorial Church, the Episcopal congregation located across the street from Thomas Jefferson's Rotunda, quite well. The son of the bishop of Southern Virginia and the brother of Henry St. George Tucker, the missionary bishop of Kyoto (and future presiding bishop), Bev Tucker had been a Rhodes Scholar at Christ Church, Oxford, and would soon take a one-year leave of absence to serve as a chaplain with the University of Virginia Hospital Unit in the First World War.[126] While a student, Powell was the president of the St. Paul's chapter of the Brotherhood of St. Andrew (an Episcopal men's organization for prayer, evangelism, and social outreach) and the superintendent of the Sunday school at the Church of Our Saviour, a nearby mission on Rio Road in Albemarle County.[127]

The spiritual side of Powell's career at the university was also fostered by some of his fellow students. He met regularly with the other young men who were preparing for the ministry. In one of their rooms they would gather for evening prayer, mutual uplift, and a short talk by one of their number.[128] When he arrived in Alexandria, Virginia, to begin three years of theological study, he was well prepared for seminary life.

The Protestant Episcopal Theological Seminary in Virginia, 1917–20

The seminary that Powell entered in 1917 was a venerable and dearly loved institution. A disproportionate share of the Episcopal church's bishops and missionaries had studied on "the Hill," as its graceful campus south of Washington was called. A force for Low Church evangelicalism, Virginia Seminary was the counterweight to New York's General Theological Seminary. Opposed to Anglo-Catholicism, Virginia's faculty and trustees were vigilant defenders of Protestant principles. In 1911 a student received a warning for making the sign of the cross in chapel. And in 1919, when Noble Powell was there, seminary authorities delivered a ruling on the acceptable range of colors for the stoles worn in chapel services: white for high festivals, black otherwise. The emphasis was on preaching, not ritual.[129] Homiletics instructors taught fledgling preachers to "'start low, go slow, rise higher, gain fire, wax warm, *quit strong.*'"[130]

Powell began his work at the seminary at a time when the normally tranquil existence on the Hill was disrupted by American entry into the First World War. Up to that point the student body had averaged about forty men. Seminarians were exempt from military service, but many felt it their duty to volunteer. During Powell's years in residence students came and went, and the number of seminarians fell to twenty-five, rising to twenty-eight in June 1919. Powell's class comprised eight students, only four of whom graduated.

Despite the unsettling effects of war, this period in the seminary's history—the first quarter of the twentieth century—was marked by steady enrichment. In these years Virginia Seminary made the transition from a diocesan to a national theological school. In 1916 students came to the Hill from as far away as Texas, Kansas, and South Dakota. By the 1922–23 academic year sixty-six seminarians were in residence.[131]

The faculty and curriculum were growing stronger as well. The famed preacher Walter Russell Bowie (1882–1969) recalled in his memoirs that when he was a student at the seminary—he graduated in 1911, six years before Noble Powell entered—the academic side of the institution was deficient. The seminary was a "'warmhearted'" place, but it did not show any sign "'that much intellectual ferment had been working.'" Biblical criticism, fresh scholarship in liturgical studies, concern about the social problems caused by industrialization and poverty—"'these seemed like sounds heard in the distance, which did not yet disturb . . . the serene assumptions of the Seminary.'"[132]

Academics improved over the next couple of decades, as the seminary added electives to its curriculum and replaced older faculty. The year after Bowie graduated, the most impressive member of the new generation of professors, W. Cosby Bell (1881–1933), began his seminary teaching career at the age of thirty. Powell studied systematic theology under him. The former rector of the Robert E. Lee Memorial Church in Lexington, Virginia, Bell thought about divine creation and personal growth in the light of scientific insights into the workings of nature. Accepting the theory of evolution with enthusiasm, he explored its implications for a Christian theology of process and human fulfillment.[133] As the historian John Booty has remarked, Bell was one of those "forward-looking, hopeful, optimistic Christians who abounded in the 1920s in America."[134]

In Powell's day, Berryman Green, the former rector of Christ Church, Alexandria, was dean of the seminary as well as professor of the English Bible and homiletics; he had twice refused election as bishop coadjutor of Virginia. Paca Kennedy, an alumnus, was professor of Greek and the New Testament; he had replaced Samuel A. Wallis, who continued at the seminary as its chaplain. A gentle man, Wallis was said to represent "the old evangelicalism at its best."[135] Wallace E. Rollins, a graduate of Yale Divinity School, was professor of ecclesiastical history; and Angus Crawford, soon to retire and be replaced in 1920 by Thomas Kinloch Nelson, taught Hebrew.[136] An alumnus recalled that "B" Green was the seminarians' spiritual father, "Pip" Kennedy discovered meaning in St. Paul when his students could find none, "Skinny" Rollins put them in touch with Augustine and Francis of Assisi, and Cosby Bell found theology in the tree outside the classroom window.[137]

Every Thursday evening in term time, a "faculty meeting" took place. At this event, members of the faculty sat together facing the students, and a seminary professor presented his ideas on some practical or devotional topic. In

1919, for instance, Dean Berryman Green spoke on "the importance of the pastoral side of the ministry."[138]

Two events occurred during Noble Powell's years on the Hill that interrupted the course of seminary life. For ten days in October 1918 classes were suspended so that students could assist in relief efforts during the influenza epidemic.[139] And on 27 February 1919 the Thursday evening faculty meeting was cancelled so that students and professors could travel to Washington, D.C., to attend the parade, led by President Woodrow Wilson, welcoming soldiers home from the war in Europe.[140]

In all of his academic work Powell performed creditably. His overall performance was of sufficiently high quality for the seminary to award him the degree of Bachelor of Divinity; he was the only student from his class to achieve that distinction.[141] He turned in especially good work in homiletics, the English Bible, and, in his senior year, ethics and church history. His undergraduate preparation in Greek proved useful, as he achieved in seminary respectable examination grades in that subject as well.[142]

Seminarians' education also took place outside the classroom. Professors, faculty wives, and matrons all attempted to give students—many of whom came from culturally impoverished homes far out in the country—training in the social graces. A priest familiar with the seminary circa 1920 said, "To the task of aiding young men to acquire social training and equip [them] for acceptable service in rectories, the households of the professors . . . devoted themselves with great singleness of heart."[143] Mrs. Brooke, a seminary matron during Powell's years, exercised a "restraining and refining influence," particularly during meals, when she helped her boys to develop the "good manners and refinement necessary in the ministerial office."[144]

Priestly formation also occurred in another way. Frequently, a bishop—the seminarian's "father in God"—felt compelled to write to one of "his boys" to remind him of his responsibilities as a candidate for holy orders. In a letter dispatched in February 1920, a few months before Powell was to graduate, Bishop Beckwith told Noble that he had seen Mr. Lowery in Lowndesboro and that Noble's former rector had mentioned not having heard from him in "many months." "My boy," Beckwith adjured him, "have you forgotten that Mr. Lowery was your Rector, as you will sometime be the Rector of others, and that there is something in the Ministry and its relationships that should not, even if it could, be pushed aside because 'I am busy.' Sit down and write your former Rector such a letter as you should; and stick close to him until your own feathers have grown. Be one to correct the 'forgettableness' . . . of the modern young man. You have a future: live up to it in 'small things.' I have too much interest in you to see you 'slip down' where you ought to be 'climbing up.'" "Are you studying the Prayer Book?" the bishop asked. "I have work for you, and I am asking you to continue the best preparation for that work. We are seeking new men, but only the best men. . . . Stick close to Alabama until you are ready to accept another shelter."[145]

Besides attending the seminary chapel and helping to conduct the services there, students took on appropriate duties in nearby missions and church-related institutions.[146] Powell appears to have thoroughly enjoyed the time he spent with his charges from Episcopal High School, whose large campus adjoined the seminary's. Elected president of the student body of Virginia Seminary, Powell was liked and respected by the high school students as well. Episcopal High School not only had a close relationship with the seminary—they were governed by the same board of trustees until 1923—but also maintained a strong connection to southern civic piety: it served for decades as a hallowed center of devotion to the Lost Cause.[147]

Alumni of the high school remembered Noble Powell more than seventy years after he taught them in a religion class or presided over their chapel services: "He taught the senior boys, about eight in the class. We met at the seminary, upstairs in Aspinwall Hall. He was an excellent teacher. He encouraged us to play baseball and football."[148] "He conducted the services sometimes. He came through with young people. You always felt good when you were with him."[149] Between 1875 and 1930 the high school held a voluntary, half-hour "Friday night meeting," which was led by Virginia Seminary students. Richard Pardee Williams, who taught at Episcopal during Powell's last year in seminary, wrote in his history of the school that "no boy could fail to benefit from [attending the Friday night meeting and] listening to such inspired young [seminarians] as . . . William Cabell Brown, Beverley D. Tucker, . . . [and] Noble C. Powell."[150]

In the fall of his junior (i.e. first) year at seminary, Powell journeyed to Philadelphia to participate in a convention of the Brotherhood of St. Andrew, where he gave a speech that was favorably received. The organizers of the convention expanded the length of time originally designated for discussion of Powell's paper, and the secretary for college work in the Brotherhood asked for permission to print it in his newsletter. "So much for the part that I played," Noble wrote home. "Now I'll tell you something that is of interest to you." He heard addresses by Bishop Arthur S. Lloyd, the president of the board of missions, Bishop Thomas F. Gailor of Tennessee, and John R. Mott. "I wish that I knew one third of an acre of ground as well as [Mott] knows the whole face of the earth. He talks about this nation and that nation just as I would talk of Tom, Dick and Harry. He certainly has the world view all right."

On this trip Noble was able to visit Independence Hall. "My, but it did make me feel like a real American." He enjoyed being able "to put my hand on the old Liberty Bell and strike it so that I could get some idea of its tone." He concluded that Philadelphia was "a tremendous city" but "too crowded"; it was "too big for me to feel comfortable there. It seemed right good to get back on The Hill here and have things quiet for a while."[151]

By means of all these varied activities, seminarians were being formed. They were endeavoring to learn, as one graduate put it, not only theology, church history, and ancient languages "but also the beauty of holiness, a sense of the solemnity of our calling, a sane and manly type of religion." Their formation attempted to plant in their hearts and minds the notion that a sound Christian character was "the highest preparation and the vital necessity for a truly successful ministry" and "that he who preaches the gospel must live the gospel."[152]

Deacon

In May 1920, shortly before Powell was to graduate from seminary and be ordained a deacon, Beverley Tucker, who was about to join the faculty of Virginia Seminary, asked Bishop Beckwith of Alabama to permit Noble to accept a call to be rector of St. Paul's Memorial Church at the University of Virginia.[153] In the Episcopal church, the diaconate, in most cases, was a transitional office, a kind of apprenticeship that had to be completed before the candidate was advanced to the next order, the priesthood. Completely under the authority of the bishop of his home diocese, a deacon typically served—"deacon" was derived from the Greek word for "servant"—in this status for a year, often under the immediate supervision of an experienced rector. A deacon was not free, in other words, to respond on his own to a call from a congregation; he had to go wherever his bishop sent him. The additional problem in Noble Powell's case was that Bishop Beckwith, who was jealous of his prerogatives anyway, had been nurturing Noble for the rigors of the Alabama mission field, not for the challenging but comparatively pleasant circumstances of a prestigious rectorate in another diocese. Naturally he was reluctant to let go of his outstanding protégé.

Tucker told Beckwith that "we all recognize [this is] a big request to make of you." He pointed out, however, that the position was unusual in that it was not "a local parish but a field that concerns the whole Church." Of the 1,562 students at the university, four hundred were "communicants or affiliates of the Episcopal Church"; these men came "from all over the country," including "a quite considerable group from Alabama."

The vestry of St. Paul's, Tucker said, chose Powell for this important work because he was young, well educated, intelligent, and capable of "reaching young men." Powell had impressed not only the vestry of St. Paul's and the faculty of the seminary but also "the boys and masters of the Episcopal High School, where he has been serving as unofficial chaplain for the last three years." Thus he was "peculiarly qualified to take up this work here." His "experience at Auburn, where he was associated with the students' Christian work," his demonstrated ability as an undergraduate at Virginia "to get hold of men through the St. Andrew's Brotherhood," and "his marked success in interesting the boys of the Episcopal High School and preparing them for Confirmation . . . have prompted us to believe that he can render a splendid service here."

Tucker acknowledged that Powell's employment in Virginia would mean a real loss for the diocese of Alabama, but he argued that "this work represents a recruiting ground for the ministry of the whole Church; . . . it is a missionary field for future leaders of the Church," and so "we cannot but ask you to give us of your best." Tucker hoped that Beckwith could see his way clear to giving his permission for Powell to transfer to the diocese of Virginia.[154]

Beckwith immediately sent Tucker a strong reply. The major point of his lengthy letter was to ask whether it was wise for Powell to turn his back on a field he had committed himself to in order to embrace a more appealing opportunity elsewhere: what effect might this choice have on the young man's development as a person and a minister of God?[155]

Parson, 1920–31

A Difficult Call

Although he eventually acceded to the requests of those who were importuning him for the services of Noble Powell, Bishop Beckwith of Alabama gave up his promising protégé reluctantly. "I have watched over him from very young boyhood," he told Beverley Tucker Jr., "and he was well trained in thought before he entered Seminary life. It would be an untold injustice to Mr. Powell . . . to be misguided in the step that leads *to his own development.*" Perhaps "in five or ten years" Powell would be ready "for the work you have in mind"—that is, after he has "met the demands that should be shouldered by every young man." To give him such a major responsibility as the rectorate of St. Paul's in Charlottesville now "would dwarf his future and arrest his development. I am writing purely from the standpoint of Mr. Powell." Bishop Beckwith had in mind for Powell "a work that will tax his every energy," in the mission field with a small salary. "I took him at his word as an Offering to the Church. . . . I have dealt with [him] as with a son; and I am sure that the hand that has guided him has been a loving hand. . . . It is a question, pure and simple, of what is best for the young man."[1]

One knowledgeable student of Beckwith's career has called the bishop "a real terror in many ways," who employed "draconian methods" to achieve his ends. Nonetheless he was also a church leader, this same scholar pointed out, who had "many good ideas," who encouraged young men such as Noble Powell to undertake ministries in colleges and universities, and who "worked hard to find clergy to go to the little places in the diocese and to get vestries to pay for them."[2]

What effect the additional service Beckwith envisioned would have had on Powell—whether improving or narrowing, seasoning or embittering— is impossible to say. At the time Beckwith was convinced, as he told Bishop William Cabell Brown of Virginia, that if Powell were "permitted to begin at the TOP, in ten years he will be broken in heart and spirit as are other young men, known to me, who were persuaded to try the same experiment."[3] Powell asked for Bishop Beckwith's "opinion and direction" in the matter and received in reply three points to consider: his development as "a future workman," his "obligations to the Mission field of the Church," and his lack of experience for the post in Charlottesville. Beckwith advised him: "I cannot think that your problem is difficult of solution."[4]

But Powell, caught "in this difficult position in which I find myself," knew otherwise.[5] Adding to the tension of the counterpoised claims—loyalty to his home diocese versus the lure of a promising new field of responsibility—was the judicious and troubling opinion delivered by the dean of Virginia Seminary, Berryman Green, who had consulted with members of his faculty. With only the best interests of the church at heart, these men acknowledged Powell's good academic record as well as his gift for working with young people, but they also gave "a decided word of caution" regarding "his youth and inexperience in the ministry." Dean Green wrote to Bishop Beckwith that he had "told Powell that his accepting such a work at this time was against my judgment, as much as I admired his capabilities. I expressed myself doubtfully also in a conversation with Mr. Tucker." Furthermore, "when it comes to Powell's duty to his own diocese, I have been decided and outspoken that it is to his bishop and diocese."[6]

When Powell decided to accept the call from St. Paul's, Beckwith sent him a letter that released him from any commitment to his home diocese. The Alabama bishop told Powell, "As I see it, you have pointedly absolved me from any further responsibility for your future development. Nothing is left me but to accept the position you have chosen for me."[7]

Powell replied as if dealing with a difficult parent, assuring Beckwith of his undying sense of obligation to the diocese of Alabama for the "inspiration" it provided his career and of his appreciation for all that the bishop had done for him. Powell also made it clear that he understood Beckwith's granting of the transfer to be the product of the bishop's own carefully considered decision: "The whole matter of my future work had, in my own mind, become such a complex one that I was not sure that my own . . . judgment was right and I was glad, therefore, that there was someone to whom I might go and it was, then, in your decision that I was content to rest." Powell closed by telling Beckwith that "whatever fruit my ministry may bear, I shall always consider it, in a large measure indeed, a ripening of the seed which you have sown in my life."[8] By turns heartfelt and shrewd, this letter no doubt attempted to provide not only a sop to Beckwith's ego but also a salve to Powell's own conscience. Years later, as bishop, Noble Powell was well known for guiding his own deacons with a loving but always firm hand.

The Opportunity in Charlottesville

The Episcopal church's successful effort to establish a parish at the University of Virginia represented a high point in the denomination's work among college students. Before the founding of St. Paul's Memorial Church, the closest Episcopal congregation was Christ Church in downtown Charlottesville, more than a mile east of the university. Robert A. Gibson, who became bishop of Virginia in 1902, realized in the early years of his episcopate that the students of the university not only needed their own church near the Grounds (as the Virginia campus was called) but also required an ecclesiastical home whose ministry would be supported by the diocese at large.[9] A parish at the university became a major goal of the diocese of Virginia and a focus of the national church's attention as well.

Gibson did not arrive at his idea for a campus ministry at the University of Virginia in isolation from the thinking and activities of other church leaders of his day. After 1900, Presbyterians, Congregationalists, Baptists, Methodists, Lutherans, Disciples of Christ, and Episcopalians, recognizing that growth in higher education would take place at the large public universities, all undertook efforts to move into this new mission field. As it evolved, this early version of campus ministry typically featured a diversity of denominational ministries coexisting without sectarian rivalry; this religious work on campus was an expression of interdenominational cooperation that reflected the larger ecumenical process then getting under way.[10]

By 1908 support provided by Christ Church, by the diocesan council, and by wealthy Richmonders enabled the bishop to move forward with his plans for a parish at the university and to appoint a priest-in-charge, Hugh M. McIlhany, who had been serving as secretary of the YMCA at Virginia. Groups of Episcopal women in Charlottesville and Richmond proved extraordinarily helpful in raising large amounts of money for a construction and endowment fund. McIlhany sent letters to alumni and other possible benefactors all over the United States, seeking support for a church that would be a memorial to the sons and daughters of the university. In 1909 an appropriate lot on University Avenue between Madison Lane and Chancellor Street was purchased for fifty thousand dollars. Recognizing that several years would be required to raise sufficient funds to realize the architect's plans for a brick edifice, the trustees of St. Paul's decided to build a temporary wooden structure instead. The first services held there, on a beautiful mid-September

Sunday morning in 1910, must have had something of the atmosphere of an open-air revival. Not only was the church filled to capacity for the main service at eleven o'clock, but the little building, erected in only thirteen days, still lacked windows and doors.[11]

Joy turned to grief when three weeks later McIlhany died from blood poisoning at age thirty-six, leaving behind his wife and five small children. Determined to press on with his plans for St. Paul's, Bishop Gibson set aside the fourth Sunday in Advent as the day on which all parishes in the diocese would take up a special offering for the nascent church at the university, to carry on the work the devoted McIlhany had begun. In December 1910 the bishop appointed Beverley Tucker Jr., a graduate of Episcopal High School, the University of Virginia, and the Seminary in Alexandria, as priest-in-charge of St. Paul's.[12]

Focusing his attention on the lives of the students (the trustees relieved him of the burden of begging for funds), Tucker fostered the growth of the St. Paul's Club, a social organization for students that, through its monthly gatherings, provided them an opportunity to form friendships with students they otherwise might never have come into contact with. And he also helped to develop the Brotherhood of St. Andrew chapter at St. Paul's, which fulfilled its mission of prayer and service by welcoming new students, by speaking with Episcopal students who were not yet confirmed about attending confirmation classes, and by sending out members of the Brotherhood to teach Sunday school or to conduct services at nearby missions.[13]

Under Tucker the St. Paul's congregation elected its first vestry, enlarged the church building, achieved a balanced budget, and commenced a building campaign. By 1918 there were 265 parishioners and sixty-three children in Sunday school.[14] After a decade of service to St. Paul's, Beverley Tucker resigned in 1920 to take up a professorship at Virginia Seminary.

During most of the period that Tucker was in charge of St. Paul's, the University of Virginia tended to the religious needs of its students not by engaging a resident chaplain but by allowing the university chapter of the Young Men's Christian Association to invite clergy of various denominations to conduct weekly services in the university chapel. The YMCA also supported students' religious lives by providing opportunities for Bible study and social service. In 1917, however, a new plan, developed by a faculty committee, went into effect. The weekly Sunday services in the university chapel were discontinued in favor of one well-attended service each term featuring a prominent speaker. In conjunction with this change, each denomination was invited to assume responsibility for providing religious services for its student members. This new approach fit well with the Episcopalians' goals for a thriving parish at the university. Tucker welcomed the plan not only as properly Jeffersonian in its method and aim but also as a better way to foster ecumenical cooperation among the denominations. "The colorless, vague religion of a college chapel," he believed, "makes not for religious unity but for religious negation." A group of pastors working together on behalf of students "will do far more to create an attitude of mutual trust and tolerance," which is the "first step toward cooperation and unity." The ideal, he affirmed, should be a "living unity," not a "dead uniformity."[15]

In accordance with the policy adopted in 1917, the clergy of St. Paul's not only provided a full range of opportunities for worship, fellowship, and service in their own parish, they also worked effectively with others, both clergy and lay people, to enhance the religious life of the university community— to enable this "living unity" to flourish. Parson Powell and the student and faculty members of St. Paul's were strong supporters of the university chapter of the YMCA. The YMCA at Virginia was one of the oldest branches in existence and comprised, proportionately, the largest membership of any state university in the country. When Powell arrived the YMCA had over nine hundred members.[16]

Housed in Madison Hall, which was located on University Avenue across from the Rotunda and near St. Paul's Church, the YMCA served as a religious and social center for students.[17] Noble Powell knew its leaders well and worked with them regularly. Moreover, the rector of St. Paul's cooperated fully with the university in the efforts it still made to offer religious programs to students. Powell, for example, would close St. Paul's Church for the annual formal religious exercises in Cabell Hall, preach in the university chapel as part of student-run services, and assist visiting clergy of other denominations who participated in services on the Grounds.[18]

An Outline of the Powell Years

Noble Powell began his work as an ordained minister at a time when his own denomination was exceptionally vigorous. The number of Episcopal churches in the United States had doubled between 1880 and 1920 (from 4,151 to 8,365), and the number of parishioners tripled (from 345,433 to 1,075,820). Because this growth required greater efficiency in the church's national operations, the denomination in 1919—having absorbed some of the era's business mentality—centralized its operations in New York City, established a new administrative organization, and launched a nationwide campaign to identify the needs of the church and to increase its financial support. In the 1920s Episcopalians would play leading roles in the early stages of the ecumenical movement.

Under Powell's leadership the Episcopal church at the University of Virginia flourished. Within a few years of his arrival, the congregation comprised over two hundred communicant members plus 250 others who considered St. Paul's their spiritual home. Parson Powell, as he was typically called during his years in Charlottesville, also ministered to over four hundred students at the university, to sixty students of the Nurses' Training School, and to patients at the university hospital. In addition, he was in charge of six rural missions in Albemarle County.[19] Years later he recalled with mixed feelings one Christmas when he held eighteen services in one day—in St. Paul's Church, in the county poorhouse, and in all the wards of the university hospital. He said he dreaded to consider what might have happened if one more person had ventured to wish him a "Merry Christmas!"[20]

Expanded, the "temporary" wooden structure held 375 people—insufficient to accommodate all those who wanted to attend Sunday services. Since the church lacked a parish hall, organizations such as the vestry, the St. Paul's Club, and the Women's Auxiliary had to meet either in Madison Hall or in parishioners' homes. All eleven Sunday school classes—sixty-five children—met in the nave of the church; the parish historian commented that this arrangement might have had something to do with the congregation's chronic shortage of teachers.[21]

In 1921, early in Powell's tenure, a fund-raising campaign of the national Episcopal church designated St. Paul's and its mission to students at the University of Virginia as one of the nationwide campaign's highest priorities. Unfortunately, this fund-raising effort failed to achieve its ambitious goals, and St. Paul's never garnered the fifty thousand dollars it had hoped to receive. Instead the vestry authorized a Richmond Committee composed of well-connected Episcopal laymen to attempt to raise the needed funds according to McIlhany's original memorial plan.[22] For five years this committee and Parson Powell solicited donations—travelling throughout the Commonwealth of Virginia and beyond, speaking to church groups, writing letters, and publishing articles about the work being carried on at St. Paul's. By 1927 they had succeeded in raising all but $25,000 of the total anticipated cost of $325,000 (including the purchase price of the property).[23]

After struggling with a number of architects and plans, the parish also succeeded in procuring a suitable design for the church building, which included a side chapel and a nave that would seat more than seven hundred. The new edifice, completed in September 1927 and featuring a graceful cupola and a portico with large white columns, fit in harmoniously with the nearby buildings of the University of Virginia. A new parish house, which included not only meeting rooms and a kitchen but also a lounge for the students and an apartment and office for the rector, had opened two years before, in November 1925.[24]

St. Paul's occupied a special place in the diocese of Virginia. The significance of its position as a church with a broad and distinctive purpose was indicated in several ways. One was the attendance by all three Virginia bishops— not only William Cabell Brown but the bishops of the dioceses of Southern Virginia and Southwestern Virginia as well—at the laying of the cornerstone of the new church in April 1926. A similarly impressive gathering took place at the dedication of the new church in September 1927. Nearly a thousand attended, including Virginia Bishop Henry St. George Tucker and Presiding Bishop John Gardner Murray.[25]

Another indication of the church's unique place was the decision by the diocese in 1924 to grant an exception to the rule barring from "parish" status congregations that lacked sufficient means to support themselves. St. Paul's, although incapable of attaining financial independence, nonetheless was allowed to advance from "mission" to "parish" status on the basis of its special role in the diocese as the large and influential parish church for the University of Virginia.[26]

As it happened, the full amount of financial support that the diocese was to provide never materialized. The seven thousand dollars the parish contributed to its annual budget was supposed to be supplemented by six thousand from the diocese—these additional funds were to be used for maintenance of the parish house, reduction of the parish debt, and support of an assistant minister. A financial crisis prevented the diocese from paying more than $1,900 in 1925, $1,750 in 1926, and nothing at all in 1927. Nonetheless, the congregation was able to support an assistant, Arthur Barksdale (Tui) Kinsolving II, who came to St. Paul's in the spring of 1924. The scion of a distinguished clerical family, Kinsolving helped with the student work, the country missions, and the Sunday school, as well as with the regular parish services. In 1927 he left Charlottesville to become chaplain at the United States Military Academy at West Point.[27]

Four years later, Noble Powell also left St. Paul's, having accepted a call to become rector of Emmanuel Church, a wealthy parish in downtown Baltimore. A dozen years later, following service as dean of the National Cathedral, Powell would be back in Baltimore as bishop of Maryland, ensconced in a large office in Diocesan House, a brownstone mansion within the shadow of the Washington Monument. In that place, where stacks of correspondence and other documents awaited the bishop's attention, nothing was more certain to bring a sparkle of delight to the light-blue eyes behind the pince-nez than an interruption by his secretary inquiring whether the bishop would like to take a telephone call from a gentleman with a southern accent asking to speak with "Parson."

Minute Particulars

While fund-raising and construction programs are important, far more so are those aspects of a cleric's work that are hidden from public view. The church historian Owen Chadwick has commented that "The key to a clergyman lies in his sacraments and his prayers, and in his pastoral care and private interviews, both of which are intimate if not under a seal and do not go into words."[28] In countless minor acts of devotion and myriad gestures small and unremarkable, the priest proves effective. The poet William Blake knew that "'He who would do good must do it by minute particulars.'"[29]

Parson Powell won hearts and heads to his cause by entering into the life of the university to an extent probably never equalled before or since. Attentive and caring, he never imposed himself upon the students but led them patiently, teaching by example more than precept, letting them grow according to their own time and interests and strengths.[30] Joseph Vaughan, a student at Virginia in the mid 1920s, said that "Rather than . . . lecturing to [the students], [Parson Powell] quietly went his way because he knew that, if he stood fast for the good and the right, the boys would seek him out, and that they did. He was the only man who was welcome anywhere in any situation."[31]

Noble Powell often played an important part as an intermediary between students and the faculty or administration. Those familiar with the history of the University of Virginia have noted that Powell took on a role similar in many respects to the function performed officially by the dean of the university, who handled most matters pertaining to students.[32] Vaughan commented that Powell "saw a great deal, told nothing, and did his best to straighten out the annoying details of student life without fanfare and meddlesomeness."[33]

During his years in Charlottesville Parson Powell not only interceded with university authorities and lent money to students in financial distress; from time to time he also found himself called upon to travel downtown to the police station to post bond for a student in difficulty. So well known did he become in the police court that on one occasion the magistrate reproached him, asking, "Where have you been, Parson? The next time you stay away so long I'm going to cite you for contempt of court."[34]

Powell enjoyed being where the students were. B. F. D. Runk, a Virginia student in the 1920s and the dean of the university forty years later, recalled the parson as "a large, well-proportioned man who had a smile on his face every time you'd see him." He "would visit teams practicing at Lambeth Field [the twenty-one-acre site of football, baseball, and track events], then stop in fraternity houses along Rugby Road and Madison Lane on his way back from Lambeth Field. He would also visit in the boarding houses. He knew [the students] well, and they got to know him and his views on things."[35]

On one of his trips to Lambeth Field, Powell did not refrain from interfering with the work of one of Virginia's legendary figures, the baseball and football coach Earl "Greasy" Neale. Early in his career at the University of Virginia, Neale was especially abusive of his players. One afternoon when Powell and others were watching the baseball team practice, Greasy roundly cursed one of his players, a first baseman, embarrassing those in attendance, not to mention the hapless athlete. Parson Powell, confident not only of his authority but also of his knowledge of a collegiate culture so different from that of a later era, walked up to Greasy and let him know that his methods were not those of the University of Virginia: "'This is not the kind of language we use. . . . I know you . . . are doing nothing more than expressing disgust at the player's mistakes, but that's not our style. Such language discredits you, your staff, your players, and the University.'" Coach Neale, surprised, tried to explain that he was merely trying to teach these boys how to play baseball. "'Greasy,'" Powell replied, "'that's not the way University of Virginia people get the job done.'" The epilogue of this story has Greasy Neale, several weeks later, observing the same first baseman miss a routine fly ball and saying to him, "'Mr. _____, I hope you won't do that again.'"[36]

If Powell supported the students, they also supported him. Sitting in his study in the new parish house one evening, the rector heard the sound of a window breaking. He soon discovered the damage and its cause: a rock with a dollar bill and a piece of paper wrapped around it. The money, said the scrawled message, was to pay for the broken window; in addition, Parson was to walk seventy-seven paces from the bottom step of the Rotunda, on a direct line from the main entrance of the Rotunda to that of Cabell Hall (at the opposite end of the Lawn). There he would find one thousand dollars in cash in a small container. He was to arrive between 11:07 and 11:17 P.M. on Friday, April 13, "and go alone." Obeying these instructions, Powell found the money, which was to be used to help pay for the new church building. This gift of the Seven Society, the most elite and secretive of the student groups at the university, was recognized with a plate on a pew in the new church.[37]

The St. Paul's rector wrote with news of this happy prank to his friend

Edward R. Stettinius Jr., whom Powell had come to know well during the period that Stettinius had attended the university (1919–24). Throughout these years Stettinius had been active in the YMCA and at St. Paul's Church; he had thought seriously of going into the ministry but eventually became chairman of the board of U.S. Steel, Franklin Roosevelt's (controversial) secretary of state, and rector of the University of Virginia instead.[38] In the spring of 1928 he was a member, with Noble Powell, of the Seven Society. "There hasn't been a gift of any kind to the church which has caused half so much comment and interest," Powell told him. "We are riding high, thanks to your generosity. We have chosen the seventh pew from the back, where the light falls most directly at the time of the morning service, for the plate." Powell went on to describe a meeting of the Seven Society: "We had a meeting of the Numerals the other night and the stunt was the main subject of conversation. The actives and the alumni think it is the finest thing that has ever been done and wanted me to thank you for it."[39]

By the time of these events, Powell was no longer living his life and carrying on his ministry as a solitary bachelor. On 21 April 1924 he married Mary Wilkins Rustin (1901–74), who had settled in Charlottesville with her mother and sister some years before.[40] The story the Powells told decades later was that the rector of St. Paul's had not paid much attention to the lovely young woman ten years his junior until one afternoon after she had been teaching Sunday school in a mountain mission south of Charlottesville. The weather that Sunday was terrible, and Noble Powell offered to follow her car in his own vehicle. Mary proceeded to drive back to town without difficulty, not realizing until the next day that her rector's car had gotten stuck; Mr. Powell had had to wait on the side of the road until he could catch a ride home with someone else.[41]

Mrs. Rustin, Mary's mother, had leased a house near St. Paul's Church and rented rooms to students. A regular attendant with her sister, Jennette, of the Friday evening tea dances at the YMCA in Madison Hall, Mary was a sociable young woman, though not particularly active in the church. Her marriage to Noble Powell, remembered a contemporary, "loomed up all of a sudden," especially to family members at home in Lowndesboro who had expected him to marry someone else.[42]

Apparently Noble had had a serious romantic involvement in Alabama with someone named Lila, which had incited the hopes of the young lady as well as Noble's family. His relatives wrote to him in the late winter and early spring of 1924 to assure him that they would take Mary into their hearts even though she was not Lila. His mother told him: "I hope and feel you did honorably with dear Lila, and I do want you happy, for this is life long." Mamie seemed surprised and disappointed, though, that her son was not going to marry Lila after all, "[but] I'm not expected to know my children's love affairs." Noble's plans, she acknowledged, "took my breath, and dazed me," but she promised she would love Mary.[43]

His sister—probably Josephine—wrote to him to say, "It hurts us so hard to know of all your trouble in this thing. But in time, all will be well. Lila is so strong and good. God will fill her life I pray with someone who loves her. . . . [I]f you will be happy, we will be content." It is clear, however, that she and her sister, Louise, liked Lila very much: "you know how we feel." In any event, she counselled her brother, "you *must* write Lila again—don't let her hear anything from just gossip." She said that they could not come to the wedding, since they lacked money and fine clothes. But they would treat Mary as "a real sister." "But if I were you," she suggested in a final word of advice, "I'd have a *very quiet affair.* It would make it less hard on her [Lila], for it would grieve her extremely to tell [her] you had a big affair, and you know it would be in all the papers."[44]

Mary Rustin impressed people with her vitality and charm, and so, at least in Charlottesville, "everyone was very pleased."[45] The wedding, a simple ceremony with few attendants, was held in the wooden church, and many who wanted to be present had to stand outside. As the couple came out, one university student heard his minister say, "I've got her now," whereupon the crowd cheered.[46] From then on, the parson and his wife presided at the Sunday afternoon teas for the boys at the university.[47]

A Wide Parish

Parson Powell's position in relation to the University of Virginia was unique among Charlottesville clergy not only because of the large number of Episcopal students in residence (over a quarter of the total) but also because other denominations had not yet built churches near the Grounds.[48] Approximately two-thirds of the undergraduates came from private preparatory schools, many of which were Episcopal in allegiance or inclination.[49] Moreover, the university at this time (1920) was a small institution—only sixteen hundred students—rendering it more likely for a strong personality to achieve a widespread influence.[50] Thus Powell was able to function as the de facto chaplain to the university.[51]

Charlottesville was a town whose southernness would have been much more apparent to the visitor in the 1920s than today. It had, as the novelist Julian Green recalled in his memoirs, only one hotel, the Monticello, which faced a neoclassical brick courthouse whose entrance was guarded by a "bronze cannon . . . dreaming of Manassas beneath the magnificent sycamore trees whose golden leaves gave the effect of sunlight."[52]

When Green began his studies at the University of Virginia in 1919, he found the town itself unappealing, "with . . . poor and dismal little houses." But the university Grounds offered a different prospect altogether—and we can imagine Noble Powell arriving a year later and taking in a similar view of his extended parish: "the closer one came to the University, the gardens, the trees and the verandahs . . . lent an air of distinction to the long avenues and spoke of a time that I had thought was long past."[53] Green admired the Rotunda and Jefferson's serpentine walls, which "meandered as if [they] were drunk."[54] The Lawn itself featured "a forest of white columns . . . Doric, Ionic, Corinthian, they rose up on all sides to such an extent that one might think it was a hallucination."[55] In warm September, "at Cabell Hall, the scent of honeysuckle hung over each window casement." In the fall, "the trees [on the Lawn] were turning gold and there was a marvelous smell of heat and dry leaves in the air."[56]

Green discovered much about the tastes and folkways of his fellow undergraduates. He soon came upon a fairly clear caste system, according to which students belonged—or failed to belong—to certain fraternities, lived in ideal or less-than-ideal circumstances, and associated with—or only regarded at a distance—the most exalted members of each class.[57] The elite belonged to the top fraternities and lived on the Lawn or the Range, the rows of small rooms that ran along the sides of Jefferson's original "academical village" and featured fireplaces and rocking chairs.[58]

Respectable alternatives to the coveted Lawn rooms included the many boarding houses near the Grounds, which typically were presided over by socially if not financially secure widows and single ladies.[59] In his first years as rector of St. Paul's, Powell stayed at Mrs. Blackford's, which was operated by the widow of the Episcopal High School principal.[60] As a student at Virginia five years earlier, Powell had roomed at Mrs. McIlhany's, run by the widow of the first priest-in-charge of St. Paul's.[61]

In time, Julian Green grew accustomed to the barbarian yelling of his peers, to the singing and shouting of his drunken housemates, to the boys' eagerness to sample "alcohol of a rather uncertain kind due to the rigours of prohibition."[62] He came to see that what students meant by the phrase "Virginia gentleman" was that "you could do whatever you wanted, except cheat." Those who were found to have violated the provisions of the revered, student-run honor code "no longer existed in the eyes of the authorities" and were forced to leave the Grounds "that same day."[63] His fellow students spent endless hours talking "quite openly" about women, occasionally referring, "in mysterious whispers," to their adventures at a notorious house in town; but virginity and ignorance about sex were common attributes.[64] Popular entertainment could be had at the downtown theatre, the Jefferson, which "was always full of students noisily expressing their opinions."[65]

Students spent time playing poker, participating in sports, attending dances and horse races, hiking in the mountains, working at part-time jobs, and reading the latest novels by John Galsworthy and Booth Tarkington.[66] One attribute that Virginia students of the twenties lacked completely was "anything remotely resembling a social conscience," a historian of the university has remarked. "Concern for the poor or the disadvantaged was almost unknown to them, and the race problem for them was virtually nonexistent. It was much the same at other institutions."[67] University of Virginia students, Julian Green observed, were denizens of a separate and distinct microcosm.[68] The university "stood on its own, somewhat disdainfully set apart from the rest of the world, for it was a little universe unto itself and one that considered itself almost perfect. . . . Both the students and the teaching staff, who all came from the South, considered themselves so far removed from the rest of humanity that it was hardly worth mentioning."[69]

A significant part of that social and cultural separation was racial. The Jefferson Theatre provided opportunities for students to have their prejudices reinforced when black-faced white performers put on minstrel shows. The student newspaper, *College Topics,* urged its readers to attend the show by "Lasses White," who "[knows] the characteristics of the real Southern darkey [and has] a natural gift for mimicry and a keen sense of humor," enabling him "to give a correct portrayal of the negro as he is known below the Mason and Dixon line."[70]

In this decade in which the Ku Klux Klan was a potent force, achieving unprecedented gains in membership and political power in southern and midwestern states, *College Topics* reported in 1921 that the president of the University of Virginia, Edwin A. Alderman, had recently thanked the Virginia Realm of the KKK for their thousand-dollar contribution to the university's gymnasium fund.[71] In 1925 members of the Washington Literary Society and the Jefferson Society found the following statement sufficiently controversial to offer it up as the topic for the annual debate between the two student groups: "Resolved, that the Ku Klux Klan is detrimental to the welfare of the American people."[72] Although the Klan did not have the support of the majority of southern Protestants, it did represent an extreme expression of a widespread antipathy during the 1920s toward "foreign elements"—including Jews, Roman Catholics, and immigrants from southern and eastern Europe—who threatened WASP hegemony. In Charlottesville the Klan was a minor presence, holding occasional parades in town and meeting a couple of times in downtown churches, but another racist organization—the Anglo-Saxon Club—received more support at the university.[73]

Solid walls of racial separation would not be breached in the 1920s in Virginia, but athletic contests did function at this time as a counterforce to the cliquishness of Virginia students. No doubt this was one reason why Noble Powell—always welcome on the players' bench—supported the university's teams so enthusiastically. Athletics could provide a sense of unity at a time when campus cohesiveness was being eroded not only by the traditional caste system but also by higher enrollments, the development of graduate and professional programs, a more diverse student population, and the growth of the elective system. A football or baseball game could provide a focal point for everyone. Athletics helped to undermine the campus dominance long enjoyed by debating societies and fraternities, thus overcoming at least for the moment time-honored lines of distinction.[74]

St. Paul's Memorial Church was not only a student parish, however; it also attracted the families of the faculty and staff of the university, as well as local professionals, such as the attorney Bernard P. Chamberlain, and others who lived nearby. As its rector, Powell came to know some of the leading figures—and the most memorable characters—in the history of the University of Virginia.

The biology professor Ivey F. Lewis served as the senior warden of St. Paul's and was also a strong supporter of the university YMCA. Powell confessed to Lewis that he was "not an intellectual" or any kind of scholar but simply a lover "of my fellow men" who wished to convey to them something of "the ethics and character of Jesus."[75] In Powell's day a proponent of eugenics who feared "amalgamation" and preached the necessity of maintaining "the purity of the white race in America," Lewis would stir up a hornet's nest in 1958–59 when he voiced vigorous opposition to the integration of St. Paul's Church.[76]

The Greek scholar Robert Henning Webb and his wife were also members of St. Paul's. Mr. Webb's retiring manner did not prevent him from giving his students vivid descriptions of the battle of Marathon or from producing earthy translations of Aristophanes.[77] Webb's classics colleague Walter A. Montgomery, who taught Latin, was a regular worshiper at St. Paul's, but he reserved a large portion of his devotion for the dead heroes of the Confederacy.[78] Other well-known faculty members who attended St. Paul's were William Minor Lile, dean of the law school and a vestryman of the parish; the astronomer Samuel A. Mitchell, who served for many years as chairman of the board of the university YMCA; and the French professor Francis H.

Abbot, a bachelor who was famous for his long courtship of Betty Booker, with whom he starred in university-produced comic melodramas.[79] Abbot sang in the St. Paul's choir with John J. Luck, a popular mathematics professor who loved poetry and painting and who, because of his ample girth, was known to the students as "Pot Luck."[80]

If the University of Virgina was, as Julian Green said, a little world set apart from the rest of humanity, then it was fortunate that Noble Powell's field of activity covered a more extensive domain. Years later Powell treasured his recollections of ministering to the rough mountain folk of Albemarle County as much as he enjoyed recalling the time he had spent with his half-pagan student charges.

Responsible for six missions in the Ragged Mountains—the setting of some of Edgar Allan Poe's short stories—Powell became accustomed to making adjustments as the situation demanded, occasionally walking ten miles over mountain roads impassable by automobiles because of snow or mud. He preached indoors and out, in all kinds of weather—to mountaineers gathered around a great log fire on the side of a hill, to another group on Christmas Day while he stood up to his knees in snow, to a congregation attending services in a corncrib while rats scurried across the floor. Powell savored the memory of presenting for confirmation the seventy-year-old patriarch of Gibson's Hollow; and he never forgot the experience of serving as preacher, chief mourner, and assistant gravedigger at a funeral at which there was only one other living person present.[81]

These opportunities arose as part of Powell's labors on behalf of the archdeaconry of the Blue Ridge during the 1920s, the heyday of the mountain mission work. At this time the archdeaconry encompassed nearly forty mission stations, eighteen of which operated schools.[82]

The archdeaconry was largely the inspiration of one man, the redoubtable Frederick W. Neve (1855–1948), a well-born Briton who, after graduating from Merton College, Oxford, turned his back on a promising career in the law to become a priest. In 1888, after serving for eight years as a curate in three English parishes, where his ministry focused on improving the lives of the poor, Neve came to the United States to be rector of two churches in western Albemarle County: Emmanuel, in Greenwood, and St. Paul's, in Ivy. A tall (six feet, four inches), ruggedly handsome young man, Neve made treks into the surrounding countryside and became convinced of the need to bring the church—the gospel and the sacraments as well as education and health care—to the isolated and impoverished people in the gaps and hollows of the nearby mountains.

In 1904 Bishop Robert Gibson appointed Neve archdeacon of the Blue

Ridge, and the enterprising priest built a network of Episcopal outposts: chapels, mission homes, first-aid clinics, clothing bureaus, and schools. The work of the archdeaconry extended from the Ragged Mountains southwest of Charlottesville, to the Blue Ridge in the west, then north for a hundred miles to the Potomac River near Harpers Ferry—an area of sixty-eight hundred square miles. Thousands of children and adults benefited from these institutions. By the time of Neve's death at the age of ninety-two, twenty-six missions existed in seven counties. Although all of the day schools had by this time either closed or been taken over as part of the state's expanded public system, the small churches of the archdeaconry ministered to five hundred families. Six priests served the missions, but most of the necessary tasks were performed by twenty-five lay workers and deaconesses.[83]

Archdeacon Neve and Noble Powell formed a close friendship that lasted until Neve's death. In the Neve Papers in Alderman Library at the University of Virginia are letters from Powell to the archdeacon expressing gratitude for the privilege of being associated with Neve in the church's mountain mission work during some of "the happiest [years] of my life."[84] "I often think," Powell wrote only a month before Neve's death, "of the happy contacts [with you] when your inspiring leadership opened my eyes to the missionary opportunities in the Church."[85]

As a graduate of the mission-minded Virginia Seminary, Powell was already aware of most of these occasions for missionary service. In a larger sense, though, he was right to credit Neve with opening the eyes of many to the opportunities residing in mission fields close to home. When Neve began his work in the 1890s, Episcopalians were vitally concerned with missions—but mainly missions to foreign lands, such as Brazil, China, and Japan. Neve awakened the interest of Episcopal men and women to the needs of a large body of people who were their own near neighbors.[86]

At the time of his consecration as bishop, Powell received a cordial message from Frederick Neve. The new bishop replied, "Your message means more to me than I can tell. You were for many years my chief and advisor in the work I was privileged to do under your direction in the Ragged mountains, and I shall ever cherish that experience." Powell went on to assure Neve that "When we speak of Apostolic Succession, you certainly are in that line if anyone is. The generations to come will rise and call you blessed because of your life and your preaching of the Gospel of our Lord Jesus Christ."[87] One of the many beliefs shared and acted upon by Neve and Powell was the conviction, stemming from the example of the English parish, that all the people in their area were in some sense parishioners and thus deserving of their attention.[88]

The one group of Episcopalians in Charlottesville that Noble Powell had much less to do with was the body of African Americans who formed what eventually became Trinity Parish. Begun in 1919 as Trinity Mission, this black Episcopal congregation was served by a senior student from the Bishop Payne Divinity School in Petersburg, Virginia, and was overseen by the archdeacon of colored work, George MacLaren Brydon, a white priest.[89] The seminarian's salary was paid for out of the diocese's colored work fund. After they had successfully established their church, the congregation of Trinity declared themselves "very grateful to the people of Christ Church and St. Paul's Memorial Church for their support and cooperation."[90]

That the white and black churches thenceforth had little or no involvement with one another is not surprising in this era of ecclesiastical segregation and white ambivalence about the recruitment of new black Episcopalians. In the 1880s, at least on some occasions, whites and African Americans had worshiped together in Episcopal churches in the South. But by the 1920s the situation was very different, as black Episcopalians were isolated in their own churches and councils. The "archdeaconries for colored work" established in Virginia in 1901 and in other southern dioceses had evangelization and the planting of new missions as their raison d'être, but white Episcopalians expressed their feelings about African-American membership in the Episcopal church by creating separate black convocations that were allowed to send only a limited number of representatives to the annual diocesan conventions.[91] African-American Protestants often decided that they preferred to join one of the independent black denominations, such as the African Methodist Episcopal church or the A.M.E. Zion church, instead of the Episcopal church.

A Walking Sacrament

The work of a priest consists in one essential though humanly impossible task: to body forth Christ in the world, to be God's representative in both sanctuary and secular city. In the English theologian Austin Farrer's memorable phrase, the priest is called to be "a walking sacrament." He it is, Farrer says, who "bears the stamp," who serves as "a token of Christ wherever he is: in him Christ sets up the standard of his Kingdom and calls us to the colours." Other people may be wiser or kinder or more helpful; a priest "give[s] his fellow Christians a right to his services. It might well be . . . that the woman next door to you has greater gifts for teaching small children than the school-mistress; but that doesn't mean you can expect her to teach your little family for you. You've a *right* to the school-mistress's services; she's given herself over to be eaten alive by the children of the place. And so with the priest: go on, eat him alive, it's what he's for."[92]

Noble Powell, ordained a priest in January 1921, exercised in relation to others what the French philosopher Gabriel Marcel termed *disponibilité:* spiritual availability, the capacity of being truly present to the other, especially to those who are in need. The rector of St. Paul's placed himself at the disposal of the people of his parish, spending himself on their behalf: go ahead, use me up.[93]

He held what students of the twenties called "gum sessions" until late at night and was at home to any student at any time.[94] The reading groups he assembled, the guest lecturers he brought in, and the wide-ranging discussions he stimulated led some undergraduates to believe that the meeting room at St. Paul's Church was as much a classroom—and as engaging—as any they attended on the Grounds.[95] The St. Paul's Club, largely Episcopal in membership but open to any student, grew from 450 members in 1921, to five hundred in 1925, to six hundred in 1927, to more than seven hundred by the time Powell left in early 1931. The Brotherhood of St. Andrew attracted fifty students to participate in its life and work.[96]

Students were not drawn to St. Paul's by the fine preaching—as rare a commodity in that place as in any other—but by Parson Powell. As James Platt (B.A., 1933) put it, Powell "wasn't an excellent preacher; he inspired people just by being there. People would've gone to be in contact with him no matter what he said."[97] Regular association with such a person—as advocates of "self-improvement" knew—could be positively formative: friendship was one of those benevolent affections that could serve as a support of conscience and a motivator of moral conduct.[98]

Men and women who knew Powell at the University of Virginia all focused on this salient characteristic; the value of the parson depended in large measure upon the character of the person. As the eighteenth-century legal scholar William Blackstone wrote in his famous *Commentaries,* a priest "is called parson, *persona,* because by his person the church, which is an invisible body, is represented. . . . He is sometimes called the rector . . . but the appellation of *parson* . . . is the most legal, most beneficial, and most honourable title that a parish priest can enjoy."[99]

Sixty to seventy years after they graduated, scores of University of Virginia alumni warmly recalled their associations with Parson Powell. He helped them find rooms when they arrived, took them to their first football games, led them in their cheers at Cabell Hall pep rallies, and enabled them to hear "bang-up preachers" like England's Geoffrey Studdert-Kennedy, the hugely popular World War I chaplain known as "Woodbine Willie."[100] The parson took students with him to Richmond and New York to help raise funds for the new church building, accompanied a group of young men interested in seminary to a conference at the Washington Cathedral, and rode with the football team on buses and trains to away games.[101] Occasionally, he even borrowed their girlfriends when he had teas for the students.[102] Supporting those who were affiliated with an institution that many—not only the acutely sensitive Julian Green—found to be "snobbish" and "a kind of prideful place," Parson Powell functioned as a vitally helpful ally and confidant.[103]

In an era of Protestant Christianity that believed, with Phillips Brooks, that preaching could best be defined as "the bringing of truth through personality," Noble Powell's personal magnetism and manifest sincerity counted for much.[104] Wholesome, muscular Christianity was the order of the day, and many students saw in their parson the epitome of what they wanted to be. They could see that the St. Paul's rector was, in their words, "accepting of himself"; they viewed him as someone who was like them but with more experience in the world.[105] Although "not a strong theoretical man," he was "steady,"[106] a "center-of-the-road man."[107] When a student asked the parson at his regular Sunday night open house to explain the doctrine of the Trinity, Powell told him, "Langbourne, see that nail on the wall? Well, hang your question up there and let it rest awhile."[108]

Alumni recalled that Parson Powell, a Low Churchman, typically wore a necktie instead of a clerical collar.[109] Although "very relaxed" with the students, "no one was respected more." He knew how to "bring up what we were all interested in" and make students feel comfortable.[110] "The look in his eyes [showed] he was at peace with the world." Consistently "gracious and well-groomed," even courtly, he made "no effort to try to impress anyone," though he was always "eager to help." He "encouraged you to think for yourself," and he made you feel "you weren't the only person who had doubts sometimes"; he helped students to see that the Bible included "legends as well as historical writing."[111] "Not an aggressive man," Parson wasn't always "reaching out to glad-hand you." He was "not out to turn the world upside down or to be satisfied with the way it is." He "communicated the idea of being candid."[112] A "very warm person with a good sense of humor," he "got along with any kind of student."[113] For many Virginia alumni, knowing Parson Powell was one of their fondest and most vivid memories from their student days in Charlottesville.

Powell was at his best in the pulpit when the strength of his personality and the power of his own plain convictions came through in his preaching. When he dealt overmuch in abstractions, so that, as one of his listeners, Clifford Stanley, remarked, "the ideas hung out there between you and him," he was apt to disappoint. A longtime professor of theology at Virginia Seminary, Stanley heard Powell preach many times in Charlottesville. He liked the parson but found him to be "not particularly profound"; Powell did not possess "a great, leading kind of mind."[114] Those who attended St. Paul's hoping to be intellectually challenged often discovered that Powell's words held little interest for them; they were more likely to find food for thought in the sermons of the Reverend William Kyle Smith, a Princeton Seminary graduate and the secretary of the YMCA at Virginia.[115] Powell's pastoral gifts and simple friendliness enabled him to "get by with a lot" as a preacher.[116]

But when Powell spoke to his people directly, almost extemporaneously, on practical Christian living, or when he "talked right to you, quietly but with emotion too," recounting in his own appealing manner the parables of Jesus or stories about the Master, then he "kept your attention; everybody listened."[117] Virginius Dabney (B.A., 1920; M.A., 1921), a student member of St. Paul's who went on to fame as a newspaper editor and author, recalled an occasion when the rector declared that "Jesus didn't gallop with the gang."[118] Powell's homiletical record was irreverently summarized one Sunday after the eleven o'clock service, when Sally Doswell, half of the elderly pair of unreconstructed Confederate sisters known as the Misses Doswell, declared to the rector, "Parson, your sermons are much like your name; sometimes they're noble, and sometimes they're just plain silly."[119]

As a priest of the Episcopal church, Noble Powell operated within a religious milieu in which everything did not depend upon the individual's immediate answer to the summons delivered in preaching. For Powell and his congregation the spiritual life comprised scripture and sacrament, prayer and praise, repentance and renewal, example and fellowship. A heart changed over time was the goal, accomplished with the assistance of divine grace, through the ministrations of the church and not without the human being's own patient striving. This form of spirituality had slow, gradual transformation as its aim, not a dramatic, emotional conversion experience. The Book of Common Prayer presented a structure to flawed human beings, a rhythm of contrition and thanksgiving; it offered a pattern of religious practice that was encouraged and supported by a primarily pastoral ministry.[120] Such was the life of worship and spiritual growth that Noble Powell participated in and fostered at St. Paul's.

A New Call

In the fall of 1930 Powell accepted a call to become rector of Emmanuel Church in Baltimore, Maryland. Earlier that year, his decade of rich experience in

Charlottesville was crowned with the birth of his and Mary's first child, Philip Noble. Soon after his son's arrival, the proud father wrote to his "dearest ones at home," letting them know that "I can't walk down the street without stopping all along to be congratulated."[121]

In his professional life also Powell had reason to be pleased. In recognition of his success in college mission work Virginia Seminary awarded him an honorary doctor of divinity degree in 1930. The University of Virginia gave him its prestigious Algernon Sidney Sullivan Medal for unselfish contributions to the welfare of the university and elected him to membership in the Raven Society and Phi Beta Kappa. But probably just as meaningful to him were the testimonials from students after they learned of his intention to leave the university—including the petition from thirty-five members of the football squad asking that he reconsider his decision.[122] The Varsity Club gave a dinner in his honor just before he left for Baltimore and presented him with a loving cup.

The student newspaper and the yearbook made much of his departure and the loss it represented. The lead editorial in *College Topics* for 3 November 1930 affirmed that "not only the members of St. Paul's Memorial Church but the whole University will be affected by the resignation" of Parson Powell. "During the years of his rectorate here, the Parson has so completely identified himself with the life of Virginia, that it is hard for anyone who has known him for any length of time to think of the University without him. In eleven years he has set a standard for future college rectors that will be either a severe handicap or a powerful inspiration to his successors." The writer observed that Powell had raised "the religious tone of the University at large" and attracted a large number of students to St. Paul's, where they "worship . . . of their own free will. One need only meet the Parson to understand one important force that draws the students to church."[123]

Corks and Curls, the yearbook, devoted an entire page to Powell in 1931. The parson's appeal to "students of all denominations [was] unbounded." The university felt the loss of "a man of the greatest personal charm as well as the highest moral fibre." Powell "found his way to the heart and soul of every member of the community as no one else has done." The parson "was at home in every gathering, intellectual, athletic or social." People sought his presence and advice when "matters of importance to the University" were being considered. "Many of the movements which have aided the progress of the University in recent years had their beginnings in the sitting room of the Parish House." Students valued him as an "intermediary with the faculty"; Powell "performed many a task which others dared not or could not undertake."

Upon leaving for Baltimore, Powell told the students that the purpose of the church was "to make them men in the true sense of the word." He spoke of real freedom as "the ability to match capacity with every opportunity in life": people who lack the capacity to do something—or have not developed the self-mastery required to make effective use of whatever talents and skills they have—will not be free to avail themselves of opportunities when they arrive. So both the church and the university, he seemed to be saying, exist to increase people's capacities to live lives that are free and abundant in good things. Unquestionably, by standing alongside them as friend and ally Powell enabled many students to realize more than they could have on their own. Thus, the student reporter concluded, "Mr. Powell will be greatly missed, not only by those who have attended St. Paul's, but by all those who have known him as friend."[124]

Powell's efforts at the university brought him wider recognition too, as St. Paul's developed a reputation as a highly successful operation—not least of all in the specific task of prompting the most promising college graduates to consider careers in the church.[125] During his years in Charlottesville, Powell began to be better known not only in the diocese of Virginia—where he was nominated for bishop coadjutor in 1926—but also in the national Episcopal church, through speaking engagements, conferences, committee memberships, and informal reports and comments.[126]

Powell's own vision was broadened during this period as he came to know many more of the church's—and some of the nation's—leading lights, chief among them the man who in 1927 succeeded William Cabell Brown as bishop of Virginia: Henry St. George Tucker (1874–1959), the former missionary bishop of Kyoto. Powell welcomed Tucker to St. Paul's Memorial Church not long after the latter's return from Japan in 1923 to fill a vacancy at Virginia Seminary in pastoral theology. Stepping in at the request of Bishop Brown, Tucker conducted a confirmation service at St. Paul's in May 1924.[127]

Charlottesville was familiar ground to St. George Tucker, who had achieved an outstanding record as a student at the University of Virginia (B.A. and M.A., 1895). A more profound thinker than Noble Powell and a bolder, more adventurous person as well, Tucker was also a more retiring figure. The two men were united, however, not only in their commitment to Christ and the church but also in the way in which they expressed that commitment: in their churchmanship both were Virginia evangelicals, Tucker (as it were) by nature and Powell by nature and adoption. Happily for them, their paths were to cross many times in ensuing years.

The one unfortunate legacy that Noble Powell left behind in Charlottesville was the debt St. Paul's Church owed on the parish house and the recently purchased rectory.[128] After whittling down the debt to twenty thousand dollars, the parish more than doubled its financial obligation by spending twenty-four thousand dollars for the rectory.[129] In the years following the onset of the Depression, fund-raising proved difficult. St. Paul's parishioners reduced the amount of their weekly contributions. To generate additional income, the church rented rooms in the upstairs of the parish house to students. In 1932 the parish cut its rector's salary by 10 percent and reduced all other expenditures by 20 percent; a year later the vestry had the parish telephone disconnected. In 1934, to raise money to pay the coal bill, members of St. Paul's held a spelling contest and charged twenty-five cents for admission.[130]

The debt, remembered a man whose father, Dr. Robert Bean, was a vestryman at the time, meant that "the church was stuck for two decades before it could do anything at all." Although Dr. Bean thought it was unnecessary, "Powell wanted a new rectory."[131] Molly Laird Gould, the daughter of William H. Laird, who succeeded Powell as rector and served until 1947, recalled that Powell was "an extremely charming man who left the church in a horrendous financial mess." Buying the rectory meant taking on a "terrible debt," which was "a burden for his successors."[132]

When Powell made the decision to ask for a rectory, the parish was in good financial condition, and it had made considerable progress on its other debt obligations. The rector undoubtedly felt that a house—which almost all parishes had in those days—would complete the infrastructure he had set out to build and also make the rectorship more appealing to his successors. After he left the parish he surely worried from time to time about the church's condition. In 1949 the Reverend Theodore H. Evans, rector of St. Paul's from 1947 to 1961, wrote to the bishop of Maryland to relieve his mind about the state of the parish's finances: "You will be glad to know that except for less than ten thousand dollars on the Parish House, St. Paul's is free of debt, and the balance is covered by pledges to be paid in the next two years."[133]

Changing Times

By 1931, when the Powell family left Charlottesville for Baltimore, the University of Virginia was beginning to change in significant ways. More students from the northeastern states were attending the university, admission requirements were raised, the first sorority opened to serve women students (who had been admitted to the university's graduate and professional schools since 1920), and new residence halls were constructed to accommodate a growing student body. In a few years the Rotunda would be deemed inadequate as the university's main library and a new facility built, named after the late President Alderman.[134]

One has the impression of a small, rather provincial institution turning a corner on the road to becoming a more diverse and estimable national university. A new journal of literature and discussion, the *Virginia Quarterly Review,* was established in 1925. And in the latter part of the decade students on the Grounds could hear lectures by some of the most stimulating thinkers of the day: Alfred North Whitehead, whose *Science and the Modern World* and *Religion in the Making* had recently appeared, soon to be followed by *Process and Reality;* Walter Lippmann, the editor of the *New York World* and author of *A Preface to Politics* and *A Preface to Morals;* and Bertrand Russell, whose liberal thoughts on marriage and morals had recently been published.[135]

The other institution that Noble Powell knew well, the Episcopal church, was also being transformed in the twenties, as was the Protestant establishment as a whole. To a large extent the special conditions obtaining at the highly traditional University of Virginia—where most of Powell's parishioners were respectful young white southern males who did not own cars—isolated him (and them) from these changes. Immigration, increasing pluralism, industrialization, and urbanization were not forces whose effects Powell had to contend with upon his arrival in Charlottesville in 1920. There he might have been more concerned with opposing the too-frequent interaction of some students with the local moonshiners.[136]

Nor do we have any reason to believe that the fundamentalist-modernist controversy, one of whose flashpoints occurred in 1925 at the Scopes Monkey Trial, caused the Parson, a southern moderate, any severe headaches. His form of ministry was personal and persistent, emphasizing a reasonable faith and a virtuous life: growing into friendship with God and one another. In 1922 Powell declared that he was neither "a 'Modernist' in the technical sense nor . . . a 'Fundamentalist.'" He said he was a "Churchman," who believed that Christ is present through the Holy Spirit in the church. A supporter of the higher criticism of the Bible, Powell referred to the historical-critical study of the New Testament and said that religious expression cannot be stationary or static; scholarship had given the theory of "mechanical inspiration . . . a mortal wound." Discussing biblical scholarship with the "average person in the pew," to whom it often comes as a shock, requires care and patience: "As shepherds of the flock of Christ we are to lead our sheep gently."[137]

Powell's manner and method made him a much more adaptable, irenic, and useful clergyman than he would have been as a revivalistic fundamentalist or a sectarian exclusivist, without compromising his Christianity or undermining the strength of his own witness. Had he been a minister in the Northern Baptist Convention or in the Presbyterian Church in the U.S.A. in the 1920s instead of a priest in the liturgy-centered Episcopal church, he would not have escaped these theological wars so easily.[138]

Episcopal clergy and lay leaders for the most part declined to be drawn into direct conflict with one another over theological modernism.[139] But as well-educated people they could not so handily dissipate the unease experienced by members and potential members of their flock who believed in science but were nonetheless discomforted by naturalistic worldviews, who concurred with Darwin's theory of evolution but sometimes felt a bit anxious regarding their own place in a cosmos apparently devoid of meaning, who accepted the historical criticism of the Bible but were not sure about some of the assertions of the Nicene Creed.

No one avoided entirely the acid effects of the religious battles of this period or the results of the other cultural changes that were taking place, including secularization and the decline of the mainstream churches' prestige and influence. In the wake of the sexual revolution of the 1920s—embraced by a postwar generation eager to accept popular versions of Freud's theories, see Hollywood movies, and escape in automobiles—the old morality came under assault, though millions of Americans were still keeping a strict Sabbath, observing personal modesty, and practicing temperance.[140]

A more subtle problem than the overthrow of conventional standards of behavior was the one represented by the publication and rise to best-seller status of Bruce Barton's *The Man Nobody Knows* (1925). Barton, an advertising executive, portrayed Jesus as a successful businessman who built up a thriving organization starting with only twelve followers: Jesus's question to his parents in the temple, "Wist ye not that I must be about my Father's *business*?" (Luke 2:49), was the book's epigraph.[141] For Powell and other leaders of a denomination that would maintain an establishmentarian ethos for another forty years, the challenge was perceiving and questioning what the commercialization of American society meant for human beings pulled by materialism and pushed by rampant competitiveness.[142]

More broadly, the urgent task for influential rectors and bishops was offering a critique of American culture that was rooted in the Christian vision, uncoupling or at least distinguishing between the cause of the church and the ambitions of the marketplace and the mighty. The First World War and concomitant social changes may actually have spurred a process of Protestant de-acculturation, enabling churches to assume a more independent stance vis-à-vis the other institutions and forces of society. Or, as the historian Winthrop

Hudson has argued, the weakening of old-line Protestantism may well have made the establishment denominations all the more vulnerable to the wiles of the secular world of business, politics, science, and the arts, permitting increasingly mobile, urban, and self-oriented Americans to slip their authentic Christian moorings.[143] In 1929 Charles Fiske, bishop of the Episcopal diocese of Central New York, lamented a situation in which "it is hard . . . to differentiate between religious aspiration and business prosperity. Our conception of God is that he is a sort of Magnified Rotarian. . . . Efficiency has become the greatest of Christian virtues."[144] In Baltimore Noble Powell would be much less isolated from all these challenges than he was in Charlottesville.

An Urban Agrarian

Powell lived the rest of his life in large cities, but for thirty years after leaving St. Paul's he spent a portion of each summer at "Briarpatch," his camp on Devil's Knob, near Love, Virginia. This way he could meet the demands of his new urban assignments while maintaining roots in well-loved soil. He always enjoyed telling people he was going to "spend the summer in Love with Mary." The cottage he had designed and helped to build, using foot-wide planks from chestnut trees cut down on the property and hauled to a nearby sawmill. The house lacked electricity but not the other requisites his wife had demanded, including a screened-in porch and running water (via a nearby spring and gravity), and it featured a large and handsome fireplace in the main room. The porch, raised twelve feet off the ground on locust poles and running across the front of the house, overlooked a broad and deep valley and the mountains of the Blue Ridge.[145]

This rustic environment—where Powell could read, grow corn and potatoes, chop wood, talk with his neighbors, and rest—suited him, as did the camp's proximity to Charlottesville. In the late 1940s he told a friend that when he retired he might buy a small house "close to the Rotunda," where he could live year-round; "the place"—meaning the University of Virginia and its surroundings—"gets on my heart and stays there."[146]

In 1930, Powell's last year in Charlottesville and about the time he bought his rural retreat, twelve southerners—including John Crowe Ransom, Robert Penn Warren, Andrew Lytle, and Donald Davidson—published a manifesto titled *I'll Take My Stand*. More poetic than programmatic, the book was a defense of traditional agrarian culture and humane values, which were under assault from the forces of the modern machine age.

The Vanderbilt Agrarians, as they were called, criticized bureaucratic centralization, mass conformity, and narrow specialization. They attacked an expanding industrial order that dehumanized workers, exploited nature, and worshiped only cash and the god of material progress. They sought a recognition of man's dependence on God and nature and valued manners, conversation, sympathy, family life, and a sense of vocation and duty. In no sense, as far as anyone knows, was Noble Powell a conscious follower of the Agrarians, but he was close enough to them in some of his attitudes that we can properly have their cause in mind when we think of a protest undertaken by Powell himself.[147]

Around 1950 the local electric cooperative—operating on the basis of funds provided by the Rural Electrification Administration, a federal program launched during the New Deal—cut down trees at Powell's summer retreat, put up an electric pole with a transformer, and installed power lines and electricity. Powell would have none of it. The authorities, he felt, should at least have sent him a postcard notifying him of their intentions. He resented the idea that the REA (their letters were on all the utility poles) could ride roughshod over rural people who had only an inexact notion of the extent of their own rights. So he went to court and sued the electric cooperative to have the lines taken out and punitive damages awarded, and he won. His lawyer, his old friend Bernard P. Chamberlain, called it "a salutary case." Powell's rural neighbors, however, were glad to get the electricity.[148]

Big-City Rector and Dean, 1931–41

Emmanuel Church, Baltimore

Emmanuel Church was located on the southeast corner of Cathedral and Read Streets, in the center of the see city of a historic diocese and at the heart of the Episcopal establishment. The stone edifice—a Gothic Revival structure erected in 1854—embodied many of the characteristics that made Episcopalianism an attractive alternative on the American religious scene. In times of war and peace, boom or bust, Episcopal churches seemed to stand for stability and refinement. An urban-based denomination, the Episcopal church in the United States had grown with the rise of the nation's industrial centers and the influx of people from the farms to the cities. Churches like Emmanuel were socially and aesthetically appealing; they drew people who were looking for sound liturgy, fine music, dignified preaching, and the society of their peers.

Situated in a fashionable neighborhood of large townhouses hard by Mount Vernon Place, Emmanuel Church was close to the Walters Art Gallery and the Peabody Institute and only six blocks north of the Roman Catholic cathedral and the Enoch Pratt Free Library. In the nineteenth century the parish had counted among its communicants many of the wealthy citizens who lived in the mansions near the Washington Monument. Louis McLane (1786–1857), the secretary of state under Andrew Jackson, and John H. B. Latrobe (1803–91), counsel to the Baltimore and Ohio Railroad and a leading philanthropist, were members of Emmanuel Church. The parish experienced the unusual honor of hosting two general conventions of the Episcopal church, in 1871 and 1892. Delegates to the latter convention—including the financier J. P. Morgan—heard Phillips Brooks preach from Emmanuel's pulpit and approved a new version of the Book of Common Prayer. Four years later, in 1896, the rector of Emmanuel baptized an infant named Bessie Wallis Warfield, who later became the Duchess of Windsor.[1]

Emmanuel's fabric was considerably improved during the tenure of Noble Powell's predecessor, Hugh Birckhead (1876–1929), who had accepted the call to the Baltimore parish in 1912. In deciding to come to Emmanuel, Birckhead, desiring to be the pastor of a flock that he could truly know, surrendered one of the most prominent posts in the Episcopal church, the rectorate of a highly influential parish several times larger than Emmanuel. For the previous six years Birckhead had served as rector of St. George's Church, Stuyvesant Square, Manhattan, where he had succeeded the famous builder of the "institutional church," William Storrs Rainsford.[2]

Like many other Episcopalians who expressed their devotion to the arts by focusing on ecclesiastical architecture and music, Birckhead possessed a well-developed taste for beauty and drama. He not only oversaw the completion of Emmanuel's 137-foot Christmas Tower, whose detailed images depicted the story of Jesus's birth, but also expanded and enhanced the chancel, creating a kind of religious theatre. There he installed a marble altar designed by Henry Vaughan, a new organ, an east window in the style of fifteenth-century stained glass, a reredos of Indiana limestone, and a carved oak pulpit. The reverential mood of the interior was reinforced by a large rood at the entrance to the chancel; the crucified Christ was shown attended by the kneeling figures of Mary his mother and John the beloved disciple. This affecting representation of divine love, an addition to the church that Birckhead particularly looked forward to seeing, he did not live to appreciate. The rood was dedicated in 1930, a year after Birckhead died while on a visit to Newport, Rhode Island, and only a few months before Noble Powell came to Emmanuel Church as rector.[3]

During Birckhead's tenure, Emmanuel continued to enjoy a reputation for its outstanding music and preaching. The rector was an eloquent speaker in his own pulpit and at the podia of other institutions throughout the United States; he was a popular choice for college and university commencements. Birckhead spoke out against indifference to the poor and for the rights of women (including the right to vote), urged blacks and whites to meet together to foster cooperation and mutual understanding, and promoted ecumenical relations between Protestants and Roman Catholics. He practiced his own ecumenism by forming a friendship with James Gibbons (1834–1921), the cardinal archbishop of Baltimore who was a noted supporter of American principles and institutions. Birckhead frequently walked down Cathedral Street and joined Gibbons for a late-afternoon stroll.[4]

On the same day that Birckhead delivered his first sermon as rector of Emmanuel Church, a young organist and choirmaster, Frederick L. (Fritz) Erickson, was commencing a forty-eight-year career in the parish. A dedicated and imaginative musician, Erickson drew thousands of people to Emmanuel to hear his work. For years the candlelight Christmas service at Emmanuel was the only one of its kind in Baltimore. With Erickson in charge of the music and Birckhead overseeing the staging, this annual service of Christmas carols became a favorite yuletide treat for local Christians of all denominations.[5] Of Erickson's achievement Noble Powell later said that many of those who came to hear his music returned to listen to more and stayed to catch perhaps just one note "'of that beautiful music for which our hearts yearn.'"[6]

In September 1930, just after the vestry of Emmanuel had extended its call to Noble Powell, the Maryland diocesan, Edward T. Helfenstein, wrote to the Charlottesville rector to let him know that the Baltimore parish presented "many opportunities": "Emmanuel Church, as you probably know, is in most respects the most important and influential one in the Diocese."[7]

In Powell's day, Emmanuel Church was, in the words of someone long familiar with its history, "*the* social parish in the city," with a congregation that comprised "the movers and the shakers." With these people Powell was a notable success. "It was difficult to follow Birckhead," this same individual pointed out, but Powell won their support. His parishioners "really worshiped their rector," and he was aided by the presence "at his side [of] Mary, a charming and genuine person who graced the rectory [and] never put her foot wrong." Powell was "the classic rector of that era. He exemplified the Gothic setting; Susan Howatch [the English author of novels featuring the Church of England in the twentieth century] would've written wonderful stuff about him."[8]

Among those "movers and shakers" were members of the vestry during Powell's years at Emmanuel. The man with whom Powell corresponded about his call to the parish was Henry D. Harlan (1858–1943), who was acting president of the vestry at the time. The former chief judge of the Supreme Bench of Baltimore, Harlan was a highly regarded figure in the community. For thirty-eight years he was president of the board of trustees of the Johns Hopkins Hospital and for thirty-nine years a trustee of Johns Hopkins University. Elected to the Standing Committee of the diocese in 1912, he was annually reelected until 1941, when he requested the convention's permission to retire.[9]

Other well-known lawyers on the vestry were Daniel R. Randall (1864–1936), who held a Ph.D. in history from Johns Hopkins and was a widely recognized authority on Maryland's past; D. K. Este Fisher (1860–1953), a founder of Gilman School and a well-known civic leader; and Robert W. Williams (1890–1983), a graduate of Gilman and Harvard University, a trustee of Johns Hopkins University and the Enoch Pratt Free Library, and a leading maritime lawyer who served as the first chairman of the Maryland Port Authority. Albert G. Towers (1873–1952), the president of the Mortgage Guarantee Company, was a former chairman of the Public Service Commission. Both he and the vestryman Cleveland R. Bealmear (1884–1947), the chairman of the Housing Authority of Baltimore, were active in city and state politics.[10]

The background of one vestry member, James A. Latané (1880–1955), must have been of particular interest to Noble Powell. The scion of a family long established in Virginia, Latané was not only the master in chancery for the equity courts of Baltimore City and for ten years the chairman of the Maryland Racing Commission; he was also the son of Bishop James A. Latané (1831–1902), a notable figure in the Reformed Episcopal church. Bishop Latané, scorning ritualism, had left the Episcopal church in 1874 and joined the breakaway Low Church movement, which sought—unsuccessfully—to unite evangelical Protestants. A powerful preacher and a devoted missionary, the senior Latané, based in Baltimore, served for twenty-two years as a Reformed Episcopal bishop.[11]

The story of the Latanés points to an important feature of Emmanuel Church's identity. In a diocese that still manifested signs of the old divisions between evangelicals and Anglo-Catholics, Emmanuel was a leading Low Church parish. The guest preacher at its first service in 1854 was the bishop of Ohio, Charles P. McIlvaine, an outstanding representative of the evangelical wing of the Episcopal church.[12]

The men who served on the Emmanuel vestry tended to hold on to their positions for long periods of time. Latané, for example, was a member of the vestry for twenty-seven years and parish registrar for thirty-six. Robert W. Williams would serve on the vestry continuously from early in the Powell years until 1959. Judge Harlan was a vestryman at Emmanuel from 1899 until his death in 1943.

More significantly, these men knew one another not simply as the result of their civic and parish affiliations but also as a consequence of their positions in society. As familiar with the Social Register as they were with the common telephone directory, they saw one another at the same clubs—Baltimore Country, South River, Elkridge, Mount Vernon, Merchants, University—and participated in the same society organizations, such as the Bachelors' Cotillion. Several were members of the Society of Colonial Wars. They lived in the same neighborhoods—typically, in Powell's day, in the suburban communities of Roland Park, Guilford, and Homeland rather than in the old urban neighborhoods of Mount Vernon and Bolton Hill. Not surprisingly, they were leaders in the diocese as well as in the parish, holding positions in the Churchman's Club, on the Standing Committee, and on the governing boards of Episcopal institutions. In politics they tended to be moderate-to-conservative Democrats (as was their rector) or, more rarely, moderate Republicans.[13]

Like his parishioners, Noble Powell was clubbable; he always protested that he was not a "joiner," but he clearly was. In Auburn he had affiliated with the Masons, and in Charlottesville he became a member of the Colonnade Club, the Varsity Club, and the Theta Chi social fraternity.[14] During his years at Emmanuel he participated in a host of civic, social, and ecclesiastical activities. He was a member, for example, of the Eclectic Club, an interdenominational group of leading clergy who gathered periodically for dinner and discussion. He served on the executive committee of the Baltimore Ministerial Association, and he was an officer of the YMCA. Diocesan conventions elected him a member of the Standing Committee and a deputy to the general conventions of 1934 and 1937. He served as president of the board of trustees of the Church Home and Hospital and as board president for a diocesan institution whose cheerless name was the Maryland Home for Friendless Colored Children. He was a member of the boards of the Church Mission of Help (an Episcopal adoption agency) and of the League of Nations Association. Active in the local chapter of the National Conference of Christians and Jews, Powell caused some raised eyebrows in 1937 when he exchanged pulpits for one service with Rabbi Morris S. Lazaron of the Baltimore Hebrew Congregation.[15]

Mary Powell also participated in a variety of social and church functions, including the Junior League, the Colonial Dames, the Daughters of the American Revolution, and the women's board of the Hospital for Crippled Children. When opportunity allowed, she tried to do some reading; in 1936 she took up a new novel by Margaret Mitchell called *Gone with the Wind*. By this time the Powells had a second son, Thomas Hooker, born in 1932.

Noble Powell was typical of those clergy who acted on behalf of society through their participation in established, mainstream organizations. Powell worked not to effect the transvaluation of values but to fix worthy principles even more securely in people's hearts. He was a keeper of standards—but only insofar as he perceived the rules and their results to be just. Where he did not, as in the exclusion of women from the National Council of the Episcopal church, he said so.[16]

In the main, though, he did not see a need for the church to array itself against the dominant norms of civilization. At the same time that the theologian H. Richard Niebuhr and his coauthors were writing *The Church against the World* (1935), Powell and his mainline colleagues were busy exercising what one historian has called "custodianship." These "agents of the Protestant establishment," William R. Hutchison has observed, were accustomed to assuming major responsibility not only for the nation's moral and religious life but for important social and educational functions as well.[17] Through at least the first two generations of the twentieth century, these denominational leaders viewed themselves as guardians of a sacred treasure. In the words of another historian of American religion, Edwin S. Gaustad, the churches of establishment Protestantism "saw the nation's destiny, the community's welfare, as peculiarly and inescapably *their* concern." The "quality of life in general, morals and manners, depended upon *their* leadership. Or so they earnestly believed and regularly assumed."[18]

As rector of Emmanuel Church, Powell ably carried out the functions of administration, liturgy, and pastoral care at which he had excelled in his previous post. He strengthened the Sunday school, held monthly meetings with a buffet supper for the young people, drew a substantial number of the men of the parish to monthly dinners featuring guest speakers, and organized a nursery class and a Boy Scout troop. The regular Sunday services included Holy Communion at 8 A.M., morning prayer (or Holy Communion once a month) at 11 A.M, and an evening service that was always well attended. There were also two weekday services of Holy Communion. At Emmanuel, Powell introduced intinction as a method of receiving the eucharistic elements; this practice had been favored when he was rector of St. Paul's in Charlottesville. During his first year in Baltimore he preached the sermon at the baccalaureate service, held at Emmanuel, for Johns Hopkins University.[19]

As a boy at Emmanuel, Huntington Williams Jr., who later became suffragan bishop of North Carolina, frequently heard his rector preach. Noble Powell, recalled Williams, had a "very effective" way of asking "a rhetorical question and then taking a nice pause while we thought about the question."[20]

The Great Depression, which by Christmas 1933 had thrown one of six Baltimore families onto the relief rolls, affected even wealthy Episcopal parishes like Emmanuel.[21] While the total number of Emmanuel's communicants during the Powell years held steady at about a thousand, the amount of money contributed dropped by 38 percent between 1929 and 1937, forcing a 10 percent reduction in staff salaries.[22]

During this difficult period of national crisis, a large minority of Episcopal clergy and laypeople swung leftward, and gatherings of the general convention and the House of Bishops adopted statements critical of capitalism and selfish profit-seeking and in favor of reforms sought by labor. Noble Powell, however, true to his roots in small-town, southern evangelical piety, refrained from speaking out directly on political or economic matters. In commenting on the story of the rich young man who could not let go of his earthly treasure (Matt. 19:16–24), Powell urged his listeners to be daring, to count not the cost, and to "make the principles of Jesus's life the principles of our lives"—but he declined to spell out in more concrete terms how Christians should go about accomplishing this task.[23]

Powell's pastoral presence, however, was surely a comfort to parishioners who worried about social unrest as much as they feared bankruptcy. Business leaders were afraid that riots would break out in the city; to help prevent civil disturbances, Baltimore banks provided money to unemployment relief funds.[24] A man who became a priest mainly through the influence of Noble Powell recalled that the rector of Emmanuel "was almost a god to people around here; he had an ability—a born instinct—to relate to people. There wasn't a warmer person in the world."[25] If the larger, public world contained discord, the church could provide a peaceful sanctuary, an island of serenity in the midst of turmoil.[26] One of Powell's most notable attributes was what Samuel Johnson called "good humour." "Without good humour," observed Johnson, "virtue may awe by its dignity, and amaze by its brightness; but must always be viewed at a distance, and will scarcely gain a friend or attract an imitator."[27]

An inability to gain a friend or attract an admirer was never Powell's trouble. While serving at Emmanuel Church, he delivered a tribute to Berryman Green on the occasion of the Virginia Seminary dean's retirement. Powell's words applied as much to their speaker as to the honoree: "Dr. Green never taught just a subject. He communicated a personality. He was his own best subject. . . . But it is as the Friend that his old students think most often of B. Green. He was, above all else, our friend. And isn't that the noblest of all: 'Ye are my friends.' Dr. Green has never been able to be an official. That has always been too menial a role for one of his lofty conception of man. He elected us to be his friends. . . . He didn't know anything about masses of men. His friendship is with individuals. He loves mankind because he loves men."[28] Powell's thoughts on friendship reflect much of significance concerning his own philosophy and practice of ministry.

Emmanuel's parishioners expressed their regard for Powell in 1935 when they installed new chimes in the Christmas Tower as a gift to their rector. Powell called these chimes one of the loveliest presents he had ever received: "Your gift is a true Christmas gift. There is nothing selfish about it. Its value is realized and its beauty appreciated only as it is used and shared by all."[29] Other members of Emmanuel revealed their admiration in more personal ways. George Wong, for example, named his newborn son Noble Powell Wong.[30]

When Powell left Baltimore in 1937 to go to the Washington Cathedral, he had to urge members of Emmanuel not to abandon the parish because he was leaving: people who did so, he said, he would have to regard as his own fail-ures.[31] And he told his parishioners that he now wished to give back to them, in trust, what they had given to him—his chimes: "As you listen to them week by week may they sing to you of the joy and happiness in my heart for the blessing that has been mine in serving here with you."[32] For the rest of their lives, Mary and Noble Powell would regard Emmanuel as their home parish.[33]

The Washington National Cathedral

Between the eighteenth-century Anglican parish church of Virginia or New England and the twentieth-century Cathedral Church of SS. Peter and Paul (the Washington National Cathedral) lay a chasm of time and taste. The gulf between the brick church of colonial days and the huge stone edifice of "the American century" separated not only two distinct architectural styles but also two sets of ideas regarding the function of a church building and the form of the people's worship.[34] Cathedrals, shunned after the Revolution as smack-ing of prelacy, started to gain favor in the 1850s, when the High Churchman James Lloyd Breck and other leaders of the "cathedral movement" preached the value of cathedrals as institutions by which Episcopalians could add dig-nity and beauty to the surrounding culture.[35]

Begun in 1907, thirty years before Noble Powell went there as dean, the Washington Cathedral reflected the ambition of the Episcopal church to be a national church capable of providing a splendid and hospitable place of worship for visitors of all denominations.[36] At the ceremony for the laying of the cornerstone of this stateside version of a fourteenth-century English Gothic cathedral, those in attendance—including much of the ecclesiastical establishment of the United States—heard a main address delivered by Pres-ident Theodore Roosevelt, the champion of aggressive American action at home and abroad. Twenty thousand people, one of the largest crowds ever seen in the nation's capital, celebrated the start of the "great church for na-tional purposes," which the federal city's architect, Pierre L'Enfant, had ad-vocated in 1791.[37]

Standing tall atop Mount St. Alban, the highest point in the city, the Washington National Cathedral, in the words of two social historians, be-came "a semiofficial repository of national pride, national hope, and national unity."[38] In the vaults of the cathedral that some called "America's Westmin-ster Abbey" reposed the earthly remains of Adm. George Dewey, hero of the battle of Manila in the Spanish-American War, and of President Woodrow Wilson, crusader for peace and democracy.[39] Even before its walls rose above the ground the cathedral had begun to serve as the place where Americans gathered to commemorate significant events in the life of their country: on the cathedral close was held the national service to observe the end of the First World War.[40]

In the cathedral's founding documents resided earnest hopes for concord among sects and nations—a mission and a challenge that appealed to Noble Powell. "Because of its broad Charter [from the U.S. Congress] and its strategic location," declared Powell, the Washington Cathedral was in a special position to bring together "Christians of all names." To Powell, the lack of unity among the various denominations coupled with "the fact that responsibility must somewhere be lodged until that unity . . . is attained" created for the Episcopal church an opportunity for ecumenical witness: "it is the privilege of the Episcopal Church to assume that responsibility," but the church must do so "with a full sense of the great trust committed to it, . . . look[ing] forward to the time when, without compromise, but with complete conviction, this Cathedral may be accepted by Christians everywhere as what it is now: 'A House of Prayer for All People.'"[41]

Before Powell became dean of the cathedral and warden of the adjacent College of Preachers, he stressed to the cathedral chapter that he would strive to make the cathedral the chief mission church of the diocese, the regular site of outstanding musical services, the center of the kind of intelligent and direct Christian interpretation that "will make the nation listen," and the focal point of church unity. "National Cathedral," he told them, must become more than "just a popular name"; the reality behind the name "must be won" and become a "spiritual fact" in a way that it was not yet. The cathedral's advantage in attempting to be a harbinger of unity was that there was "no other place on the American continent where it is possible to do anything *nationally*." The cathedral could become a "conference ground for other faiths." But above all, Powell said, "the primary stress [should] be on the spiritual side of the Cathedral's life. This [is] to take precedence over everything else, and nothing else [should] interfere [with it]."[42]

Powell's approach to the deanship was summed up in a few lines he wrote to a canon of the cathedral in 1938: "While I appreciate fully the vital importance of organization, nevertheless, we must give first place . . . to creating friendly contacts and keeping in its primary place the spiritual side of our work."[43] As dean and later as bishop, Noble Powell humanized administration. His own relentless commitment to the job at hand, his intelligence and good judgment, and his formidable leadership skills drove him and his programs forward. But his love of people and his simple friendliness, his kindly use of humor and his self-confidence mixed with honest humility carried others—from canon precentor to herb shop volunteer—along with him.

Caring more about people than about organization, Powell kept himself and others focused on the principal goals of the cathedral without having to preside over endless meetings about management objectives. Sincere words of praise and gratitude accomplished more for him than the language of bureaucracy could have. Powell knew how to summon forth the best efforts of his colleagues, who recognized his integrity and welcomed his joyful spirit.

Characteristic aspects of Powell's personality were represented in letters he wrote to friends and family shortly before his installation as dean. To an old friend in Charlottesville he said, "I don't know what sort of a Dean I am going to make, but I hope I shall continue to be human—that's the one requirement. I do get a great kick out of life and if one person knows it I am really delighted."[44] A letter from about the same time to his family in Lowndesboro contained a mixture of humility and pride: "It is a most wonderful opportunity on Mt. St. Alban but I feel so puny and tiny when I think of myself in it. It is without doubt, the most strategic and important place in the American church and I feel dumb and numb when I think of myself there with all that will be on my shoulders." He assured his Low Church kinsmen he would not allow himself to be tempted by the trappings of office: "I have . . . the right to put on all the dog in the world in the way I dress. But I have an idea it is expensive and I would be more comfortable in what I am accustomed to so will hold to that."[45]

Limited funds during the Powell years meant that greater progress was made in realizing such intangible values as goodwill and sound learning than in furthering the construction of the cathedral, which was only a little more than one-third finished when Powell arrived on the close. The apse, the sanctuary and great choir, and the north transept had been built; the crossing was largely finished, and three crypt chapels were in use. Toward the end of Powell's tenure, work commenced to complete the north porch.[46] At the end of World War II the cathedral still lacked a south transept, towers, and almost all of its nave.

Since 1920 plans for the cathedral had been prepared by the Boston architectural firm of Frohman, Robb, and Little, who succeeded the original architects, George F. Bodley and Henry Vaughan. Philip H. Frohman was a dedicated servant of the cathedral, but his highly deliberate manner often frustrated his ecclesiastical superiors. "I had an epistle which should have been in five volumes from Frohman about the south transept steps," Dean Powell complained to one of his canons. "Thank him for his letter, if you see him. I haven't time to write. If he wrote less and worked more, I would not have to write so much apologizing for our delays."[47]

Despite the lack of major progress in construction, Powell was witness to a number of important events in the history of the cathedral, including services at which the carved rood screen, the Aeolian-Skinner great organ, and—two weeks after Germany invaded Poland—the children's chapel were dedicated. He also took part in the dedication service for the carved stone tomb of Lt. Norman Prince (1887–1916), the courageous aviator who helped to found the Lafayette Escadrille, a group of American flyers who served with the French army before U.S. entry in World War I. Surmounting the Prince sarcophagus was the heroic figure of a uniformed young airman standing on the back of a powerful eagle in flight. Participating with the dean and the bishop of Washington in this service were Maj. Gen. Adelbert de Chambrun of France and Gen. John J. Pershing, who had commanded the American Expeditionary Force in Europe.[48]

On 22 October 1941 Noble Powell had the honor of taking part in the service in which his friend Henry St. George Tucker was installed in his new chair in the cathedral. Powell's assignment was to greet Tucker at the south door before the presiding bishop was officially escorted to his stall. The general convention of 1940 had passed a resolution designating the National Cathedral as the seat of the presiding bishop, whose administrative offices remained in New York City.[49]

At the time of this service, which was attended by over two thousand people, Tucker had more on his mind than the enhanced authority and prestige of the presiding episcopate. Committed throughout 1939 and into 1940 to U.S. neutrality in the European conflict, by early 1941 he had come to see Hitlerism as a malignancy that had to be removed by force of arms. In the summer of 1941, in a shortwave broadcast to the English-speaking peoples of the world, Tucker said that Americans realized they must aid Great Britain even if that assistance led to Americans' joining the fight.[50]

For their part, Mary and Noble Powell were especially concerned about the plight of British refugee children. In 1940, during the harrowing months of the battle of Britain, Powell attempted to make arrangements for scores of these children—from the preparatory school of Winchester Cathedral—to be accommodated on the grounds of the Washington Cathedral. He and Mary wanted to take one or more British children into their own home for the duration of the war.[51] Noble Powell entreated a friend in England, the distinguished Oxford University theologian Leonard Hodgson, to make inquiries about helping "some boy around eight to eleven" who needed a safe home.[52]

Powell believed that "England is fighting the battle for the best which the world has known. I would that America might help far more." Like Tucker, he knew the sympathy of the American people was "overwhelmingly for England." He told an English chaplain in September 1940 that "the splendid courage and confidence which [the British people] are showing will, regardless of what the outcome may be—and we are confident that in the end Britain will win—adorn a bright page in the annals of mankind." Three times daily "our prayers are ascending for you in the Cathedral."[53]

Failing to secure a boy from England, the Powells set aside the amount of money they would have spent to care for the child and used it on behalf of the British people. Mary became absorbed in putting together "Bundles for Britain," while her husband continued to hope the United States would do more to support the United Kingdom.[54]

Powell's position in Washington during these years of excitement and anxiety must have made him unusually aware of any event of national or international significance.[55] As the dean of the Washington Cathedral, he was surrounded by people who represented—or at least had once been part of—the country's civil, military, and ecclesiastical power structure. John J. Pershing, promoted to general of the armies after the First World War, had become an Episcopalian while serving in the Philippines, where he came under the influence of Bishop Charles Henry Brent; in Powell's day he was one of the Washington Cathedral's most vigorous supporters. Another chapter member who devoted much time to the cathedral was the Philadelphia lawyer and former U.S. senator George Wharton Pepper (1867–1961), who has been described as "the grandest of grand old men: his last two names belonged to the oldest families in Philadelphia."[56] He was the cathedral's chief lay representative and fund-raiser. William R. Castle, the former undersecretary of state, was also an active member of the cathedral chapter.

The thirty-member council of the Washington Cathedral included the Methodist statesman John R. Mott, who in the late thirties found time for cathedral business in between his trips to international ecumenical conferences. In Mott's view, this worldwide ecumenical activity was all part of "that for which this great Cathedral will increasingly stand": the desire of Christians "to draw together in ever closer understanding, fellowship and unity."[57] From Mount St. Alban, Mott believed, the call to unity might be heard more clearly than from any other place in America.[58] Other council members included the liberal theologian William Adams Brown, a Presbyterian who, like Mott, was a prominent figure in international ecumenism, and the Baptist Douglas Southall Freeman, the editor of the *Richmond News-Leader* and biographer of Robert E. Lee.

Andrew W. Mellon, a Presbyterian, died only a few months after Powell assumed the deanship; he had served as treasurer of the cathedral and was a generous patron. The chaplain of the United States Senate, ZeBarney T. Phillips, was a member of the cathedral chapter as well as rector of the Church of the Epiphany in Washington and president of the House of Deputies of the general convention; he would succeed Powell as dean in November 1941. Powell's faithful colleague Anson Phelps Stokes (1874–1958) had served as a top-level administrator at Yale University for two decades before becoming canon residentiary of the cathedral in 1925. An active proponent of urban renewal and interfaith cooperation, Stokes was the son of a rich New York banker who had devoted his leisure time to sailing the seas, founding the Metropolitan Museum of Art, and fighting Tammany Hall.

Eleanor Roosevelt, an Episcopalian, was the honorary chair of the women's committee of the cathedral, which had undertaken the special task of providing the funds for completion of the north porch. Roosevelt heard Dean Powell preach in April 1938—not at the cathedral but at the Knights Templar service on Easter morning at the Arlington National Cemetery. She referred to his sermon in her "My Day" column: "[Dean Powell] emphasized the thought that the story of the Resurrection meant the seeking of Jesus and that He was not to be found in death, but in life where people experience all of life's joys and sorrows."[59]

But the people that Powell most enjoyed working with were the priests who came to Washington for a week of study and spiritual refreshment at the College of Preachers.

The College of Preachers

A participant in the first conference held at the College of Preachers in June 1925, Noble Powell soon became a member of its council of advice, an informal group that lent support to the warden of the college, Philip M. Rhinelander, the former bishop of Pennsylvania. Powell's early and close involvement with the College of Preachers, as advisor and occasional conference speaker, meant that he was well known to the leadership of the Washington diocese years before he moved to Emmanuel Church in Baltimore. Henry St. George Tucker and Leonard Hodgson were also members of the advisory council, as was Albert Lucas, the headmaster of St. Albans School and later Bishop Powell's archdeacon in Maryland.

By the time Powell succeeded Rhinelander as warden in 1937, nearly three thousand clergy, in groups of fifteen to twenty, had enjoyed the experience of taking part in a week of postordination training at the college. There they worked on their preaching, subjecting their efforts to useful critiques, and followed a simple rule of prayer and study away from the radio and the interruptions of parish life. Powell's own preaching benefited from the repeated opportunity to offer and hear criticism of sermons at the college.[60]

In 1929 a gift from the New York layman Alexander Smith Cochran had provided for a stately building for the college on the cathedral close. Although the college had an academic as well as a spiritual purpose, the college and cathedral shared the same larger goal: to serve as a unifying force in the church.[61]

Powell won wide recognition for the quality of his work as warden of the College of Preachers. By the time he left Washington he was one of the best-known and most highly respected clergymen in the Episcopal church. During his four years at the college, many present and future leaders of the Anglican Communion—including Stephen Bayne, J. W. C. Wand, and Donald Coggan—passed through its stone portals and participated in its programs.[62] Impressive men also worked with Powell on the staff of the college, preeminent among them the Reverend Theodore O. Wedel (1892–1970), a Yale Ph.D. who had served as secretary for college work on the National Council of the Episcopal church. Wedel became the director of studies at the College of Preachers in 1939 and three years later succeeded Powell as warden, holding that post until retiring in 1960.[63]

Episcopal Elections

When, in early 1937, a nominating committee of the diocese of Michigan wanted to shortlist him for bishop coadjutor, Noble Powell had no difficulty making up his mind to turn them down. Michigan held little appeal for him, and by this time he was on his way to Washington.[64] Two years later, when Louisiana elected him bishop, he had a tougher time deciding. Chosen on the fifth ballot in April 1939, he had mixed feelings about the call. He had not sought the post, and he was reluctant to leave his work at the cathedral and particularly at the College of Preachers when he still had much he wanted to accomplish.

But becoming the bishop of a southern diocese—Louisiana's first diocesan was Leonidas Polk, the "fighting bishop" of the Confederacy—interested him considerably. Moreover, the opportunity to get out from under the authority of James E. Freeman, bishop of Washington, and run his own diocese pulled this planter's son toward accepting.[65] Bishop Freeman (1866–1943) had a sizable ego and a need to control. An in-house history of the cathedral used such adjectives as "large," "forceful," and "hard-driving" to describe him. In 1936 Freeman had maladroitly pushed aside Powell's predecessor, George C. F. Bratenahl, as the longtime dean approached his seventy-fourth birthday. The bishop's friendly biographer described Freeman's preaching style in a way that suggested there was more drama than depth in his art.

Possessing a booming voice and employing increasingly vigorous gestures in the pulpit, Freeman clearly enjoyed playing the showman.[66]

Powell declined the Louisiana election, citing his desire to complete a program for the expansion of the College of Preachers.[67] But an additional reason for refusing was the split in the Louisiana diocese. By the fourth ballot, Powell, the Low Church candidate, had the solid support of the laity; but the clergy were evenly divided between him and the Baltimore High Churchman Don Frank Fenn. Following a brief recess, delegates elected Powell on the next ballot. Historians of the Episcopal church in Louisiana have concluded that Powell "feared he would find too divided a diocese to serve effectively."[68]

Another probable factor that would not have been stated publicly was the weakness of the Episcopal church in Louisiana relative to the denomination's position in Virginia and Maryland, where, as a proportion of the general population, Episcopalians were roughly three times more numerous than in Louisiana. The following September, Louisianans again elected Powell their bishop, and again he said no. Two years later, when a strong call came from the diocese of Maryland, he accepted.[69]

4

Bishop, 1941–63

Indian Summer

Often referred to as "the last bishop of the old church," Noble Powell flourished during the final years of a cultural and ecclesiastical epoch distinguished
by personal authority and widespread social cohesion.[1] In temperament and
outlook he could not have been better suited to his era. The mood of the
period was conservative, marked, in the words of one commentator, by "an
unself-conscious rootedness in the traditions of society"; but the times were
dynamic as well, full of hope and anxiety.[2] Following the trauma of the Second World War and in the face of fresh threats posed by the Soviet Union,
people longed for stability, normalcy, and fellowship. This desire to find a
place in the world, to belong, worked in favor of the traditional denominations, with their friendly, energetic, businesslike clergy.[3]

As a result, higher percentages of Americans attended church than ever
before,[4] and church membership grew in the 1950s at a faster rate than the
national population.[5] "Faith" became the weapon of choice in a spiritual arsenal that political leaders from the president of the United States to the may-
ors of small towns turned to in their crusade against all those forces—especially idolatrous Communism—that threatened the American Way of Life.[6]

In the booming suburbs, young families in tract houses embraced a gen-
eralized civic piety along with television, labor-saving appliances, shopping
malls, and a higher standard of living. Denominations as well as individuals benefited not only from economic growth and rising levels of dispos-
able income but also from the popular culture's commitment to traditional
values and the nuclear family. New settlements of growing families meant
new churches, which functioned as safe, moderately challenging environ-
ments for the nurture of children and parents together.[7] Mainline churches
enjoyed the experience of this "American high," absorbing the era's confidence and fighting against its fears—of war, of economic depression, of
crime and delinquency, and of anomie.[8]

By 1960, toward the end of Powell's episcopate, one in eighty-six Americans was a member of the Episcopal church, the highest communicant-to-general-population ratio since the denomination's organization following the American Revolution.[9] The baptized membership of the church in the diocese of Maryland increased by 40 percent during Powell's years in office, to almost sixty-seven thousand; and the number of diocesan clergy grew from 127 to more than two hundred.[10] During this same period Powell confirmed close to thirty thousand children and adults—"a wonderful potential," he declared, "for the Kingdom of God."[11]

Following the Second World War the Episcopal church in Maryland and throughout the United States was revitalized not only through membership growth and building campaigns but also through renewed attention to liturgy, theology, and Christian education. The fifties and early sixties were an Indian summer for the mainline churches in America and certainly for the Episcopal diocese of Maryland. The season was late autumn, but the weather most days was calm and mild, the atmosphere warm and hazy.

A constitutionally cheerful man in an optimistic era, Powell was, many Marylanders have observed, the right bishop for the postwar period. Well grounded in tradition, he was at the same time hopeful and forward-thinking.[12] Marylanders—clergy and laypeople and seminarians—were proud of their bishop and trusted him implicitly; they respected his authority and relished his presence among them. "People easily called him 'our beloved bishop,'" a later Maryland diocesan recalled, "and they meant that."[13]

The Diocese of Maryland

To be bishop of the diocese of Maryland—which extended, as Powell put it, "from the sparkling waters and silver sands of the Chesapeake to the verdant valleys and dazzling snows of our Western Mountains"—was especially satisfying.[14] Ninth in an illustrious line of diocesans that stretched back to Thomas J. Claggett, the first Episcopal bishop consecrated on American soil, Powell included among his predecessors the renowned High Church leader William Rollinson Whittingham, many of whose initiatives and episcopal concerns foreshadowed Powell's own a century later.[15]

A less-well-known diocesan, William Paret, had a long and important episcopate (1885–1911), during which he helped to overcome disruptive divisions between High and Low Church factions in the diocese and devoted himself to church work on behalf of the poor and African Americans. Paret's successor was John Gardner Murray, bishop from 1911 to 1929 and the first elected presiding bishop of the Episcopal church in 1925; in this role Murray provided solid spiritual and administrative leadership.

In Maryland Bishop Murray's archdeacon for the country churches was the genial and straightforward Low Churchman Edward Trail Helfenstein, who became diocesan just as the Depression was beginning and who served to the height of the Second World War, proving to be as unlucky in the temporal lot he drew as his successor, Noble Powell, was fortunate. During these years of stress and deprivation, it was all Bishop Helfenstein could do to hold his diocese together. Into old age he struggled on, and in the end patience and resolve—virtues cultivated in his cherished garden—won the day, and his last utterance before he died was "victory."[16]

The clergy who served under Powell also included some notable figures. From the outset of his episcopate he worked with a dedicated corps of priests, some of whom had national reputations. Don Frank Fenn, a theologically conservative churchman, was rector of the Church of St. Michael and All Angels, a large Anglo-Catholic parish in downtown Baltimore.[17] In 1941 Arthur Barksdale Kinsolving was still holding forth at Old St. Paul's, and Theodore Parker Ferris had not yet left Emmanuel for Trinity Church, Boston. Cedric E. Mills, who later became the first bishop of the Virgin Islands, was rector of one of the nation's most historic African-American churches, St. James's, Baltimore, which was founded in 1824 and guided in the first half of the twentieth century by George Freeman Bragg Jr.[18]

During his episcopate, Powell had the satisfaction of leading not only such parochial luminaries as the Baltimore rectors Harry Lee Doll (Old St. Paul's) and Bennett Sims (Church of the Redeemer) but also a host of less prominent but equally well-rounded and effective men. These priests had entered the ministry at a time in the life of the nation when a career in the Episcopal church, notwithstanding the miserable salaries, was still an attractive option for the best and the brightest.

The Second World War and the Immediate Postwar Era

Powell's years as bishop may have included a long stretch of Indian summer, but they began in a wintry season of exhaustion and dread. "Among many of our clergy," Bishop Helfenstein reported in 1941, "there is a spirit of defeatism."[19] Neither a defeatist nor a utopianist, Powell was one of those clergymen who had benefited from the annealing experience of national trial. A younger bishop, John Maury Allin, said that Powell was typical of many of the bishops of the 1940s and 1950s who had come through the Depression: they had a perduring strength, an uncommon wisdom and stability, that served the church well.[20]

The Second World War brought a shortage of clergy for parish work and

a flood of servicemen and workers into Maryland's camps, military instal-
lations, and factories. It placed heavy demands on some parishes and clergy,
often the smaller churches lacking adequate facilities and funds. But the war
gave a big boost to the economy and converted Baltimore into a thriving
arsenal of democracy. The Bethlehem-Fairchild shipyards, for example, hired
forty-seven thousand workers to build nearly five hundred ships; workers
poured into the city from the rural South, some renting rooms in twelve-hour
shifts. In Essex and Middle River, east of Baltimore City, residents lived in
neighborhoods called Victory Villa and Aero Acres, and were among the fifty-
three thousand employed to build bombers in a Glenn L. Martin aircraft
plant. When the war ended, people worried about whether the jobs would
last and about the intentions of a new enemy.[21]

Speaking to his diocesan convention in 1945, Powell acknowledged these
anxieties of the postwar era: "A new world is being born now, not in the
morning of new hope and fresh energy, but in the night of doubt, puzzle-
ment, perplexity, and disillusionment. The dust of a crumbling civilization
is in our eyes and throats. Its noise is like thunder in our ears." People, he
said, "have always known they needed a Saviour," and recently they believed
they had found one in knowledge: "Let a man know the truth," they thought,
"and his life would be full." Human beings discovered amazing facts but
"harnessed [them] not to salvation but to destruction."[22]

Two years later, as Americans were approaching the height of their commitment to science as an answer to human problems, Powell spoke to his
diocesan convention about the incapacity of science and technology to effect peace and brotherhood: "Today we are disillusioned, and this failure of
science to save us has done something to our hearts and minds." If "technical progress" has helped "to make mankind one," it has done so at the cost
of further dehumanization. More valuable than the power to transmit information from one end of the earth to the other, he said, was the capability of
having something "worthwhile to say"; and more important than the achievement of travel to distant corners of the planet at high rates of speed was "what
kind of man makes the trip."[23]

Powell was also deeply concerned about another persistent theme addressed by popular and highbrow writers of this era: the individual versus
the crowd. "Jesus didn't gallop with the gang," he had told students at the
University of Virginia, and thirty years later he continued to worry about the
dangers of social conformity, the threat to the self posed by commercial culture, big government, and the huge organization.[24]

These larger worries were set aside for a time in 1946 when Geoffrey Fisher, archbishop of Canterbury, made his first visit to the United States and

included Baltimore on his itinerary.[25] Fisher addressed the general convention in Philadelphia; his visit made American Episcopalians more aware of their relationship to the worldwide Anglican Communion. On 18 September 1946 he and Bishop Powell rode to Baltimore from Philadelphia on a special car of the Baltimore and Ohio Railroad. They were met at Mount Royal Station by a welcoming committee of clergy and laity that included the governor of Maryland, a United States senator, and the mayor of Baltimore. That night, following Fisher's remarks to a packed hall, a festive dinner was held in the Sheraton-Belvedere in honor of the archbishop.[26] Well-attended diocesan celebrations were a regular feature of the Powell episcopate.

Following the contentious general convention of 1946, which had turned down union with the northern Presbyterians, Powell began convening a group of up-and-coming clergy from around the country to examine problems and questions facing the church during the period of transition from the presiding episcopate of Henry St. George Tucker to that of Henry Knox Sherrill. This group, which called itself "The Thirty," met annually for several years and helped to unify the church's younger leadership.[27]

"Looking back over the years," commented one former member of The Thirty, Bishop John Seville Higgins, "I see Bishop Powell as one who might well have been elected Presiding Bishop and given the Church outstanding leadership in that position. Bearing, character, looks, compassion, faith—he had it all."[28]

Powell was mentioned by some in 1946 as a possible successor to Henry St. George Tucker as presiding bishop, but he would not have been excited by the prospect.[29] For Powell and Episcopalians generally—especially in these years—the diocese was the real center of church life, or, more accurately, the diocese and the parish together, for this denomination always had a strong congregationalist streak in its makeup. Although committed by its constitution and canons to a unitary form of government in which legal sovereignty resided in the triennial assembly known as the general convention, the Episcopal church in the United States functioned as a confederation of dioceses. The diocesan bishop stood for the church universal and provided within the diocese a special focus, a sign of unity; he personified the church as a whole and represented its continuity across time and space. Therefore to him, the personal bearer of apostolic ministry, was entrusted the power of conferring ministries through ordination. Similarly, he alone had the authority to confirm, because the confirmand was admitted to the whole church, not to a local Christian group. Anglicans stressed common worship and sacramental unity more than doctrinal conformity, and the bishop was the key sacramental person.[30]

To Noble Powell, then, the presiding episcopate would not have seemed a promotion. Most Episcopalians probably did not even know the name of their presiding bishop—and Powell already held a post that combined all the things he loved, including opportunities to build the church and to care for its people. Powell chaired or served on various boards and committees of the national church; but to him, a southerner, the local reality was the truest and the most rewarding. Once installed in office he had no desire to go elsewhere.

The diocese of Maryland provided him with challenges sufficient to the day. By the late 1940s and early 1950s Powell's own remarks reflected the mixture of hope and hard-nosed realism that pervaded the religious discourse of the era. Preachers recognized the turmoil in the present and reasons for people to be afraid, but they also began to point to the promises that existed alongside the problems of the day. In 1950 Powell said Americans were living "in the midst of what is perhaps the vastest revolution in the history of mankind. . . . This fact presents us with two possibilities—tragedy and opportunity. . . . [I]f we Christians are alert and accept our chance, the Gospel of Jesus Christ can be woven into the fabric of the garment of life of tomorrow."[31]

The Bishop Claggett Diocesan Center

Powell always saw a basis for hope in the young people of the church. He cared about no aspect of his work more than he cared about the two diocesan schools, Hannah More Academy and St. James School, which he labored mightily and successfully to save and strengthen.[32] And in 1950 the diocese came into possession of a piece of real estate that would serve well as a church camp and conference center for young people and adults.

Located seven miles south of the city of Frederick and comprising almost three hundred acres, the grounds had been the site of a year-round farm school for less-fortunate boys. Somewhat improved but still appealingly rustic, the property opened as the Bishop Claggett Diocesan Center in 1952. Five years later, more than four thousand members of the Episcopal church in Maryland gathered at Claggett on Diocesan Family Day and attended the dedication of an outdoor altar, which contained a stone or brick from every parish and mission in the diocese as well as a tiny bit of marble that Powell had picked up years before from the floor of the Colosseum in Rome. The altar's backdrop was the Sugar Loaf Mountains—"truly," Bishop Powell said, "a reredos fashioned by the Hand Divine!" Its cross, silhouetted against the mountains, was made from two cedar trees that had been planted on the grounds of the episcopal residence in Baltimore by Bishop Helfenstein.[33] "I long," Bishop Powell said one day, "to look over the ramparts of heaven and listen to laughing children on the grounds of Claggett."[34]

The Episcopal Advance Fund

Fund-raising campaigns, such as the one launched by the diocese of Maryland in 1958 for a revolving fund for new churches, also reflected the era's hopes for the future. Churches across the United States spent $935 million on new church buildings in 1959, up from $409 million in 1950 and $26 million in 1945.[35] Led by the prominent Baltimore lawyer Carlyle Barton and based on an extensive survey of the Maryland diocese carried out several years before, the campaign for the $1.7 million Episcopal Advance Fund was undertaken to meet three objectives: to construct new churches and to provide additional facilities for existing churches in areas where the population was burgeoning,[36] to contribute to the needs of the national church, and to build a new diocesan center on the grounds of the recently consecrated Cathedral of the Incarnation.[37]

While these plans proved to be overly ambitious, the diocese was able to assist some new congregations in the construction of facilities. The Advance Fund provided a church building for Holy Trinity, in the Essex–Middle River area, and for new structures in more than a dozen other locations, from Anne Arundel County, south of Baltimore, to western Maryland's Garrett County. And the diocese made gifts to the national church. But not enough funds were raised to build a diocesan center on the cathedral close, so the old mansion downtown, at 105 West Monument Street, was renovated.[38]

Ecumenism

The last five years of Powell's episcopate saw dramatic new opportunities open up in the field of interchurch relations, and he regarded his ecumenical work as one of his most important episcopal achievements. Brought up in the practical ecumenism of Lowndesboro and actively committed to interfaith cooperation since his days as a student lay reader, Powell became more deeply engaged in such work during his tenure at the Washington Cathedral and later as bishop. Disappointed in 1946 when negotiations for union with the northern Presbyterians failed to achieve their goal, Powell accepted the judgment of the majority of his colleagues that the final report of the joint commission contained ambiguous language and had been presented to the general convention without sufficient time provided for its careful consideration. He was willing to be patient, however, believing that unity "must come in God's way, it must come in accordance with the will of Christ, it must come when our minds, our hearts, and our hands are knit together in mutual understanding and trust and love and purpose."[39]

Historians of American Christianity generally agree that defeating the distrust and allaying the antagonism between Protestants and Roman Catholics has been the most important ecumenical development since the Second World War. Bad feelings and mutual suspicion persisted well into the postwar years and ended only in the early sixties.[40]

Noble Powell, however, enjoyed unusually close and affectionate relations with Roman Catholics in Maryland well before the breakthroughs of the Second Vatican Council (1962–65). He undermined hostility and misunderstanding by cultivating friendships with Catholic leaders, including the archbishops of Baltimore: Michael Joseph Curley (1921–47), Francis Patrick Keough (1947–61), and Lawrence Joseph Shehan (1961–74). After Powell's death, the Diocesan Council rightly remarked that "Long before the balmy days of the Ecumenical Movement, which is a popular cause today, Noble Powell, through the proffer of his own warm friendship, drew men of diverse Faiths into a warmer fellowship."[41] A strong rapport and friendship developed between Powell and Archbishop Keough, who made certain that the bishop of Maryland was given the front pew as his honored guest at the dedication of the new Cathedral of Mary Our Queen in November 1959.[42]

The man who became the first rector of that cathedral, Monsignor Thomas A. Whelan (1906–87), was a key figure in the activities of the archdiocese for many years. When asked in 1979 who among all the persons he had known "stood out in their character, their ideas and their effect on you," Whelan named Keough and Shehan—and Noble Powell, whom he had met forty years before. Born into a socially prominent Baltimore family, Whelan was a graduate of Calvert and Gilman schools and Princeton University; his mother, whose family were Episcopalians, had attended Emmanuel Church when Powell was rector there in the thirties.

"Bishop Powell," Whelan told the interviewer, "used to write me frequently about different topics. [He] was certainly to me a great influence . . . one of the most charitable, kindest men that I have ever met." Whelan recounted an interesting exchange the two men had around 1958: "[When Pope John was elected, I met] Bishop Powell . . . on Cathedral Street and he said, 'Tom, this is one of your greatest Popes.' I thought he was faking. I said 'Bishop, this is an old man from no particular region.' He said, 'You mark my words— he'll be one of your greatest Popes.' That proved to be right. Bishop Powell, to me, had great insight into character." When Powell retired, Monsignor Whelan gave a luncheon in his honor in the rectory of the Cathedral of Mary

Our Queen. "I look back on that," he said, "as one of the most pleasant experiences of my life."[43]

In the fresh ecumenical climate of 1963 Bishop Powell could tell his annual convention, the last he would attend as diocesan, that "Christians must rejoice that in this critical year in man's existence there should be one of the calibre and character of His Holiness, Pope John XXIII, in the great place of leadership he occupies." Then he mentioned a small but—in those early days of Anglican–Roman Catholic ecumenicity—significant event: "We rejoice that recently, here in Maryland, we were privileged . . . to be part of a history-making gathering when His Excellency the Archbishop of Baltimore graciously accepted an invitation to speak to our Clericus."[44] Building on the friendships he had established and nurtured over the years and moving in the midst of unprecedented opportunities for dialogue, Bishop Powell broke new ground in January 1963 when he prevailed upon Archbishop Shehan (he would not receive his cardinal's hat until 1965) to address the Clericus, the clergy group of the diocese. In an interview conducted at the time Powell said, "Efforts toward unity are not the concern of officials only. They must be part of the concern of everyone who accepts God as our Father, Jesus Christ as our redeemer, and the Holy Spirit as our sanctifier."[45]

After Shehan spoke to the Episcopal clergy of the diocese of Maryland, Powell wrote to thank him: "Would that I could command words adequate to express the gratitude which is in my heart for your abundant kindness and rich friendship! Your prophetic insight . . . was a joy to us all. Your presence was a blessing to us. What a magnificent sense of humor you have, and we treasure, above all else, your frank honesty. . . . You have done us good, and you have advanced Christian understanding and comradeship, and in so doing you have made new friends."[46] Later in the year Powell addressed a letter to Shehan, "Your Excellency (and my beloved friend)."[47]

By the end of his episcopate Powell could look back on all the changes in interchurch relations that had taken place and note the "very marked increase in contacts of all kinds" between the major church groups in recent years. "Relationships here have been extraordinarily successful. No one can ever know the influence that John XXIII had."[48]

Following his retirement Bishop Powell became, in 1964, the first Protestant to receive the Andrew White Medal from Loyola College of Maryland. Saluted by the Baltimore school as an outstanding proponent of ecumenism,[49] he was also cited for "his long service to the spiritual welfare of the people of Maryland."[50] Later that year Powell was the featured speaker at the Archdiocesan Unity Commission.[51] And, only a few months before he died, he was named a trustee of Good Samaritan Hospital, a Roman Catholic institution in Baltimore. Cardinal Shehan attended Bishop Powell's funeral in November 1968, and Mary Powell wrote to him afterwards expressing warm thanks for his friendship.

An editorial in the *Baltimore Sun* got it almost right when it said of Bishop Powell at the time of his retirement: "When the good news of Christian reunion began to ring he stepped forward like one who had long been waiting in happy anticipation."[52] In fact Powell had been waiting but also acting, reaching out and making friends in his own quietly effective way.

Civil Rights

In 1942, in his first episcopal address to the Maryland diocesan convention, Powell took up the theme of interracial cooperation: "we as Christians must be doing all in our power to right this situation [of tension between the races]. He who broke down 'the middle wall of partition' is the Lord of us all." Powell said that "As Christians, we cannot recognize these distinctions save as each group is able, through its obedience to Jesus Christ, to . . . bring its own contribution to the healing of the nations. Christians must set an example. We must, with unremitting zeal, work for that condition 'where there cannot be Greek and Jew . . . but Christ is all and in all.'"[53]

During his years as bishop, Powell, a racial moderate, made a contribution to social harmony and integration. But by the end of his long episcopate, in the summer of 1963, he found himself on the sidelines, watching as less patient forces in church and society passed him by. A proponent of gradual change, Powell could not bring himself, a septuagenarian son of the evangelical South, to embrace the newer methods of direct confrontation and civil disobedience. Nor could he place much hope in the long-term success of federal efforts to achieve a good society, believing that transformation must take place within the hearts and minds of human beings and their communities. Like many Americans in the early 1960s, including Massachusetts-born John F. Kennedy throughout most of his presidency, Powell could not descry the crucial role that only the federal government could play in establishing the basic conditions of racial justice.

Looking back on this era from the vantage of the present, admirers of Bishop Powell might wish that he had been more inclined to "get out in front," more willing to expend some of the capital of personal authority he had so impressively accumulated over decades as a churchman in positions of prominence. Anyone who has read Martin Luther King Jr.'s "Letter from Birmingham Jail" cannot help viewing Powell's devotion to moderation, order, patience, and peace from the critical perspective of that now-canonical text. Even in Powell's own time, his coadjutor, Harry Lee Doll, grew impatient with his senior colleague's refusal to assert himself more boldly on behalf of equal rights and a just society. During his own tenure as diocesan, from 1963 to 1971, Doll, following the course of events in the national church, would assume a much more prophetic stance than did the more priestly figure that preceded him, putting at risk his own prestige and threatening to disturb the tranquillity of a fairly conservative, semisouthern diocese.

After both men were long dead, Maryland Episcopalians could still be found speaking of each bishop as having been just the right person for his era. The historian disposed to counterfactual flights of fancy, however, might suggest the appeal of the opposite scenario: Doll to shake up the complacent fifties and Powell to steady the tempest-tossed church of the late sixties. But such imaginative speculation in this case is neither plausible nor productive, failing as it does to reckon seriously with the intricate ways in which the constituents of history shape and influence one another.

When Powell did address racial matters in his public utterances, he tended to do so in fairly general, nonprescriptive terms, similar to those he used at Emmanuel Church during the Depression when he dealt with the nation's economic crisis. But some of his statements on race still carried weight. One of his best efforts came in early 1951 in Alabama.

Beginning a series of Lenten sermons at Christ Church in Mobile, Powell told the congregation that he intended to speak with "complete and brutal frankness" on the subjects of racism and nationalism, which, he averred, were crucifying Christ all over again in the present day. Emphasizing the cause of "common humanity," Powell said that we cannot live in a dreamscape, looking "with equanimity on the present situation in the world." We must not pretend that things are getting better; in fact, they are getting worse, and "the cause [is] within ourselves." The "crucifixion of Jesus is going on today." The "same elements" that "howled around Pilate's judgment seat" are in our midst. Those who clamored for the death of Jesus were "the very best people of their day . . . the bulwarks of orthodoxy." But "they kept themselves apart [and] considered themselves superior to other people."

In our own time, Powell continued, some people feel that their own race is the highest, but "Jesus died to show that God was the Father of all mankind and that every creature stands equal before his Creator." Those who "separate themselves from their fellow men and say they are better than others," those that "divide their lives into sacred and secular compartments and refuse to mingle religion and life," and those who waste time on trivial matters and refuse to "step out on the road to adventure in the search for new truths" are still "driving nails in the cross of Jesus."[54]

In the diocese of Maryland, Powell brought in African-American clergy to missionize and staff black churches. The Reverend Robert M. Powell, an African-American priest, said, "[Bishop Powell] was proud of the fact that I was the first black priest ordained in Maryland in fifty-some years. He looked upon me, as he often said, as his son. He appointed me his chaplain, and he provided great support for the Lafayette Square Community Center [of which Robert Powell was director from 1958 to 1963]." Father Powell would have liked to see the bishop "take a personal stand" on civil rights and "encourage it to happen," but the bishop only assured him that "integration will come; let us do it gradually."[55]

One of the bishop's closest friends and advisors was Cedric Mills, an African-American priest who served as rector of St. James's, Lafayette Square, from 1940 until 1963. "Bishop Powell," Mills recalled, "was for civil rights, but he wanted to keep things on an even keel. He favored desegregation, but his attitude was moderation."[56]

According to the Reverend Charles W. Fox Jr., a longtime African-American missionary and vicar in the diocese of Maryland, Bishop Powell's "dream was that the Episcopal church would grow among black people." The bishop was "open to change, but [he wanted to know] what do you put in the place of the establishment? If you tear down the establishment, then what? You have to have a plan of what you're going to build. So, change so that you can rebuild."[57]

Halfway through his episcopate Bishop Powell provided a clear and beneficial response in the face of unrest provoked by the U.S. Supreme Court decision *Brown v. Board of Education.* In late September 1954 the school board of Baltimore City reaffirmed its decision to end segregation in the city school system. This statement led to the picketing of several schools and to an ugly prosegregation demonstration by hundreds of working-class white students and some parents at a large high school in south Baltimore.[58] The mayor, Thomas J. D'Alesandro Jr., called for "cool heads and calm" in the midst of a "serious situation." During these unquiet days city police thought it prudent to provide escorts for black workers from several places of employment, including Southern High School and South Baltimore General Hospital.[59]

Expressing respect for the rule of law, nineteen civic, religious, and labor organizations came out in support of the school board's policy. Bishop Powell added his voice to those who, in the nation's northernmost southern city, were calling for peaceful compliance with the Supreme Court decision. According to an account in the *Baltimore Sun,* "Bishop Powell said the admonition to 'love thy neighbor' should not be forgotten." The *Sun* quoted Powell's comments at length:

We cannot get away from the truth in [the command to love our neighbors] and be a people devoted to justice and able to enjoy the rights which have come to us from the past. Our rights are guaranteed to us by law. It is a law-abiding citizen who respects the rights of others and thus preserves the freedom which he enjoys. Only a disciplined people can be a free people. This is a time of social change when our citizens must be serious and sober in all our thinking and acting. It is particularly important that parents of children in our schools should so discipline themselves as to set a worthy example to their children. Only so can we provide for our children a way of life which we would have them enjoy—a way of peace and justice and right. Now is the time when every citizen of Baltimore should be sure that he has no part in tarnishing the good name of our community or depriving our children of their rightful heritage of true democracy.[60]

Maryland's educational, religious, and political leaders—including the governor, Theodore R. McKeldin, a strong proponent of civil rights and a good friend of Noble Powell's—worked together effectively to make certain that the state would comply peacefully with the desegregation order.[61] As the U.S. Civil Rights Commission observed in 1961, Baltimore was the only southern city to have acted in accordance with *Brown*.[62] At the time of Bishop Powell's retirement, an editorial in the *Evening Sun* noted his contribution in this matter: "He has spoken out bluntly and forcefully at critical times such as those which followed the historic desegregation decision of the Supreme Court in 1954. And because his was the persuasive voice of a man of great conscience and conviction as well as that of a spiritual leader his counsel has been heeded."[63]

Throughout the rest of the 1950s Powell continued to speak of Christian brotherhood, and he talked knowingly of the "millstone" of "old prejudices, most of them born in other days," which "hang . . . about our hearts."[64] "Not only is a follower of Christ committed to love his neighbor," the bishop told the diocesan convention in 1958, "but to show this love in action. The people of God, individually and collectively, are called upon to see that all those in need have opportunity to live a fuller life."[65]

An occasion for religious people to demonstrate collectively on behalf of social justice—love in action—arose in the summer of 1963 on Independence Day. The protest at Gwynn Oak Amusement Park, just west of Baltimore City, occurred during a period of greatly heightened interest in civil rights on the part of white Americans. The spectacle of police dogs and fire hoses being trained on nonviolent demonstrators in Birmingham, Alabama, the preceding spring had been telecast around the world, causing not only an explosion of concern nationwide about racial injustice but also the

Kennedy administration's first significant moves to address the problem of discrimination.

Maryland law permitted the owners of Gwynn Oak, who said that integration would mean "financial suicide," to exclude African Americans from their sixty-five-acre park. To challenge this practice, the Congress of Racial Equality organized a nonviolent protest that included hundreds of participants, black and white, from New York, Philadelphia, Baltimore, and Washington, D.C. The demonstration had the backing of such groups as the Americans for Democratic Action, the Maryland Council of Churches, the NAACP, and the Urban League.[66] "It was," as one clergyman-participant remarked thirty years after the event, "Baltimore's last great civil rights campaign."[67]

The *New York Times* reported that Gwynn Oak "was the first time that so large a group of important clergymen of all three major faiths had participated together in a direct concerted protest against discrimination."[68] Among the clergy present were Dr. Furman L. Templeton, the black chairman of the National Presbyterian Interracial Council; Rabbi Morris Lieberman, of the Baltimore Hebrew Congregation; and Monsignor Austin J. Healy, of the archdiocese of Baltimore. The leadership of the protest included two high-ranking officials of old-line Protestant denominations: Eugene Carson Blake, the stated clerk (chief executive) of the United Presbyterian Church in the U.S.A. and acting chairman of the race commission of the National Council of Churches, and Bishop Daniel Corrigan, the head of the Home Department at the Episcopal Church Center in New York. The following month Blake would stand alongside Martin Luther King Jr. in the March on Washington, and three years after that he would become general secretary of the World Council of Churches.[69] Corrigan would go on to fame as one of the bishops who ordained the women known as the Philadelphia Eleven, whose irregular ordinations to the priesthood in 1974 pushed the Episcopal church to approve women's ordination two years later.

Shortly before the Gwynn Oak demonstration Blake gave a reason for his own involvement: "'We can no longer let the burden of the day be borne alone by those who suffer the discrimination we contest. We who are white have been at best followers, certainly not the leaders. If I am asked why we are here today, I will gladly answer. I will be considerably embarrassed, however, if I am asked why we are so late.'"[70]

When the protestors attempted to enter the amusement park, 283 of them were arrested for violating a state trespass law, while a crowd of about a thousand whites shouted such taunts as "Dump 'em in the bay!"[71] Blake and Corrigan were among the thirty-six clergy who were hauled to the police station. The police also arrested three Episcopal priests from New York, including Daisuke Kitagawa, the executive secretary of the Divison of Domestic Mission. Bishop Corrigan said of his role in the day's events: "'I suppose it's just a matter of putting our bodies where our mouths have been. Negroes working for their rights have been wondering, "Are you with us or aren't you?"'"[72]

The Gwynn Oak demonstration received national and international press coverage and made Blake, Corrigan, and their allies the representatives of a higher stage of commitment to racial equality by mainline denominations. "Members of the ecclesiastical establishment," Blake's biographer observed, "had at last placed their . . . reputations on the line for social justice."[73] A large photograph of Blake being put in the back of a patrol wagon was published on the front page of the *New York Times* with the caption "Setting an Example."[74] *Time* magazine printed the same picture but with a different legend underneath: "The Timidity Is Gone." Both captions signified the dawning of a new era of denominational involvement in campaigns for social justice.[75]

Of course these church leaders, including Corrigan and Kitagawa, were national officials, out-of-towners who did not have local constituencies to answer to.[76] Where was Noble Powell in all this? Civil disobedience was a hard concept for old-line church executives to embrace. Participation in the Gwynn Oak demonstration meant breaking the law, and churchmen such as Powell worried about the danger of encouraging lawlessness among blacks and whites. Their opposition to civil unrest following the *Brown* decision had been based not only on their commitment to brotherhood but also on their belief in order and the rule of law as the only structure within which true freedom can flourish.

Powell thought that the church had a role to play in social betterment, but, true to his heritage, he tended to favor a more individualistic and incremental approach to righting wrongs in society. "You and I are the Church," he told the diocesan convention of 1960, "and as such we are everywhere in contact . . . with the world." How can the church influence society? "When a Christian enters a shop or a factory, a home or an office, a school or an industrial plant; when he walks and rides abroad, the Church is in intimate contact with the world."[77]

Even after his retirement, when Powell noticed a situation that did not seem right—a man sentenced to twelve years in prison for stealing to feed his family, for example, or three African-American men condemned to die for a rape that evidence suggested they did not commit, or abuse of prisoners at the Baltimore City Jail—he would act behind the scenes to try to correct injustice.[78] He was no hidebound conservative; he spoke out on the issues of the day and of the need for Christians' collective action to bring about a more just society. But his preferred mode of conduct was essentially evangelistic: spread the gospel message, lead people to Christ—to the adventure of a triumphant friendship in which sinners' hearts are conquered and their wills transformed by divine love.[79] We tend to forget that up until the March on Washington in 1963, not only senior white churchmen but also many—probably most—African-American clergy in Baltimore and elsewhere rejected King's tactics as too radical; the ordained minister's job was preaching, not agitating in the streets, engaging in civil disobedience, and getting thrown in jail.[80]

Besides these larger differences of approach with the Gwynn Oak protesters, Powell had a specific grievance concerning the methods of the New York Episcopalians who had come down. His handwritten journal entry for 4 July 1963, the day of the Gwynn Oak demonstration, reads: "At home all day preparing to move [out of the Bishop's House]. Had long conversation with Bishop Corrigan about a demonstration parade. Quite frank with him about coming into my diocese without knowledge of his presence. He is here for the civil rights demonstration. . . . Corrigan represented that the P[residing] B[ishop] had sent him. I did not go."[81]

Powell was in high dudgeon because Bishop Corrigan had come into "his" diocese without providing what he felt was proper notification.[82] Corrigan (1900–94) was well known to Powell; they had met at the College of Preachers in 1940. Four years later Powell was instrumental in bringing Corrigan to the diocese of Maryland to be rector of Grace and St. Peter's, a large church in downtown Baltimore, where he would remain for four years. In 1947 Corrigan served as president of the Clericus.[83]

A man who was a priest in the diocese in 1963 said that Powell was "livid" about another bishop coming into the diocese without his permission; the "courtesies had been violated." And many Maryland priests, he remembered, felt the same way their bishop did, some calling the interloper "Wrongway Corrigan."[84] None of the Episcopal clergy in Maryland participated in the demonstration. "The local priests were upset," another priest recalled; "why didn't you tell us? Neither of our bishops was informed. It was a canonically illegal act, a technical invasion of the diocese, [and a] personal affront."[85]

Beyond the omission of those courtesies that any southerner would deem essential to the maintenance of the fraternal bonds that enable civilization to endure—and permit bishops to work together harmoniously for the good of the whole body of Christ—another factor was probably at work in Bishop Powell's response to Gwynn Oak. Father Charles Fox gave this explanation of why Powell felt frustrated and angry: Corrigan was not only "making him look bad, coming into the see city [without his permission]"; he was also making Powell look as though he was "not taking a stand either way. He was hurt."[86] Bishop Powell, a consummate politician who eschewed conflict, must have sensed at about this time that the old sources of authority were starting to lose some of their potency.

Eight weeks after the Gwynn Oak protest, the historic March on Washington for Jobs and Freedom took place. At 7:30 on the morning of the march, at the Church of the Redeemer, Harry Lee Doll, the bishop coadjutor, presided at a service of Holy Communion for those who would shortly board two buses for the nation's capital. A few hours later, these clergy and laypeople from the Free State would march with a quarter-million other Americans to the steps of the Lincoln Memorial and hear King deliver his "I have a dream" speech. Bishop Doll badly wanted to join them on this trip but remained in Baltimore, in deference to his diocesan.[87]

The rector of Redeemer, Bennett Sims, recalled this day as representing a turning point in the life of the Episcopal church: "All in all it was fairly easy to be an ordained minister until the 1960s. Then everything changed when Martin Luther King, Jr., forced us to pay attention to the civil rights movement." "Change," Sims observed, "always arouses conflict in an institution with roots deep in tradition, and the civil rights movement was among the first of the convulsions of change in the modern church that have been with us ever since."[88] Starting in 1963, the Episcopal church moved from disputes over matters that were "hopelessly trivial," such as vestments and altar furnishings, to a concern for justice in society and in the church.[89]

Bishop Powell's attitude toward the march and proposed legislative remedies was clearly stated in a letter to a student at Virginia Seminary in September 1963: "It is mighty easy for us to use our feet, but when it comes to our heads and our hearts, that's another matter. Legal enforcement is not going to solve our problem. We seem to have forgotten all about prohibition, but the same principle is involved in both situations—legal enactment which is going to resolve our problem, and that just does not work out."[90] Powell's was a widely held view at this time, and the comparison to prohibition was common.[91]

"[Bishop Powell] was the quintessential southern gentleman," recalled a former Baltimore rector and social activist who had known the bishop since Powell's days at Emmanuel Church in the thirties. "[He wasn't] ready for the confrontations of the early sixties. He was in a dreadful bind; he wanted to be on the side of the angels. Privately, in conversation, his approach was, it takes time, go slow." While Powell "was bitterly opposed to discrimination,

I'm not sure he would have had the radar to pick up the more subtle forms of discrimination."[92]

Retirement

When his seventy-second birthday arrived and his denomination's rules required him to step down as bishop of Maryland, Noble Powell did not want to retire.[93] And no wonder: the church was his life, and the years of his episcopate, though full of challenges and hard effort, had been happy ones.[94] "Those were great days," one of his fellow bishops recalled, "just before everything fell to pieces."[95]

Whittingham served to seventy-four years of age, Paret to eighty-four, and Helfenstein retired at age seventy-eight. Therefore when the time came for Noble Powell to leave office, he complained about a church law whose purport was to declare him to have attained "constitutional antiquity and chronological senility."[96] Diocesan clergy noticed a profound sadness that came over him at the time of his retirement.[97]

It was Bishop Powell's last year in office: Maryland Episcopalians were travelling to Washington to march for civil rights, the (final) disestablishment of mainline Protestantism was under way, California's Bishop Pike was stirring the pot of theological controversy, and the folk singer Bob Dylan was reading the signs of the age, observing that indeed "the times they are a-changin'." Powell's successor, Harry Lee Doll, would be installed as bishop of Maryland in the fall, on 22 November 1963.

5

Dénouement, 1963–93

Final Years

Of the psychologist Erik Erikson's three desiderata for a happy life—work, play, and love—Noble Powell all but collapsed the last two into the first. "He ate, slept, and breathed the episcopate," said a clergyman who knew him well.[1] What the land had been to Shell Powell, the church was to the planter's son. One acquaintance said that the bishop had "wanted to die in his boots, before he left office."[2] Many people remarked the onset of a pronounced physical decline shortly after Powell left Diocesan House for good. "It was as if someone had stuck a pin in him," one priest said.[3] "I saw Bishop Powell the day he retired and again three months later," another clergyman recalled. "I never saw such a change [in a person]. He became suddenly a very old man. As dean and warden he had had great pressure on him; it was an impossible job. He never really learned to relax. [The effect of retirement] was like letting air out of a balloon. I never saw anyone go down so far so fast. After a year it was worse. It seemed fantastic."[4]

In retirement, Powell from time to time took services, served as guest preacher, or substituted for the diocesan bishop at confirmations. He attended Episcopal conventions and the board meetings of various institutions—the diocesan girls' school, for instance, and the church's adoption agency. Calling upon his wide circle of friends, he provided valuable assistance to the development office of Church Home and Hospital. And he particularly enjoyed visits with his grandchildren: his son Philip and his wife, Margie, had three daughters—Priscilla, Mary Blair, and Margaret—and a son, Philip Noble, who was always called "Nobie." When Nobie was about six or seven, he received a bit of extra tutoring from his grandfather, who would read to him and help him with his arithmetic.[5]

Notwithstanding these occasional diversions, Bishop Powell, suffering more and more from painful and crippling osteoarthritis, often felt lonely and ignored. Three years after stepping down, he lamented his situation in a letter to a priest in the diocese: "I find I miss very much because of retirement; in the nature of the case I am largely out of touch."[6] Two years later, after months of illness, he announced, "I'm ready to die now."[7]

If there was a measure of human ego at work in the active diocesan's reluctance to depart center stage and go into retirement, there was also a longing to be of service that persisted to the last. In Church Hospital, on Broadway in east Baltimore, the venerable prelate, dying, his body and mind enfeebled, received the blessing of a priest he had ordained almost a quarter-century before. Then, moving as if to try to get out of bed, he entreated the clergyman, *"Let me know what I can do for you."*[8] Not many days later, on the evening of Thanksgiving Day, 1968—an *annus horribilis* almost wholly alien to everything Powell represented—he finally succumbed.[9]

Legacy

Powell's most significant contribution to the diocese of Maryland was a characteristic element that suffused his entire episcopacy: the manner in which he fulfilled the office of pastor, coupled with his consistent emphasis on friendship as a way of expressing the Christian life. These qualities, embodied by him and remembered by many, constitute his richest legacy. The attitude and action of the pastor, the distinctive traits of Christian friendship, undergirded all his other achievements. Broken and flawed though the witness of any bishop will be, Powell as winsome shepherd of his flock was virtually nonpareil.

In 1958, when the annual convention of the diocese of Maryland was about to elect a bishop coadjutor, Powell reminded the delegates of "the essential duties lodged in the Episcopate." Although "the Church is a big business," he told them, "let us be sure that we never come to think that [a bishop] is primarily an executive or business administrator. His duty is to shepherd the flock, to devote himself to study and prayer and meditation, bringing forth heavenly treasures . . . out of God's great revelation of Himself, and sharing these with the pastors of the flock."[10]

A major part of Powell's role as shepherd of the clergy was to remind them of their own duty as pastors. On the occasion of Don Frank Fenn's retirement, Powell told a true story about the time he was meeting with a group of candidates for ordination and urging them to remember "the indispensable character of the pastoral office." One of the young men, "fresh out of Seminary," was "captivated by the charm of ecclesiastical organization": secretaries, filing cabinets, telephones, committees, office hours, and so forth.

The young man, in an effort to support his view of the ministry as essentially parish administration, cited Don Frank Fenn, noting that "the Rector of the great Parish of St. Michael and All Angels could not possibly exercise a pastoral ministry" in the old-fashioned sense the bishop was emphasizing. The ministerial candidate's "illustration," observed Powell, was "unfortunate." "That very afternoon, a hot July one it was, just before I met with these young men, I was driving . . . to my office . . . [and] saw Dr. Fenn say good-bye on the porch of a home to a mother and her three children, go down the steps, pass two houses, and start up the steps of the third. In season and out, he has, as a representative of the Lord of Lords and King of Kings, ministered to his flock."[11]

Powell's achievement was not only to unite a large jurisdiction that was full of actual and potential divisions—urban and rural, high and low, traditional and liberal—but also to vitalize this diocese through a ministry that was primarily personal and pastoral. Much more sympathetic to the insights and traditions of his High Church clergy than was the dogmatically Low Church Ned Helfenstein, Powell also worked for unity by declining to seek the appointment of an assisting bishop for a geographical region (such as western Maryland) and by refusing to countenance threats of heresy trials against clergy of questionable orthodoxy.[12]

When he retired he expressed regret that "'my high hopes at my consecration were destroyed in the acid of everyday life.'"[13] But perhaps there was more modesty than accuracy in this assessment, for the good that Powell accomplished was done by "minute particulars" in the midst of common life. An editorial in the *Evening Sun* displayed better perspective on Powell's career when it asserted that "Differences of doctrinal or liturgical or worldly viewpoint notwithstanding, people hearing him preach or meeting him went away feeling they belonged almost to a single common pastorate."[14]

Powell believed that none of his duties as chief pastor was more crucial than the selection, placement, and guidance of parish ministers.[15] For the good sense and devotion he brought to this task he enjoyed a strong reputation among his brother bishops as someone who "took care of his clergy."[16] He knew how to "line up the place and the person."[17] Early in his episcopate there was a national shortage of priests; around the time of his retirement the opposite problem began to appear.[18] Throughout these years Powell worked to improve clergy salaries and pensions and many times gave seminary students and clergy financial assistance out of his own funds.[19] When he felt that he had failed to provide adequate support—when a priest had to be deposed or, worst of all, when a rector committed suicide—Powell was, naturally, devastated.[20]

In an era that still reposed great faith in personal authority, those who wished to go to seminary knew that their futures depended on the judgment of this one man: "You say you want to do good?" he would ask would-be clergymen. "Go think about it, and come back in a year and we'll see; you might want to be a doctor or a lawyer by then." Deacons knew who was in charge of their diaconal careers; Bishop Powell made it clear there was just one human being to whom they were accountable: "Now, God has called you to be a deacon. We don't know yet if he's called you to be a priest."[21] New rectors received from him carefully chosen words of encouragement and direction: "Take it quietly, patiently, lovingly, and with Christian joy in your heart, and God can then use all of you for His glory."[22] Or, more bluntly: "Now, don't stir up more snakes than you can dispatch."[23] And rectors in difficult cures found their hearts lifted and their vision clarified as the result of a visit from their bishop.

"I have to deal with human nature," Powell remarked; "they wear a round collar, but they're still human."[24] And this bishop understood human nature, among other things.[25] "He knew you better than you knew yourself," one clergyman remarked.[26] "Bishop Powell," another priest said, "was always drawing you a little higher than where you were."[27]

Writing of bishops in the 1990s, a time when their authority was no longer widely acknowledged and their role no longer seemed clear or their function relevant, James C. Fenhagen, the former dean of the General Seminary, discussed the decline of bishops as significant forces in the life of the church. In too many instances the bishop had become a remote figure, according to Fenhagen, no longer well connected to the clergy and the congregations.[28]

But, more positively, Fenhagen recalled an occasion in his own early career as a priest when a bishop's involvement—in this case, the applied wisdom of Noble Powell—made all the difference: "I will always remember a visit made to me by my bishop while serving in my first parish just two years out of seminary [in the 1950s]. I was involved in a conflict situation that I wasn't sure how to handle." Fenhagen had mentioned this problem to his bishop several weeks before, but nothing further was said, and he expected no response. Then "one weekday afternoon the doorbell rang and I opened it to see the bishop standing there. . . . He had been in the area and had remembered our very brief conversation. He proceeded to spend an hour with me and then went by to see the Senior Warden of the parish."

Thus, Fenhagen said, "began a process that was immensely healing. I was in a large diocese and I had no reason to expect such a visit. But it was a visit that had an immense effect on my ministry. I felt heard, and I felt a sense of partnership that has forever shaped my understanding of what episcopacy is about." Since that time, Fenhagen has received support from "diocesan staff and colleagues. . . . But that visit was special because of its quality and because of the sacramental relationship it represented. I was not in need of pastoral care, but of spiritual wisdom."[29] Powell was a model of the bishop as pastor in an era that was less confused about the function and status of a bishop. Unglamorous, undramatic, and largely hidden from public view, the patient nurture of the sacramental relationship, Powell believed, was of the essence of episcopal ministry.[30]

It would be a mistake to deduce from anything that has been said so far that Noble Powell was simply an affable, storytelling bishop with good pastoral skills. He did have a fine, frequently self-deprecating sense of humor. He might, for example, tell about the time in western Maryland that he was the passenger in an automobile that was waiting at a railway crossing. Powell told the driver a long story, only to find that his efforts at conversation had been for nought when the caboose finally went by and the man behind the wheel declared, "Seventy-six cars!"[31] Powell was amiable and hard-driving, approachable and strict, optimistic about the future and realistic about human sinfulness, open and guarded, sociable and alone. He blended in one person his mother's graciousness and his father's austerity. Clergy called him "Bishop Powell," never "Noble"; and generally he was the one to tell the humorous stories while you listened.

A statement adopted by the Diocesan Council upon Powell's death spoke of the affection people had for him but went on to point out that "'He was not . . . an easygoing, hail fellow well met. His own self-discipline was very exacting and he expected a high standard of discipline from other men, and, because of the person he was, he inspired them with the desire to live up to his expectation.'" Only on rare occasions, "'when reprehensible conduct was willful, careless, or caused by disregard of other people, did his wrath descend. Then it was sudden, cold, and as incisive as a surgeon's knife—and often as healing. No one who felt it ever forgot it nor gave cause for it again.'"[32]

An example of Powell's authority and the respect people accorded him occurred at the time of the election of a suffragan bishop in 1955. Powell requested that there be silence during the voting and the counting of ballots, so that the election might be the result of the work of the Holy Spirit rather than of ecclesiastical politicking. During the counting of votes, delegates prayed and listened while Powell read from scripture and delivered meditations on the readings.[33]

Bishop Powell's pastoral relationships were rooted in an authority that was grounded in all three of the ways in which the German political economist Max Weber observed that leaders may gain and exercise legitimate authority. Powell was aware of his appropriation and use of all three. He had, first of all, a thorough knowledge of—and willingness to employ—the constitution and canons of the Episcopal church. Weber called this type *legal* authority, for it is based on rules having to do with the office of those in power.

Obedience may also be owed to leaders on the basis of *tradition,* such as the highly meaningful—to Episcopalians—tradition that bishops in the historic episcopate participate in an unbroken apostolic chain that links them with the original followers of Jesus. The postwar era was a time when people were generally well disposed toward tradition, including traditional institutions and their representatives.

Finally, there may be devotion to a leader on *charismatic* grounds, because of his or her personal sanctity or exemplary character or, when charisma is routinized, because of the sacred gift bestowed through the laying on of hands, as in episcopal ordination. These three kinds of authority, as represented, are ideal types; in actual practice each may function in a nonpure form and in combination with others.[34]

In Powell's case, authority rested not only on a canonical and traditional footing, both of which were important, but also on the power of his personality and character to inspire confidence and on the appeal of his deep-seated spirituality.[35] Powell played a pastoral role among his fellow bishops—his equals in rank—that was based almost entirely on this kind of personal authority. His peers went to him readily for help and ideas. "He was not a bit condescending but [adopted] a pastoral stance toward bishops and fellow clergy," one of his brother bishops remarked. "He was very open, not withdrawn, always willing to listen, talk, share confidences. He was a very much loved man. Noble Powell was noble—just what his name implied."[36]

Younger bishops coming into the House of Bishops could find it "intimidating," remembered one who had had that experience. And "some bishops were arrogant and cold. The older bishops tended to be lofty. But Noble Powell was very gracious; he [manifested] warmth and kindness. He was very democratic and welcoming to new, frightened bishops. It stood out with me. I really loved him."[37] His peers also appreciated and respected Powell because he did not "speak at the drop of a hat" but "spoke only when he had real involvement in the topic, and then quietly and without flourish."[38]

The spiritual foundation of Powell's authority contained some slightly surprising elements. That self-control was a watchword of this admirer of Robert E. Lee was to be expected. Powell did preach and live a disciplined life and consistently made clear to ordinands that they should as well, providing them with clear rules about how they should conduct themselves.[39]

Nor are we surprised to find those who knew him speaking after his death of a "real life of prayer" evident behind and beneath his conduct of Quiet Days and retreats.[40]

Less predictable, however, was Powell's deepening Catholic sensibility. As the years passed he came to a "high" view of the church and the sacraments and especially of the historic episcopate.[41] "I'm as Catholic as any man," he would remark.[42] Although he never became fond of Anglo-Catholic ceremonial practices—bells, adoration of the reserved sacrament, chasubles, prostration by ordinands, the missal, and so forth—he loved both Mount Calvary, a historic Anglo-Catholic parish, and Emmanuel, his old Low Church parish; and he regularly made his confession to a priest.[43]

"Bishop Powell did not wear a cope and mitre except for the sisters at All Saints' Convent [in Catonsville]," said a priest that had served under him. "But once at a clergy retreat at Claggett, when the leader couldn't show up, Bishop Powell led meditations on the Virgin Mary. Sitting there, just talking, he presented magnificent ideas and concepts on the nature of Mary—to great depth. I hadn't thought he functioned at that theological level. The jaws of the High Churchmen just dropped. Bishop Powell was more Catholic than the Catholics!"[44]

Powell's life was noble and sacrificial, but it took its toll on him and his family. Being the "fiduciary of a thousand trusts," as one acquaintance characterized him, meant responding to constant claims on his attention and maintaining a grueling schedule of travel and appointments.[45] His journals reveal a nonstop round of activities day and evening, virtually seven days a week. After a visitation in western Maryland he would not hurry back to Diocesan House. Instead, as one priest said, "he'd rap on the door and stop in at every rectory along the way; they were a buggy ride—about ten miles—apart. He'd make a pastoral call, stay half an hour or so."[46] On Monday mornings he would come into the office totally spent, then somehow become rejuvenated when the first visitor arrived. How he found time for reading, reflection, and writing is a mystery. Twice in the 1950s, however, he was hospitalized briefly for exhaustion.

Powell's fellow bishop Edward Welles, a former member of The Thirty, looked back on his own career and acknowledged that "the most serious mistake of my episcopate" was "sacrificing the children and family life."[47] Too often when one man tried to hold together an entire diocese the diocesan family took precedence over the nuclear family. There is some humor but more pathos in a published statement Mary Powell made about her experience travelling by sea with her husband to the 1948 Lambeth Conference. The crossing took "six wonderful days," she told readers of *The Maryland Church-*

man, and these days were "enjoyed to the full, especially by me perhaps, for never in the 24 years since we've been married have I known just where I could find my husband. (I'm hoping I'll not have to wait another 24 years to acquire him again!)"[48] Once, when a clergyman telephoned the episcopal residence and asked if the bishop was there, Mary Powell replied, "Are you kidding?"[49]

She and her husband hosted such functions as luncheons in the Bishop's House for the Clericus. A gracious lady who enjoyed cooking and entertaining, she helped to make the clergy feel that they were part of the diocesan family. Mary Powell also took an active interest in beautifying the grounds around the cathedral and the Bishop's House.[50] But by and large her husband fulfilled his episcopal duties without her, while she carved out her own life, spending time with her friends in Baltimore society, travelling, and taking relatively little part in diocesan affairs.[51] The couple's marriage was solid, even if their relationship was not particularly intimate; perhaps Mary and Noble did not have enough in common.

Relations among members of the Powell household tended to be decorous and reserved—even, in the words of Tom Powell, "cool and distant."[52] Neither of the boys grew up questioning or consciously resenting his father's consuming devotion to duty, however, and both went on to enjoy productive lives and careers. A graduate of Phillips Andover Academy and the University of Virginia who also earned a degree at Johns Hopkins in mechanical engineering, Philip (b. 1930) worked for many years in technical sales, representing companies that dealt in specialized mechanical equipment. His younger brother, Tom (b. 1932), educated at Gilman, Princeton, and the Hopkins Medical School, had a private practice as an orthopedic surgeon.

Of the two sons, Philip more nearly resembled his father and probably enjoyed a closer relationship with him. He remained an active churchman, while his brother did not. Having emerged early on from what he called the "strait-laced" world of his parents to become a thoroughgoing skeptic, Tom Powell traced the origins of his break with Christianity to a high school physics class, which prompted him to think seriously about an approach to truth rooted not in faith but in empirical evidence. Although he always felt as if he should not disturb his father's peace of mind with an account of his unbelief, he was sure that by the end of his father's life the bishop was aware of his doubts.[53] In his last years, Noble Powell expressed regret that he had not taken more time to get to know his sons when he was younger. "I waited too long," he is reported to have said; "I don't know my boys."[54]

While visitations took Powell away from his family at home almost every Sunday of the year, the people in the larger diocesan community warmly looked forward to these appearances by their bishop. In Powell's day the action of confirmation still bore a partial resemblance to a classic rite de passage and thus carried somewhat more weight than it later did, because until the changes of the 1970s confirmation brought with it full membership in the church and permission to partake of the Holy Communion. However impaired its theology, the older understanding of confirmation as a completion of baptism meant that young people could look forward not only to making a public and (more or less) mature affirmation of their faith but also to crossing over from the social group of childhood to a new identity within the church.[55] This change in status had to compete for attention with other, less formalized and more secular markers of the passage into adulthood—such as obtaining one's driver's license, going away to college, turning eighteen, and losing one's virginity—but to many young people and their families confirmation was still significant and memorable.[56]

When Powell was bishop, the ritual process surrounding and incorporating the event of confirmation seemed to commence not with the beginning of the official rite but with the bishop's arrival at the church or rectory. Even before he ambled up the nave in his rochet and black chimere to occupy the bishop's chair, he had an effect. His presence changed the atmosphere in the parish house or undercroft or vestibule.[57]

The congregation would attend to the sermon with more care than usual. By the time he was bishop, Powell had evolved into a distinctive and highly effective preacher. Working from a few notes rather than reading from a manuscript, Powell would recast the language and themes of the Bible into straightforward terms, illustrating his points by means of stories and characters and images, preaching his sermon in a clear and quietly dramatic way.[58] Carefully prepared and structured, his sermons were often in the exhortatory mode, but Powell urged his listeners through a style of delivery that was never admonitory or ostentatious. He would sketch, for instance, memorable word pictures of two exemplary characters, one proud and the other praiseworthy, and then ask—not tell—his hearers which one they should take to heart: "Or shall we be like. . . ?" In the manner of Anglican preachers before him, he regularly appealed, calmly but piercingly, to the conscience and the will of each member of the congregation.

Powell was less interested in abstract thelogy than he was in theological "knowledge carried to the heart."[59] Dedicated to gradual nurture and character formation in the bosom of the church, Powell himself, so far as we know, never experienced an emotional conversion experience but rather, to paraphrase 2 Timothy, was acquainted since childhood with the holy scriptures and continued in the wisdom he had learned.[60] His characteristic theological mode was one that today we would call a "spiritual" or a "practical" theology: a theology of the Christian life that aimed at the upbuilding, the patient influencing, of his flock. Devoted to the Bible and the Book of Common Prayer, Powell was an orthodox, mainstream, trinitarian Christian thinker, one not usefully typed according to any of the prevailing schools of academic theology. What he did to real effect was to convey theology through enactment, through vivification, through the personal, persuasive language of faith. Frequently able to bring fresh life to old teachings, Powell helped his listeners to see themselves in new roles and thus to better understand what it meant to view life through the lenses of faith.[61]

The meaning of the sacramental rite of confirmation was associated, then, with all the words and actions of the bishop, observed during the visitation and encountered afterwards in memory. When, with his large hands pressed on top of the confirmand's head, the bishop recited in his soft Alabama accent the brief prayer—"Defend, O Lord, this thy Child with thy heavenly grace; that *he* may continue thine for ever; and daily increase in thy Holy Spirit more and more . . ."—it sounded right: the boy or girl could intuit that this bishop was not simply going through the motions but truly wanted, through the agency of the Holy Spirit, to strengthen him or her for coming battles against the principalities and powers of a fallen world.[62]

Characteristic features of the diligence and *disponibilité* that Powell displayed in his life are reflected in a thank-you letter the bishop sent to a ten-year-old boy on Christmas Day 1964. A couple of weeks before, Bishop Powell had been to the boy's parish for confirmation. On this occasion the young fellow, coached by his mother, had given him a present, a block of the rather hard-to-find Peter's chocolate, the bishop's favorite candy. When the bishop left it behind, the boy fetched it and took it to him. Powell wrote:

> It was so good to see you when I was there for Confirmation. And you were good to give the alluring package to me. As you know, I left it and was going back for it when you were so good as to bring it to me. It went under our Christmas tree and this morning I opened it and found the delicious candy which you so thoughtfully gave to me. I do appreciate it greatly. When I saw the candy, I thought of King David when he asked for a drink of water from the well in Bethlehem. Two of his soldiers faded away in the darkness, went to Bethlehem, and brought the water. King David was filled with reverence for their fine spirit and said the water was evidence of their love. I take it in that same way, and I thank God for our friendship, shown in the fine gift you have made.[63]

Even the child could sense that the quality of the thanks—not to mention the proffered parallel from 2 Samuel 23—far exceeded the value of the offering and the minimal effort required for its retrieval. Besides surmising that he had been set an example by someone whose standards were still far beyond his own reach, the boy was pleased to have Bishop Powell's friendship, which was presented in the letter not as something offered but as something assumed.

The leitmotif of Noble Powell's entire career, friendship was a way of life that the bishop not only wrote about but enacted on a daily basis. Others have theorized about friendship; Powell lived it, following in the footsteps of his Lord. The gospel, as various authors have noted, began with friendship; and at the end of his earthly career Jesus gave to his friends his body and his blood in bread and wine, making his companions one with himself and sharers in his own destiny.[64]

Powell consistently spoke of a Christian's relationship with Jesus Christ as "a transforming friendship," which was fully engaged not in isolation from other selves, as part of a solitary spiritual quest, but in response to others. He noted that Jesus's own followers entered into this life more deeply as they sought to share him—his love, his power, and his life. "There is no other [relationship] in all history like it," Powell believed; "Life knows no equal prize." Consider "what it did for that little company of disciples. Once they were convinced—and they were not easily convinced—that He is the Truth for life, they became other men. That fear which sent them into hiding was transformed into courage. . . . Their uncertainty and doubt were, by the alchemy of His love, changed into radiant assurance and blazing faith. The lips which were silent in the hiding place now proclaim in the market place that Christ is Lord."

What changed these men, Powell continued, was a "triumphant friendship." The only sensible explanation they could give for their new lives was that "they had been with Jesus." "This friendship changed a renegade tax collector into a chronicler of eternal truth; changed a narrow nationalist into a preacher of the universal love of God; changed an accessory to murder into a bearer of life; changed a rich and luxurious and spoiled young son into the little brother of the poor." What "the world needs today," Powell said, is "this transforming friendship."

Christ called us, Bishop Powell told the diocesan convention in 1960, to be "fishers of men," not "keepers of an aquarium." "Too often [we in the church] fail because we have not the compassion of Jesus Christ. The good fisherman breaks his net because he drags it through the ooze and the stones and the mud on the bottom of the sea where fish are to be found. The true missionary . . . breaks his heart because he enters deeply into the sins and sorrows and tragedies of those whom he would bring to Christ." The "power of Christ" flows through us into others as we share their pain and grief and loneliness and fear. "The more Christ-like we are, the more compassionate we are, and the more compassionate we are, the truer we are as bearers of the good news of the Gospel. These men, Simon called Peter, and Andrew, his brother, were Christ's net. They were cast into the world to catch men for the Kingdom of Heaven. Today, you and I are His net, cast into the world."[65]

Certainly Noble Powell possessed that "affability of speech and manner" that Cicero and other writers on friendship have deemed necessary for its commencement and growth, but to Powell friendship obviously meant much more than a genial manner.[66] Friendship in his view was also richer and more challenging than the bastardized forms of Christian fellowship that American churches of the 1950s were offering in advertisements aimed at young couples seeking new social connections.[67]

Powell had in mind a friendship that was truly transformative, in which the individual's misguided will comes more and more to be aligned with the will of Christ. "When [a person] yields himself to the friendship and fellowship of Christ," Powell said, "he ceases to be a self-centered man and becomes a God-centered man. . . . The one in fellowship with Christ . . . begins to see the larger significance of his own life. . . . Conversion brings [here Powell cited the philosopher Josiah Royce] a new center of loyalty," and this new focus gives the Christian "a great, absorbing passion which draws all his being together and gives it a goal." Labor and even suffering on behalf of this cause are transmuted into "works of love."[68]

In his 1961 convention address Powell provided a dramatic example of what he meant by Christian friendship as a companionship in love. Recounting the story of Telemachus, he told of how one day this "humble, Asian monk" stepped into "the vastness of the Roman Colosseum," which was "crowded with people come to see a gladiatorial combat." Telemachus watched the contest, and his experience "filled his heart with horror. . . . With the crowd, he left behind this place of butchery, but he did not leave behind the effect which that butchery had on him." After witnessing the bloody combat, the monk could not rest. But "what could he do against the customs of the mightiest of . . . empires? Nothing, if alone. He went back to that horrid spectacle. This time, not alone," but "in the conscious companionship of the Son of God. The roar of the crowd swelled its passion for blood—the gates were opened. The gladiatorial horror began again." Then, "rising from his seat, he sprang into the arena and sought to separate the contestants. The howling mob rose to its feet and stoned him to death. But is he gone?" Powell asked. "No. Telemachus, his deed, his death, mark the evening of the gladiatorial shows. What can one person do? No one knows until in conscious companionship with God's Son he dares everything for that righteousness which is Jesus Christ our Lord, who braved the cross that we might live."[69]

From time to time Christian theologians have criticized friendship as a relationship that, in its particularizing tendencies, is significantly different from and less than the universal, need-oriented attitude and action that agapic love displays. In Powell's conception, however, there was no conflict between *philia* (Christianly understood) and *agape.* He used to tell a story about Phillips Brooks that expresses the understanding of Christianity that both men shared. A salesman called on Brooks to sell him a special limited edition of a book. "He thought to clinch the sale," Powell said, "by telling Phillips Brooks that there were only one hundred people who would be able to possess the volume." But the salesman "mistook his man. 'Take it away,' replied Brooks. 'I want nothing that may not be enjoyed by every man.'"[70]

Central to Powell's understanding of Christian friendship was his belief that Christ died for all. Friendship with Christ—a companionship in love and a school of compassion that Powell saw as the most joyful adventure a person could embark upon—is not restricted, therefore, to a select group of alluring, specially privileged people. Friends are set apart because they share the same hopes and desires, but those who are transformed by friendship with Christ long not for the happiness of a few but for the well-being of all.[71]

Friend and Peer

"Guide and shepherd as he was to his own communion," remarked a *Baltimore Sun* editorial after Powell's death, "[his] informal charge was as wide as the general community."[72] The chief pastor of a church whose legal establishment in colonial Maryland dated from 1702, the Episcopal bishop continued to be a preeminent spiritual leader in the state for several decades following the demise of Protestant cultural hegemony in the 1920s and 1930s. In many areas of the United States, but especially along the eastern seaboard, the Episcopal bishop was a familiar presence in the secular metropolis— though in some cities eclipsed by or, as in Baltimore, sharing his status with his Roman Catholic counterpart.[73]

In this era an Episcopal diocesan was the friend—and the peer—of company presidents and United States senators, an official offerer of prayers at gubernatorial and mayoral inaugurations and at the commencements of leading universities, and a deliverer of Christmas messages broadcast on radio and televison. Except in Anglo-Catholic dioceses where Protestants could not identify with the Episcopal church or its bishop, Protestants of many denominations trusted the Episcopal bishop to be their representative. And of course the diocesan's unofficial prestige and authority were considerably enhanced if, as in the case of Noble Powell, they were reinforced not only by a cooperating cultural milieu but also by superabundant stores of personal charisma and energy.[74]

The forties and fifties were a time when a highly disproportionate share of America's political leaders belonged to the Episcopal church. Franklin Roosevelt, Thomas Dewey, and Robert Taft were Episcopalians, as were Maryland Governor William Preston Lane Jr. and Senators Millard Tydings and J. Glenn Beall. Powell was especially close to Governor Lane. The bishop's almost exact contemporary, Lane was a graduate of the University of Virginia and a veteran of the First World War who was decorated for unusual valor. Active in Episcopal church affairs, he served as a delegate to the 1958 general convention and as a trustee of St. James School.[75] As one man who was acquainted with Powell and Lane recalled, "They were the two greatest storytellers I've ever known. And they were great friends of one another. Bishop Powell had a wonderful sense of humor; he exceeded Governor Lane."[76]

All of these friendly contacts were instances of the relationships that composed and helped to maintain the American establishment, which, as one historian has pointed out, "was a personal network as well as a congeries of institutions."[77] This establishment network also connected religious leaders to the upper echelons of business: "Episcopalians ruled," another historian has remarked, "from the corporate board rooms of the Northeast."[78] Each year during the week before Christmas, Powell called on dozens of Baltimore business leaders in their offices: "He'd just walk down Charles Street [the central north-south thoroughfare]," one businessman recalled, "and visit, regardless of religious denomination; he had entrée."[79]

A man who knew the bishop well pointed out, however, that Powell's salutations "didn't stop with the businesses. He visited the head of the University of Maryland and the president of Johns Hopkins University. Then he'd go through the Pratt [the central branch of the Enoch Pratt Free Library] and the YMCA, and he also went through the hospitals—University Hospital, Johns Hopkins Hospital."[80] "Bishop Powell was 'downtown,'" a clergyman of the diocese recalled; "he knew everyone."[81]

Powell was a regional representative of an elite that believed in its ability and duty to serve the denomination, foster religious unity, and contribute to the welfare of society.[82] In the postwar years, the white male leaders of mainline Protestantism were in charge to an extent they never would be again.[83] In Powell's case, establishment contacts and prestige not only enabled him to have an influence on such major public events as the desegregation of Baltimore schools and to work behind the scenes for the public good but also to win support for such diocesan enterprises as the Episcopal Advance Fund and St. James School. The son of a company president recalled that Powell's practice of visiting downtown offices "was not only a *Christian* act but a *smart* one. . . . His support among Baltimore's leaders, including my father, was strong."[84] Of course, participation in this informal entente resulted not only in the achievement of some worthy goals but in other things being left undone and unsaid.

Christ above Culture

In H. Richard Niebuhr's well-known typology setting forth the variety of ways in which Christians interpret and deal with the dominant culture, Powell probably came closest to embodying the Christ-above-culture perspective.[85] He found much in American culture to appreciate, indeed to love, and reveled in his daily concrete experience of life in this world. He expressed gratitude for his country's noblest principles and for the best values of the South, enshrined in such institutions as the honor system of the University of Virginia.[86] He not only admired such august personages as the Founding Fathers and Robert E. Lee but also respected the leading politicians and businessmen he knew well.

For the most part, therefore, Powell saw Christianity more as a perfecting than a contradiction of the ideals of western civilization, much as medieval Christian thinkers understood divine revelation to add to the truths discovered by the natural powers of discursive thought or the ethical demands of Christ to transcend the natural-law principles perceived by human reason. Obedience to the way of Christ, he knew, is more challenging and infinitely more satisfying than any other adventure a person could embark upon, but it is a way that leads into and embraces this world of everyday experience.[87]

Surely Powell's support of civilization's ideals was made more confident by his belief that its worthiest standards were rooted in the transformations wrought by the coming of Christianity. To the extent that every culture, including his own, worshiped the social deities rather than the One beyond the many and honored power and self-assertion instead of patience and self-sacrifice, he was inclined to criticize society's pretensions.

Although he had no essential quarrel with the basic institutions of American life, Powell knew that all human endeavors were marred by sin, especially the sin of pride, manifest in narrow thinking of all kinds—in racism, in nationalism, in technological overreaching, and in soul-killing bureaucratization. He had a strong antimaterialist strain in his makeup. Thus he saw

Christ not simply as above culture but also, to employ Niebuhr's term, as the transformer of culture, although clearly Powell's willingness to support rapid or extensive change was restrained by an inherently conservative attitude toward tradition and method.[88]

Like the Protestant leaders of his native state in the days of his youth, Powell favored the more limited and localized efforts represented in the institutions and reforms of "social Christianity" over the broader critique of the injustices of modern industrial society offered by proponents of the social gospel. Unlike many of the early advocates of the social gospel, whose ministerial careers, like his, were built upon an active commitment to the pastoral office, Powell did not enter into a serious, sustained confrontation with the corporate character of sin or launch an assault on the socioeconomic sources of human suffering.[89]

A vision of the church as social crusader did not play a major role in the ecclesiology of this bishop, whose early formation took place among the Baptists and Methodists of rural Alabama; his position was more one of "let the church be the church." In addition to the two attitudes already noted, there was in Powell a "dualistic" strain: he recognized an opposition between Christ and culture. This approach refuses, in Niebuhr's words, "to accommodate the claims of Christ to those of secular society." Powell felt the polarity and tension between Christ and cultural life that ought to exist between conscientious Christians and the powers of this world; he looked to a redemption that lay beyond history.[90]

Nevertheless, to a considerable degree Powell's outlook as bishop did dovetail with the dominant temper of his times. Obviously this was an era in which an Episcopal bishop's capacity to function, enjoy recognition, and perhaps even bring some influence to bear beyond his own denomination was bolstered by a cooperating social environment: authority and atmosphere went together. As James Griffiss, a priest who served under Powell during this period, has pointed out, the postwar years offered, despite the fears induced by the cold war, a sense of security, which "derived from a society that was centered in the church and a political order which was reasonably stable." Houses of worship were full, money was starting to flow in for construction and new programs, college students still turned to the churches for guidance, and religion held people's interest as an intellectual as well as a spiritual topic. Anglicans such as T. S. Eliot and W. H. Auden "were for many people living examples of the harmony of religion with the arts and the intellectual life." It was "intellectually and socially 'respectable' to be religious."[91]

During Powell's years in office, Griffiss observed, social norms and spiritual values "were still fairly clear," but with this clarity sometimes went a rather self-satisfied attitude of moral superiority. The church of the 1940s often appeared to be "a bastion of political and social conformity." In most parishes, Griffiss remembered, "the biblical words of judgment about conformity to social mores spoken by the [Hebrew] prophets . . . and by Jesus . . . were either not heard or were interpreted away." Preachers rarely took on racial and economic injustice, and the fact that "all churches in Baltimore were racially segregated never caused most Christians any problem whatsoever. The church was simply a part of what we later learned to call The Establishment."[92]

As bishop, Noble Powell displayed many of the strengths and some of the weaknesses of the Episcopal establishment in his day. No doubt having this combination of attributes in mind as he penned sentences suited to the occasion of Powell's retirement, the editor of the *Baltimore Afro-American* observed that the Maryland diocesan "was a tall man with a soft answer," a leader who "never lost his temper," though there were times when "We thought he should have because we had lost ours." The editorial noted that, during the years of Powell's episcopate, the writer had been anxious for positive change and from time to time had pressed the bishop with questions about the pace of integration in the Episcopal church: When was the church going to integrate its schools and homes for unwed mothers? When would the Episcopal church elect a black bishop? When would black and white Episcopal rectors exchange pulpits during Lent? Eventually some significant changes did come to the Episcopal church. Now, the writer said, choosing his words carefully, "We salute [Bishop Powell] as a gentle, patient, comforting disciple of his Lord, who kept the respect and affection of his people in . . . difficult times."[93]

By the end of Powell's episcopate, the reluctance of mainline churches to denounce the status quo had roused the ire of such social critics as Gibson Winter, an Episcopalian who wrote in *The Suburban Captivity of the Churches* of "the deformation of Protestantism." By this phrase Winter, who had served as a parish priest in the suburbs, meant religious life that existed only to address "a private sphere of symptoms rather than a public sphere of values."[94] Religion, he claimed, had been reduced to the function of personal and emotional adjustment; the residential parish was now a private island. The church ought to become involved in "the renewal of the metropolis."[95] By the time Powell left office, a religion that had been gaining power in all its forms—popular, elite, and ecclesiastical—was increasingly coming under attack by religious academics, whose jeremiads provided an intellectual foundation for the wholesale assault of the later sixties.[96]

It was symbolically fitting, albeit horrendously unfortunate, that Powell's successor, Harry Lee Doll, should be installed as diocesan on the day that John F. Kennedy was assassinated. The murder of the thirty-fifth president is often taken to mark the beginning of that period of social upheaval known as "the sixties," a decade of disarray that, as a cultural phenomenon, lasted until about 1973.[97] Harry Lee Doll (1903–84) served as bishop of Maryland until 1971, when he resigned his office at age sixty-eight, four years earlier than church law required. His guiding theme was the church as a family, but after eight years as paterfamilias he had had enough.[98]

The happiness of his years as suffragan (1955–58) and coadjutor (1958–63) had been undermined to some extent by a diocesan who was benign but autocratic, reluctant to share the responsibilities of the diocese and to delegate important functions, even to another bishop. Moreover, Powell tended to regard Doll as a good-hearted but weak person, in need of guidance. The two bishops enjoyed a cordial but rather formal relationship, Doll always addressing his senior by his title, while wishing that Powell would tell him to call him by his Christian name.[99]

Toward the end of his time as Powell's deputy, Doll sometimes felt restrained and frustrated, and on rare occasions he would unleash his anger on innocent third parties. A difference emerged between the two bishops—though not one that was ever expressed in a direct confrontation—which had to do not only with specific issues, such as the methods to be employed in the civil rights struggle, but also with attitudes toward social transformation in general. Politically Doll was no radical, but he was more open to change than Powell was. In February 1961, for example, in the weeks following JFK's inauguration, Doll told the annual convention of the diocese of Maryland that "We must give thanks to God . . . that we live in this time of unrest and upheaval . . . , [when] the Church of the Living God is mightily challenged by the customs and mores of the world. . . . [We must] rethink our offensive against the world, being ready to discard many of our traditional patterns for new ones."[100] It is hard to imagine Bishop Powell addressing the matter of the church's responsibility in those terms.

In the first year of his episcopate Doll declared that civil rights "'was perhaps the greatest religious issue of our time, not only in this nation but in the world.'"[101] He put his beliefs into practice when in January 1966 he testified in favor of an open-housing ordinance that was being considered by the Baltimore city council. These hearings in the War Memorial building were made particularly memorable by the response of a hostile crowd of white people, who hurled boos, jeers, and catcalls at him from the public gallery.[102]

As diocesan, Doll expressed a commendable impatience on behalf of the rights of African-American citizens and the downtrodden. He also made significant strides in developing the ecumenical relationship that Bishop

Powell had begun with the Roman Catholic archdiocese and Cardinal She-han.[103] Doll was effective too in implementing a more democratic approach to diocesan administration. And he led the diocese in support of a new prayer book and women's ordination; his and Delia's daughter Chotard became a priest and was one of the first female candidates for episcopal office in the United States.[104] "Harry Lee Doll performed nobly as bishop," Bennett Sims remarked. "He was a moral hero, [who] provided prophetic leadership that [his successors] have carried on."[105]

Doll's days as diocesan occurred during one of the most traumatic pe-riods of the nation's history: eight years marked by war, assassinations, ur-ban riots, and all manner of assaults on traditional institutions. By the end of his tenure in office the diocese of Maryland had begun to suffer the loss-es in money and membership that afflicted the denomination nationwide. At this time, one priest remembered, Doll "agonized over the fact that we were not meeting our national church apportionment. [There was a] de-cline in church support [caused by] two factors combined: demographics and protest." It was part of "what was going on in the culture," a "revolt against authority."[106]

By 1967—the start of the "second sixties"[107]—the civil rights movement had been transformed by the rise of "black power" and a new militancy, which stressed economic and political self-determination.[108] In the wake of the Episcopal church's boisterous special general convention in South Bend, Indiana, in 1969, Harry Lee Doll, an unwavering supporter of the presiding bishop, John E. Hines, sustained fierce attacks on his leadership.

Attempting to defend the special convention's decision to make two hun-dred thousand dollars available to a group understood to be indirectly asso-ciated with James Forman's bold "black manifesto," which demanded mil-lions from mainline churches in "reparations," Doll endured an evening of withering criticism and revilement in a meeting at the Church of the Redeem-er in Baltimore. Interviewed at the time of his retirement, Doll recalled that "'there were at least 1,000 people [there], and never in my life have I felt such a wave of pure hatred flow up to me as there was that night.'"[109] The rector of the parish, Robert P. Patterson, described Doll "sitting in a chair in front of the altar." After he "made a presentation, people began to yell. You could see the man just visibly slump with despair." The abuse did not let up for some time afterwards: "He'd be called in the middle of the night repeated-ly," Patterson recalled. "He was bowed but never beaten. He never became hostile himself. He absorbed it. [At the end], he was tired; he had fought the battles long enough."[110]

Establishment's End

Although the Episcopal establishment never exerted its influence through the sheer force of overall numbers, its decline is partly indicated by the denomination's membership drop after 1965. From 3.64 million members in 1966, the church fell to 3.04 million in 1980 and to 2.5 million in 1993. This loss was unprecedented, having come after almost two centuries of growth. In Noble Powell's last year in office, 1963, there were nearly sixty-seven thousand baptized persons and forty-one thousand communicants in the diocese of Maryland; in 1993 there were some forty-seven thousand baptized persons and twenty-nine thousand communicants.[111]

In the 1960s and 1970s, people's attitudes toward institutional affiliation—including membership in mainline religious bodies—underwent an important shift. "The decade of the sixties," wrote the historian Sydney Ahlstrom, "was a time . . . when the old foundations of national confidence, patriotic idealism, moral traditionalism, and even of historic Judaeo-Christian theism, were awash."[112] All of the major institutions of society came under attack in these years—the federal government, corporations, the military, universities, as well as churches—but the sufferings of mainline Protestantism turned out to be chronic. "Religion was different," one historian has observed, "only in how far and fast it fell in perceived cultural significance, and perhaps also in how seriously this sense of malaise was internalized in the life of the institutions of organized religion."[113]

For old-line denominations such as the Episcopal church, the shattering of the fifties-era religiocultural synthesis of beliefs and national ideals meant a loss of prestige, clout, and drawing power. The coherence and dominance of American culture-religion gave way under the pressure of a series of events—Selma and Birmingham, foreign war and domestic dissension, the rise in drug-related violent crime, treachery in high places—which revealed that not everything was right in God's New Israel. The body politic contained some major character flaws, and the nation's civic faith and old, elite sources of authority received a drubbing.[114] In the mainstream churches the process of actively confronting the political and social questions of the era, such as race and war, often disrupted the internal harmony of the denominations themselves, causing some members to withdraw their support.[115]

Also at this time, as American religion became much more pluralistic (a religious diversity augmented by an influx of non-Protestant immigrants), the psychology of religious folk became highly individualistic and church membership notably fluid.[116] Living in a mobile and atomistic society, Americans grew accustomed to shopping for the religious product that appealed to them at the moment. Denominations—brand names—held far less significance than previously.[117] Many people paid more attention to the theological families— liberal, conservative, charismatic, and so forth—to which their congregations belonged than they paid to denominational affiliations.[118] In many cases the roots that anchored congregants to their churches were shallow and easily disturbed. By the late 1970s roughly half of all adult Episcopalians had not been raised in the Episcopal church. Moreover, religious belonging no longer received the social support it had enjoyed in the 1950s. Becoming a Presbyterian or an Episcopalian or a Congregationalist meant much less than it once had as a sign of upward mobility.[119] Fast-growing evangelical Protestantism had become a respectable alternative to the mainline.

Undoubtedly, the largest portion of those individuals who abandoned the Episcopal church did not join another church but drifted into secularity— but a secular realm with a difference, permeated by sacred themes, images, and rituals. A diffused spirituality and a variegated religiosity were increasingly the order—or disorder—of the day.[120] "[I]t has become clear," one scholar of religion has noted, "that secularization does not entail the progressive demise of religion in general but a transformation of its form. In a secularized or secularizing society, religious activities . . . become a matter of . . . voluntary affiliation instead of an automatic cultural assumption or obligatory public duty."[121]

Many people who would have described themselves as "very spiritual" disaffiliated with the Episcopal church and other old-line denominations because they no longer felt they needed the guideposts of organized religion to pursue their journeys. These churches were bound to have less appeal in a society that had become "posttraditional." To an unprecedented degree, everything, including career and religion and personal identity, was now a matter of choice and not a given. The postmodern self was unabashedly protean. In a fast-paced, ever-changing technological age, family and heritage and custom no longer exerted the influence they had in the past, even in the South.[122] And concepts like "sin," "atonement," and "salvation" became less comprehensible in a culture whose beliefs were many and varied and whose values tended to be relativistic. Citizens participated in a public life that was post-Christian and were prone to err on the side of nonjudgmental acceptance of a variety of "lifestyle choices."[123]

Erosion of the Protestant mainline brought with it a decrease in the appeal of the ordained ministry as a career, a decline in the caliber of seminary graduates, and a falling off in the quality of preaching.[124] With mixed results, commissions on ministry took over from diocesan bishops the leading role in appraising those who wished to go to seminary. By various means, the church made proceeding to holy orders frustratingly difficult for some of its most desirable candidates.[125]

When Noble Powell was in Charlottesville he played a major role in recruiting promising candidates for the ministry. Starting in the 1970s, the Episcopal church consistently neglected the nation's colleges and universities. Few denominations had a stronger office of college work than the Episcopal church in the decades immediately following World War II. But this emphasis declined markedly during the era of the Vietnam War.[126] Among mainline denominations the Episcopal church was not alone in having abandoned this effort, and the problem was not soon rectified. In 1993 one observer declared that the commitment of American denominations "to the mission field of campus ministry" was "anemic."[127]

In some ways, the effects of Protestant cultural disestablishment were salutary. American popular culture—including the information and entertainment media—provided little support for those who sought to practice their faith in more than a superficial manner. Consequently, as secularity exerted its steady pull, Episcopalians found themselves, on the eve of the third millennium, no longer members of a popular in-group but of a religious body that required a more conscious effort to join and be part of. In this sense, the Episcopal church came to resemble something closer to a "gathered community," whose values no longer largely and, as it were, automatically overlapped with those of a unified American culture.[128] Granted, this church community still demanded relatively little of its initiates, but more of a commitment was required to be a member than in the days when belonging was a matter of social expectation.

Bishop Powell would have been heartened to see that large numbers of people who were not Episcopalians realized the value of some Episcopal institutions. Undoubtedly one of the chief reasons that church-related schools met with such marked success in the latter decades of the twentieth century was that the same secular currents that drew Americans away from liberal Protestantism's receding shore swirled around and propelled them toward Episcopal boarding and day schools. The challenge of secularism and the widespread perception of a loss of "traditional values" helped to strengthen Episcopal institutions that were neither altogether within nor completely outside the Episcopal church. For thousands of young people in the last decades of the twentieth century, these schools represented the only serious introduction to the Episcopal church—or even to Christianity—they would receive.[129]

In financial terms, these schools and their counterparts at the other end of the age range—Episcopal retirement centers—were enjoying a level of success that many struggling parishes could only envy. By the mid 1970s most of the churches in the diocese of Maryland that had received assistance from the Episcopal Advance Fund found themselves unable to pay off their loans. Consequently, the diocese awarded them the money outright as grants. Otherwise, as the bishop at the time remarked, these churches would have been kept in perpetual mission status, unable to undertake any programs or outreach of their own, busily holding bazaars and bake sales to pay off the interest on their loans.[130] Meanwhile, plans were begun in the late 1980s to devote a section of the property of the Bishop Claggett Diocesan Center to the development of an ecumenical retirement community, to be managed by an Episcopal agency.

Scholars have noted that the religious depression of the 1960s—the third disestablishment—lasted longer and had a more significant impact than the downturn of the late twenties and early thirties.[131] As the Protestant establishment increasingly found itself sidelined, the Episcopal bishop found his or her authority diminished in church and society. Part of this change was brought about by the churches themselves. Not only in religion but in education and family life the old formality and hierarchy broke down, and less-patriarchal styles came to the fore.[132]

Noble Powell was bishop during an era that encouraged the emergence of strong, highly visible leaders, who had personal relationships with their executive counterparts in business, education, and government. By 1970, toward the end of Harry Lee Doll's period in office, challenges had arisen throughout society to that older style of charismatic leadership. The expanded use of task forces and consensus building seemed preferable to the benign rule of a commanding presence at the top. Mainstream Protestant denominations democratized their administrative functions, emphasizing an egalitarian rather than an authoritarian management structure. As a result, church governance became more anonymous and bureaucratic; individual powerhouses had less opportunity to arise or preside. The new approach to leadership, which highlighted the image of the church as the people of God, strived to give recognition to the ministry of all baptized Christians and provided wider opportunities for women and members of minority groups to participate in decision making.[133]

These leadership changes incorporated many worthwhile elements, but, as Jim Fenhagen has noted, by the 1990s bishops often seemed remote figures, their authority no longer widely acknowledged, their role no longer clear. In many dioceses bishops in the last quarter of the twentieth century presided over their jurisdictions like chief executive officers over a corporation. With bigger staffs they oversaw dioceses with fewer Episcopalians in a manner that could seem more bureaucratic than personal, more businesslike than pastoral.[134]

Episcopal bishops lost authority within the larger society as well. With the Protestant "intactness" of the fifties gone, church leaders no longer had broad influence beyond the boundaries of their own denominations.[135] The mainline could not confidently shape or engage the culture the way it once had.[136] In Maryland the Episcopal bishop was no longer the widely recognized personage he was in Noble Powell's day. Also, owing to changes in the economic and political spheres, where complex and impersonal bureaucracies came to dominate the scene, later bishops could not establish the range of relationships with other leaders that Powell enjoyed in an era that offered more opportunities for nonutilitarian commerce between persons.[137]

A Life in the Church

Although the times had changed, history did not continue to move always in the same direction. By the 1990s Christians in a troubled society—one marked by violence and the neglect of children, the decline of kinship and the loss of a sense of place—were giving fresh consideration to such Powellian themes as the vices and virtues of everyday life, the reality of sin, the theology of friendship, and the centrality of the pastoral ministry.[138] Powell's incarnationalist theology, emphasizing the joy of the gospel, the beauty of the natural realm, and the rich possibilities of creaturely life lived in the presence of God, still resonated.[139] His was a Christocentric theology that had a place for evil but stressed the goodness of the created order and humans' use of reason and conscience within it.[140]

Powell's thought and work always had a place for the action of the church in the world, but he doubtless would have agreed with the theologian who averred that the church has a unique role to play in shaping hearts and minds, thereby affecting people in the most fundamental ways: the church's "public role as an institutional actor has far less potential than does its indirect role as shepherd of souls."[141] Duncan Gray Jr., a hero of the civil rights era and later bishop of Mississippi, pointed out in 1972 that while the parish church had taken a good bit of abuse in recent years and was considered by some to be outmoded and dead as an instrument of social transformation, it still had an essential task to perform in precisely this area, because "legal action . . . does not get to the heart of the matter: the matter of the human heart."[142]

In the Episcopal church, at the best of times, the wayward heart is informed and guided by the sound words and right conduct of persons who stand for a distinctive way of life. As many writers have observed, Anglican-

ism is not defined by confessions or systematic theologies but is characterized by an ethos, a vision. Robert Runcie, the 102nd archbishop of Canterbury, said that Anglicanism has "a 'sensibility,' a way of understanding that
works almost by instinct." And the religious lives of Anglicans, Runcie noted, are largely shaped by other individuals, by those "whose lives of prayer
and scholarship, pastoral zeal, prophetic insight or artistic achievement have
been grounded in the scriptures and the liturgy as tradition has handed them
down to us."[143]

As the "or" in Runcie's comment indicates, one gifted person is less likely
to possess talents omnifarious than to excel in a more limited range of activities. This was true of Noble Powell. One occasionally misses in his life story the
manifestation of greater intellectual depth or of a more critical edge; at times
he seems too passive—too shy of risk—in his response to large-scale injustice.
Surely one regrets to discover a marked imbalance between his personal and
professional lives, to find such a compulsive, if not prideful, attachment to his
office as to suggest a failure not merely to value the restorative properties of
leisure but to grasp the theological importance of letting go. In sympathy with
the children who listened to him preach in the garden at Mockingbird Place,
later generations might admire the way Powell took to his role but wish he had
more often ventured to lay aside the mask of command.

To some extent, however, Powell's deficiencies were but the defects of his
virtues, and certainly the overwhelming majority of those who encountered
him found it hard to feel anything but gratitude for the gift of the abound-
ing presence of one who so transparently had their own best interests and
the welfare of the church at heart. For thousands of people of all backgrounds
who dealt with him as parson, dean, or bishop, he was the kind of influential figure that Runcie points to. Gracefully exercising his own talents, Powell drew each person "a little higher than where you were," humanized administration, practiced patience and civility, and applied spiritual wisdom.
What made him so striking was a peculiar capacity to provide a link between
the common life of the individual and divine things. This rare quality meant
that many of those who knew him found themselves engaged by a transforming friendship.

Notes

Introduction

1. See Joan Didion, "James Pike, American," in *The White Album* (New York: Simon and Schuster, 1979), 51–58.

2. "Tribute to James A. Pike," *America,* 20 September 1969, 178.

3. Julian N. Hartt, *Theological Method and Imagination* (New York: Seabury, 1977), 253.

4. William Faulkner, "Address upon Receiving the Nobel Prize for Literature," December 1950, in *Essays, Speeches, and Public Letters,* ed. James B. Meriwether (New York: Random House, 1965), 120.

5. Daniel J. Singal, *The War Within: From Victorian to Modernist Thought in the South, 1919–1945* (Chapel Hill: University of North Carolina Press, 1982), 17–18, and "Towards a Definition of American Modernism," *American Quarterly* 39 (Spring 1987): 9.

6. Singal, *War Within,* esp. 3–10, and "Towards a Definition of American Modernism," 7–26. The modernism I am outlining here is not to be confused with theological modernism, or liberalism, which arose at about the same time and evinced some similarities but was essentially a different phenomenon.

7. See Singal, "Towards a Definition of American Modernism," 14, 21.

8. This emphasis on personality contrasts sharply with the modernist program of depersonalization. See T. S. Eliot, "Tradition and the Individual Talent," in *The Norton Anthology of English Literature,* vol. 2, ed. M. H. Abrams (New York: Norton, 1968), 1807–14.

9. See Singal, "Towards a Definition of American Modernism," 10.

10. Alasdair MacIntyre, *After Virtue: A Study in Moral Theory,* 2d ed. (Notre Dame, Ind.: University of Notre Dame Press, 1984), chap. 10.

Chapter 1: Formation, 1891–1920

The epigraph is taken from Charles M. Beckwith to Dr. Harry T. Marshall (University of Virginia), 6 May 1920, Old Clergy Files, Birmingham Public Library, Birmingham, Ala. (hereafter BPL).

1. Thus from the beatings and murders of African Americans did Lowndes County derive its sinister nickname. Michael T. Kaufman, "Gary T. Rowe Jr., 64, Who Informed on Klan in Civil Rights Killing, Is Dead," *New York Times,* 4 October 1998, nat. ed., 44; Mary Stanton, *From Selma to Sorrow: The Life and Death of Viola Liuzzo* (Athens: University of Georgia Press, 1998), 5–6, 21–22, 29–30, 128–30; Juan Williams, *Eyes on the Prize: America's Civil Rights Years, 1954–1965* (New York: Viking, 1987), 284; Charles W. Eagles,

Outside Agitator: Jon Daniels and the Civil Rights Movement in Alabama (Chapel Hill: University of North Carolina Press, 1993), xii, 89, 99–102, 113–17; *The Jon Daniels Story: With His Letters and Papers,* ed. William J. Schneider (New York: Seabury, 1967), 11, 39; Glenn N. Sisk, "Social Aspects of the Alabama Black Belt, 1875–1917," *Mid-America* 37 (January 1955): 44.

2. The development in the 1790s of an inexpensive cotton gin that could efficiently separate the fuzzy seed from the short lint of the upland-grown, green-seed cotton enabled producers of these shrubby plants to compete effectively for the expanding British market for cotton staple. Unlike rice and indigo, cotton could be cultivated relatively easily and inexpensively, and once harvested it was cheap to store and transport. Technological advances, the increasing demand created by British textile mills, and the formal organization of new territories in the South sparked the rise of the American cotton kingdom. After 1815 a great migration took place from the Atlantic-seaboard South to the Southwest, as small farmers and large planters participated in the rush to acquire land and reap profits from cotton. In only ten years, from 1810 to 1820, the population of Mississippi and Alabama exploded from 40,352 to 222,311. John B. Boles, *The South through Time: A History of an American Region* (Englewood Cliffs, N.J.: Prentice-Hall, 1995), 150–53, 171; Virginia Van der Veer Hamilton, *Alabama: A Bicentennial History* (New York: Norton, 1977), 3–4. By 1840 Lowndes County was the seventh most populous in the state. Large numbers of people moved in after initial obstacles had been overcome: the Creek Indians were driven out, and pioneer settlers solved the problems of working the sticky clay soil and digging adequate wells for drinking water. Eagles, *Outside Agitator,* 91.

3. Throughout the antebellum period the slaveholding planter class of the Alabama Black Belt was one of the most politically powerful elites in the United States. C. Vann Woodward, "Look Away, Look Away," *Journal of Southern History* 59 (August 1993): 498. See also Eagles, *Outside Agitator,* 92–93. Eagles points out that most members of the "planter aristocracy" of antebellum Lowndes County were only moderately prosperous farmers making their way in a rough frontier society. Hayneville was a gambling town where men gathered on the town square to wager on cockfights or ventured indoors to try their luck in any of eight betting parlors.

4. Population Index, State Census, 1855, Lowndes County, Alabama Department of Archives and History, Montgomery. In Lowndes County, 60 percent of white farmers owned slaves; nearly 80 percent of these owned fewer than thirty slaves. In 1860 the county's population consisted of 8,362 whites and 19,340 slaves. Eagles, *Outside Agitator,* 92.

5. Frank Howard Hawthorne, *Kissin' Kin and Lost Cousins* (Montgomery, Ala.: n.p., 1989), 351–56; certificates issued to Seymour Powell, 1824, 1825, 1834, by the General Land Office of the United States, Louise Campbell Forward Collection, Mobile, Ala. (hereafter LCF Collection). Noble Powell was born on a Tuesday morning at the home of his uncle, Cecil D. Whitman (1841–1915), in Lowndesboro.

6. Virginia Van der Veer Hamilton, *Seeing Historic Alabama* (Tuscaloosa: University of Alabama Press, 1982), 139 (quotation); Eagles, *Outside Agitator,* 93; Hamilton, *Alabama,* 109.

7. Thomas McAdory Owen, *History of Alabama and Dictionary of Alabama Biography,* vol. 2 (1921; Spartanburg, S.C.: Reprint Co., 1978), 911. In 1860 the Black Belt contained 12.2 percent of the white population of Alabama; in 1900 it contained only 7.5 percent. Whites left for a variety of reasons, including fear of the large population of black freedmen (who outnumbered whites four to one), the wish to escape hard manual labor, and the desire for greater social and employment opportunities elsewhere (including the iron

and steel industry of Birmingham). The limitations of life in the Black Belt—inferior schools, bad roads, poor health care, and all the inconveniences of rural life—increasingly made such an existence seem provincial and undesirable. A growing sense of "relative deprivation" combined with the reality of economic uncertainty to drive many people away. Sisk, "Social Aspects," 31–33; Eagles, *Outside Agitator,* 103–4. Sharecroppers operated 90 percent of the farms in Lowndes County, and 90 percent of these tenants were black. They struggled within a system of debt peonage that was little better than slavery. In 1903 a United States district attorney said that the center of the South's peonage system was Lowndes County. Eagles, *Outside Agitator,* 90, 96–97. See also Howard N. Rabinowitz, *The First New South, 1865–1920* (Arlington Heights, Ill.: Harlan Davidson Inc., 1992), 17–18; Paul E. Mertz, "Sharecropping and Tenancy," in *Encyclopedia of Southern Culture,* ed. Charles Reagan Wilson and William Ferris (Chapel Hill: University of North Carolina Press, 1989), 29–31.

8. A relative recorded a favorable description: Shell Powell's plantation "ranked among the best in the neighborhood—the yield of cotton was above the average—his stock was in good condition—his cabins comfortable—and his tenants were industrious and contented." He "owned a pretty home [Mockingbird Place] on the Ridge, presided over by a lovely wife and three sweet children." Miss S. C. (Cakie) Cilley, "Garfield" (a "true story"), Lowndesboro, handwritten manuscript, ca. 1898, LCF Collection. See Grady McWhiney, "The Revolution in Nineteenth-Century Agriculture," in *From Civil War to Civil Rights: Alabama, 1860–1960,* ed. Sarah Woolfolk Wiggins (Tuscaloosa: University of Alabama Press, 1987), 109–32.

9. About twenty years after receiving it, Shell gave the book to his son, Noble.

10. Louise Howard Powell Mitchell (hereafter LHPM), notebook of jottings and reminiscences (1992–93), in the author's possession. See Ted Ownby, *Subduing Satan: Religion, Recreation, and Manhood in the Rural South, 1865–1920* (Chapel Hill: University of North Carolina Press, 1990), 106–10, 134.

11. Roberta Meadows McGavock (Lowndesboro, Ala.), telephone interview with the author, 19 January 1993.

12. LHPM notebook.

13. Edward L. Ayers, *The Promise of the New South: Life after Reconstruction* (New York: Oxford University Press, 1992), 15.

14. C. Vann Woodward, *Origins of the New South, 1877–1913* (Baton Rouge: Louisiana State University Press, 1951), 185; Wayne Flynt, *Alabama Baptists: Southern Baptists in the Heart of Dixie* (Tuscaloosa: University of Alabama Press, 1998), 207.

15. LHPM notebook; LHPM, interview with the author, Spanish Fort, Ala., 18 January 1993. In 1919 the citizens of Enterprise, in Coffee County, Alabama, erected the Boll Weevil Monument, commemorating the passing of the all-cotton system of farming and the beginning of greater prosperity through diversification. Owen, *History of Alabama,* vol. 2, facing p. 1344. See also Douglas Helms, "Boll Weevil," in *Encyclopedia of Southern Culture,* ed. Charles Reagan Wilson and William Ferris (Chapel Hill: University of North Carolina Press, 1989), 32; Leon F. Litwack, *Trouble in Mind: Black Southerners in the Age of Jim Crow* (New York: Alfred A. Knopf, 1998), 175–78.

16. Telephone interview with Roberta Meadows McGavock, 19 January 1993; Deed Record Book BB, 342–43, Lowndes County Courthouse, Hayneville, Alabama. See Eagles, *Outside Agitator,* 95.

17. Boles, *South through Time,* 223–24; Flynt, *Alabama Baptists,* 39–41, 239–43.

18. Interview with LHPM.

19. Annie Brown Baker, interview with the author, Lowndesboro, Ala., 19 January 1993.

20. LHPM notebook. In 1920 Mamie travelled north to attend her son's graduation from Virginia Theological Seminary in Alexandria.

21. LHPM notebook.

22. It was not at all unusual in the Deep South for local professional men to be planters as well.

23. In the 1880s, as the historian Wayne Flynt has observed, Alabama Baptists "seized on the [alcohol] issue with a passion." See Flynt's thorough discussion of the temperance crusade in *Alabama Baptists,* 184 (quotation), 186, 209–19.

24. Interview with Annie Brown Baker.

25. Hamilton, *Alabama,* 122.

26. Eagles, *Outside Agitator,* 103.

27. Roberta Meadows McGavock, interview with the author, Lowndesboro, Ala., 11 May 1994.

28. Telephone interview with Roberta Meadows McGavock, 19 January 1993.

29. LHPM notebook. McGavock, who spent much time at Mockingbird Place, remembered that it was "Noble's mother [who] made him a black preacher's gown; he'd wear it and preach to white and colored children in the yard." Interview with Roberta Meadows McGavock, 11 May 1994.

30. Interview with LHPM. "The town just loved him," Louise said; "he had a dedicated life."

31. Interview with Roberta Meadows McGavock, 11 May 1994.

32. Interview with Annie Brown Baker.

33. LHPM notebook.

34. Interview with Roberta Meadows McGavock, 11 May 1994. This recollection may be somewhat faulty; see chap. 2.

35. LHPM notebook.

36. William Alexander Percy, *Lanterns on the Levee: Recollections of a Planter's Son* (1941; Baton Rouge: Louisiana State University Press, 1973), 48; Charles L. Hein, interview with the author, Upperco, Md., 22 April 1994.

37. LHPM notebook.

38. Ibid.

39. Interview with Roberta Meadows McGavock, 11 May 1994.

40. See James W. Ely Jr., "The South, the Supreme Court, and Race Relations, 1890–1965," in *The South as an American Problem,* ed. Larry J. Griffin and Don H. Doyle (Athens: University of Georgia Press, 1995), 128–29.

41. Boles, *South through Time,* 420; William Warren Rogers, Robert David Ward, Leah Rawls Atkins, and Wayne Flynt, *Alabama: The History of a Deep South State* (Tuscaloosa: University of Alabama Press, 1994), chap. 19, "The Defeat of Reform."

42. Hamilton, *Alabama,* 40, 96; Eagles, *Outside Agitator,* 98–99. Eagles notes that many illiterate blacks and poor whites were disfranchised as the result of a new and complex voter registration and election law passed by the state legislature in 1893. The law assisted conservative Democrats in their effort to block the Populist challenge and retain power. See also Litwack, *Trouble in Mind,* 225–28, 363–70.

43. Hamilton, *Alabama,* 88; Sisk, "Social Aspects," 47. See also Litwack, *Trouble in Mind,* 283–312.

44. Eagles, *Outside Agitator,* 100. Eagles also reports that two black men were lynched in Lowndes County in July 1917, and no one was ever punished for these murders either (101–2).

45. Ibid., 99, 100 (quotation).

46. Silas Emmett Lucas Jr., telephone interview with the author, 11 July 1992.

47. John Egerton, "The End of the South as an American Problem," in *The South as an American Problem,* ed. Larry J. Griffin and Don H. Doyle (Athens: University of Georgia Press, 1995), 266; Sisk, "Social Aspects," 43; Joel Williamson, *The Crucible of Race: Black/White Relations in the American South since Emancipation* (New York: Oxford University Press, 1984), 28–29; Flynt, *Alabama Baptists,* 237–39, 302–5, 353–54.

48. John B. Boles, "Evangelical Protestantism in the Old South: From Religious Dissent to Cultural Dominance," in *Religion in the South,* ed. Charles Reagan Wilson (Jackson: University Press of Mississippi, 1985), 27, and *South through Time,* 241–42, 427; Edward R. Crowther, "Holy Honor: Sacred and Secular in the Old South," *Journal of Southern History* 58 (November 1992): 619–36; Samuel S. Hill Jr., *Southern Churches in Crisis* (New York: Holt, Rinehart and Winston, 1966), 29–30; Norman A. Yance, *Religion Southern Style: Southern Baptists and Society in Historical Perspective* (Danville, Va.: Association of Baptist Professors of Religion, 1978), 12, 17, 28–31; Rufus Spain, *At Ease in Zion: Social History of Southern Baptists, 1865–1900* (Nashville: Vanderbilt University Press, 1967), 209–14; John Lee Eighmy, *Churches in Cultural Captivity: A History of the Social Attitudes of Southern Baptists* (Knoxville: University of Tennessee Press, 1972); James J. Thompson Jr., *Tried as by Fire: Southern Baptists and the Religious Controversies of the 1920s* (Macon, Ga.: Mercer University Press, 1982); Kenneth K. Bailey, "Southern White Protestantism at the Turn of the Century," *American Historical Review* 68 (April 1963): 619, 628; Flynt, *Alabama Baptists,* 254–56, 288–90.

49. Daniel Lee Cloyd, "Prelude to Reform: Political, Economic, and Social Thought of Alabama Baptists, 1877–1890," *Alabama Review* 31 (January 1978): 48–64; Spain, *At Ease in Zion,* chaps. 6–8; Flynt, *Alabama Baptists,* 155, 195–97, 219–28.

50. David B. Chesebrough, *"God Ordained This War": Sermons on the Sectional Crisis, 1830–1865* (Columbia: University of South Carolina Press, 1991); Ayers, *Promise of the New South,* 170; Wayne Flynt, "Alabama," in *Encyclopedia of Religion in the South,* ed. Samuel S. Hill (Macon, Ga.: Mercer University Press, 1984), 18–21, "Dissent in Zion: Alabama Baptists and Social Issues, 1900–1914," *Journal of Southern History* 35 (November 1969): 524–40, and *Alabama Baptists,* chaps. 6–7; Hill, *Southern Churches in Crisis,* 112; Yance, *Religion Southern Style,* 31; Kenneth K. Bailey, *Southern White Protestantism in the Twentieth Century* (New York: Harper and Row, 1964), 12, 20, 36–43; Eighmy, *Churches in Cultural Captivity,* 69–71, 93; Paul Harvey, *Redeeming the South: Religious Cultures and Racial Identities among Southern Baptists, 1865–1925* (Chapel Hill: University of North Carolina Press, 1997), chap. 7.

51. Flynt, "Alabama," 18–21, and *Alabama Baptists,* 230–31, 257, 288, 293.

52. Charles Reagan Wilson, introduction to *Religion in the South,* ed. Charles Reagan Wilson (Jackson: University Press of Mississippi, 1985), 9–10; Flynt, "Alabama," 17, 18; Keith Harper, *The Quality of Mercy: Southern Baptists and Social Christianity, 1890–1920* (Tuscaloosa: University of Alabama Press, 1996); Ayers, *Promise of the New South,* 181.

53. Ayers, *Promise of the New South,* 160, 180.

54. Hill, *Southern Churches in Crisis,* 115, 172–73; Harper, *Quality of Mercy,* 117; Flynt, *Alabama Baptists,* 237–39.

55. David L. Holmes, *A Brief History of the Episcopal Church* (Valley Forge, Pa.: Trinity Press International, 1993), 128–29.

56. Murphy feared that if the worst abuses of the capitalist system were not eliminated, social disorder might result. Shocked by the mistreatment of children in the textile mills of Montgomery, he persuaded the Alabama legislature to set the minimum age of child workers at twelve and to limit their work week to sixty hours. Murphy's conservative reformism was also reflected in his stance on racial matters. Although he supported segregation and a subservient role for blacks, he protested against the denial of blacks' basic rights to earn a living and to receive an education (at least in good moral habits and industrial skills). A benevolent paternalist, he established missions in Montgomery's African-American neighborhoods, clubs for young people, and a society to study issues concerning race. Williamson, *Crucible of Race,* 415–21; Hugh C. Bailey, *Edgar Gardner Murphy: Gentle Progressive* (Coral Gables, Fla.: University of Miami Press, 1968); Daniel Levine, "Edgar Gardner Murphy: Conservative Reformer," *Alabama Review* 15 (April 1962): 100–116; Ronald C. White, "Beyond the Sacred: Edgar Gardner Murphy and a Ministry of Social Reform," *Historical Magazine of the Protestant Episcopal Church* 44 (March 1980): 51–69; Woodward, *Origins,* 353, 416–19; Singal, *War Within,* 31–32; Flynt, *Alabama Baptists,* 280–81; Gardiner H. Shattuck Jr., *Episcopalians and Race: Civil War to Civil Rights* (Lexington: University Press of Kentucky, 2000), 18–19.

57. Albert Burton Moore, *History of Alabama and Her People,* vol. 1 (Chicago: The American Historical Society, 1927), 440–41; Flynt, "Alabama," 11–12, 17; Ayers, *Promise of the New South,* 161.

58. Boles, *South through Time,* 225–26; Ownby, *Subduing Satan;* Daniel Walker Howe, *Making the American Self: Jonathan Edwards to Abraham Lincoln* (Cambridge, Mass.: Harvard University Press, 1997), 114–17.

59. Richard M. Weaver observed: "Superficially, the difference between a backwoods convert, with his extraordinary camp-meeting exhibitionism, and the restrained and mannered Episcopalian of a seaboard congregation, seems very great. Yet it must be borne in mind that despite the different ways they chose to assert religious feeling, both were inimical to the spirit of rationalism. And if the spirit of rationalism is looked upon as the foe of religion, then it must be admitted that orthodox Christianity was as safe in the hands of one as the other." Richard M. Weaver, "The Older Religiousness in the South," *Sewanee Review* 51 (Spring 1943): 238–39.

60. Ayers, *Promise of the New South,* 167; Hill, *Southern Churches in Crisis,* 21, 23–24; Bailey, "Southern White Protestantism," 619; Charles Reagan Wilson, "The Religion of the Lost Cause," *Journal of Southern History* 46 (May 1980): 232; Flynt, *Alabama Baptists,* 168. Some ecumenical small-town southerners would avoid the Episcopal church, however, finding its services too stiff, formal, and ritualistic; see Ownby, *Subduing Satan,* 127–29.

61. Mrs. Henry Howard (Flo) Meadows, "Lowndesboro Baptist Church, 1852–1988," mimeographed, 1988, LCF Collection.

62. Interview with Annie Brown Baker.

63. Stuart X. Stephenson, "Church Plays Major Role in Life of Lowndesboro," *Montgomery Advertiser,* 18 January 1964.

64. Qtd. in Stephenson, "Church Plays Major Role in Life of Lowndesboro." Lowery was called "minister-in-charge" rather than "rector" because St. Paul's was an "organized mission" of the diocese rather than an independent parish; and, of course, "*priest*-in-charge" was too High Church an appellation for this time and place.

65. See Michael T. Malone, "High Church/Low Church," in *Encyclopedia of Religion in the South,* ed. Samuel S. Hill (Macon, Ga.: Mercer University Press, 1984), 323–24.

66. Walter C. Whitaker, *Richard Hooker Wilmer, Second Bishop of Alabama: A Biography* (Philadelphia: George W. Jacobs and Co., 1907), chap. 15. See also Charles Reagan Wilson, "Baptized in Blood: Southern Religion and the Cult of the Lost Cause, 1865–1920" (Ph.D. diss., University of Texas at Austin, 1977), 59–60, 183; Gillis J. Harp, "Richard Hooker Wilmer," in *American National Biography,* vol. 23, ed. John A. Garraty and Mark C. Carnes (New York: Oxford University Press, 1999), 551. Bishop Wilmer was a noted apologist for the Lost Cause.

67. Barbara Brandon Schnorrenberg (Birmingham, Ala.), telephone interview with the author, 24 July 1997; *National Cyclopedia of American Biography,* vol 13 (New York: J. T. White, 1892–1985), 503.

68. See Flynt's substantial treatment of "black separation" in *Alabama Baptists,* 133–42.

69. Meadows, "Lowndesboro Baptist Church." See Spain, *At Ease in Zion,* chap. 2.

70. Meadows, "Lowndesboro Baptist Church"; see Ownby, *Subduing Satan,* chap. 8, "The Revival Meeting."

71. According to its chief interpreter, the two major institutional shrines of the Religion of the Lost Cause were the University of the South (Sewanee, Tennessee) and Washington and Lee University (Lexington, Virginia). The former, an Episcopal college and seminary, employed as members of its faculty several ex-Confederate generals as well as a former captain in Lee's Army of Northern Virginia: William Porcher DuBose, who possessed one of the finest theological minds of his era. Wilson, "Religion of the Lost Cause," 235–36. See also Wilson, "Baptized in Blood," 41–53. On the University of the South and its associations with the Confederacy, see also Will D. Campbell, *And Also with You: Duncan Gray and the American Dilemma* (Franklin, Tenn.: Providence House Publishers, 1997), 71, 236–37; Gaines M. Foster, *Ghosts of the Confederacy: Defeat, the Lost Cause, and the Emergence of the New South, 1865–1913* (New York: Oxford University Press, 1987), 48.

In Alabama Baptist preachers regularly expressed their devotion to the Lost Cause; see Flynt, *Alabama Baptists,* 191–93, 200–201; Rollin G. Osterweis, *The Myth of the Lost Cause, 1865–1900* (Hamden, Conn.: Archon Books, 1973), chap. 10, "With Benefit of Clergy: The Ministers and the Myth."

72. Peter W. Williams, *America's Religions: Traditions and Cultures* (New York: Macmillan, 1990), 265. See John B. Boles, "The Discovery of Southern Religious History," in *Interpreting Southern History: Historiographical Essays in Honor of Sanford W. Higginbotham,* ed. John B. Boles and Evelyn Thomas Nolen (Baton Rouge: Louisiana State University Press, 1987), 534–35; Wilson, "Religion of the Lost Cause," 219–35.

Wilson points out some distinguishing marks of southern civil religion: southern civil religion and the Christian denominations supported one another; southern civic piety differed from the national civil religion in stressing moral virtue and an orderly society more than democracy; southern civil religion was less liberal, less tolerant, less optimistic, and more homogeneously Protestant than its national counterpart; and the Religion of the Lost Cause—the form of southern civic piety that developed in the decades following defeat in the Civil War—furthered Protestant ecumenism by providing a common spiritual activity in which virtually all Protestant ministers could take part (232–33).

73. W. J. Cash, *The Mind of the South* (New York: A. A. Knopf, 1941), 111. See James L. Roark, "'So Much for the Civil War': Cash and Continuity in Southern History," and Lacy

K. Ford Jr., "Commentary," in *"The Mind of the South": Fifty Years Later,* ed. Charles W. Eagles (Jackson: University Press of Mississippi, 1992), 85–111.

74. Noble C. Powell (hereafter NCP) to "My dearest ones at home" [sisters, mother, friends in Lowndesboro], 3 February 1936, LCF Collection.

75. In 1900, in the south central region of the United States, including Alabama and Mississippi, only 15.5 percent of the population lived in urban areas. By comparison, in the north Atlantic division (from Pennsylvania to Maine), 68.2 percent of the population lived in urban areas. In the north central division the figure was 38.5 percent, and in the western division 40.6 percent lived in urban areas. William J. Cooper Jr. and Thomas E. Terrill, *The American South: A History,* 2d ed. (New York: McGraw-Hill, 1996), 484.

76. Cash, *Mind of the South,* 189. Mockingbird Place is a fairly modest, though very handsome, dwelling. Most of the houses along Lowndesboro's main road are antebellum mansions, reflecting the prosperity of an era in which the Black Belt was one of the wealthiest regions of the United States.

77. See ibid., 15.

78. Thomas L. Connelly, *The Marble Man: Robert E. Lee and His Image in American Society* (Baton Rouge: Louisiana State University Press, 1977), 100–101; Williamson, *Crucible of Race,* 26–28. William Alexander Percy (1885–1942), of Greenville, Mississippi, said that his father read Sir Walter Scott's *Ivanhoe* "once a year all his life long" (*Lanterns on the Levee,* 57).

79. This book might well have been one of those on the approved list of the United Daughters of the Confederacy, an organization that played a major role in promoting the Religion of the Lost Cause. Founded in 1894, the UDC pressured public school boards and those in charge of private schools to adopt books from its list of recommended texts. Wilson, "Religion of the Lost Cause," 235, and "Baptized in Blood," 211–12, 216–22; Cameron Freeman Napier, "United Daughters of the Confederacy," in *Encyclopedia of Southern Culture,* ed. Charles Reagan Wilson and William Ferris (Chapel Hill: University of North Carolina Press, 1989), 706; Thomas L. Connelly and Barbara L. Bellows, *God and General Longstreet: The Lost Cause and the Southern Mind* (Baton Rouge: Louisiana State University Press, 1982), 30; Osterweis, *Myth of the Lost Cause,* chap. 9, "Winning the War in the Classrooms."

80. On the significance of this event, see Foster, *Ghosts of the Confederacy,* 98, 100–103.

81. Connelly, *Marble Man,* 100; see also Wilson, "Baptized in Blood," 65–67.

82. Mary L. Williamson, *The Life of General Robert E. Lee, for Children, in Easy Words, Illustrated* (Richmond, Va.: B. F. Johnson Publishing Co., 1895).

83. Philip N. Powell, interview with the author, Baltimore, Maryland, 11 March 1992. See Connelly and Bellows, *God and General Longstreet,* chap. 3, "Robert E. Lee and the Southern Mind."

84. See Cash, *Mind of the South,* 49. Louise recalled that "We called our servants 'Uncle' and 'Aunt.' Our parents would leave us with them as much as mother and father. Not one of the people on my mother's or father's side was mean to the darkies." LHPM notebook. On white southerners' positive (and paternalistic) attitudes toward the devout and devoted "old Negro," see Litwack, *Trouble in Mind,* 184–96.

85. Ayers, *Promise of the New South,* 134; Woodward, "Look Away," 493; Bertram Wyatt-Brown, *The House of Percy* (New York: Oxford University Press, 1994), 270.

86. Clifford L. Stanley, telephone interview with the author, 1 February 1992. Stanley knew Noble Powell at the University of Virginia in the early 1920s. For a cogent interpre-

tation of the ways in which a reverential attitude toward the past could facilitate adjustment to present strains and contribute to a positive outlook on the future, see Foster, *Ghosts of the Confederacy.* The author demonstrates how, circa 1890–1910, Confederate traditionalism, including the various celebrations of the Lost Cause, helped southerners accept defeat, negotiate a difficult period of social change, rejoin the Union, and support the emergence of the New South.

87. The novelist Walker Percy, in his introduction to *Lanterns on the Levee,* by William Alexander Percy, wrote of the reputation of paternalism and noblesse oblige as "dirty words." "But," he asked, "is it a bad thing for a man to believe that his position in society entails a certain responsibility toward others? Or is it a bad thing for a man to care like a father for his servants, spend himself on the poor, the sick, the miserable, the mad who come his way? It is surely better than watching a neighbor get murdered and closing his blinds to keep from 'getting involved.' It might even beat welfare" (xiii). But, as Bertram Wyatt-Brown has commented upon these remarks, "In a sense [Percy] was begging the question. The problem was not the appropriateness of an abiding sense of responsibility. Instead, it was the often blind, dictatorial, father-knows-best aspect of the patrician's role to which a democratic society could no longer defer." Wyatt-Brown, *House of Percy,* 327.

88. Richard M. Weaver, "Aspects of the Southern Philosophy," in *Southern Renascence: The Literature of the Modern South,* ed. Louis D. Rubin Jr. and Robert D. Jacobs (Baltimore: Johns Hopkins University Press, 1953), 16, 19.

89. Hill, *Southern Churches in Crisis,* 111. Like Thomas Paine and many others, Powell would have drawn the primary distinction not between government and the individual but between government and society. "Society," Paine wrote, "is produced by our wants, and government by our wickedness; the former promotes our happiness *positively,* by uniting our affections; the latter *negatively,* by restraining our vices. . . . Society in every state is a blessing, but government . . . is but a necessary evil." Thomas Paine, "Of the Origin and Design of Government in General, with Concise Remarks on the English Constitution," in *The American Intellectual Tradition: A Sourcebook,* vol. 1, 2d ed., ed. David A. Hollinger and Charles Capper (New York: Oxford University Press, 1993), 122.

90. Powell's ambivalence toward traditionalism and modernization roughly paralleled the attitudes of proponents of the New South creed, and his devotion to hard work matched their commitment to industriousness.

91. Bailey, "Southern White Protestantism," 623; Hill, *Southern Churches in Crisis,* 25, 28, 30; Flynt, *Alabama Baptists,* 159, 163–68, 243–50, 254–55, 260–66. Richard M. Weaver observed that "Among all classes in the South an opinion obtained that religion should be a sentiment. Where the people were refined, the sentiment was refined; where they were demonstrative and disorderly, it was likely to be such. . . . [I]n the sphere of religion the Southerner has always been hostile to the spirit of inquiry. . . . His was a natural piety, [which did not express itself] . . . in an ambition to perfect a system" ("Older Religiousness in the South," 242, 248).

92. LHPM notebook.

93. Howe, *Making the American Self,* 3–5, 9–13, 21, 38, 47, 116, 122, 249–50, 268–69.

94. Louise wrote that "Noble read medicine under the beloved physician Dr. Philip Noble Cilley." LHPM notebook. Starting in the 1930s, newspaper articles about Noble Powell regularly referred to his having studied medicine for at least a year before going to Auburn. To this writer's knowledge, however, no contemporary evidence of such study exists.

95. As Louise put it, becoming a doctor "did not fire his soul." LHPM notebook.

96. Noble Powell is not mentioned in the records of Auburn University. His name does not show up in any of the places—individual name cards, grade reports, sign-in registers, yearbooks, lists of club members—where it normally would have appeared if he had been a regularly enrolled student. He seems to have been an employee of API who sat in on classes. The university has maintained what it believes to be complete records of students from Powell's years in Auburn (1911–15). Beverly Powers (Auburn University Archives), telephone interview with the author, 17 September 1992.

Powell provided confirmation of this interpretation of his record in a letter to Dean J. M. Page of the University of Virginia in the summer of 1915. In this letter, Powell mentions the academic course he completed in the public school of Lowndesboro as well as the work he carried out as an investigator for the Department of Entomology at API; but he not only fails to indicate any academic work completed at API, he specifically claims, "I have never attended college"—and then mentions having read, "in spare time," history, English literature, psychology, and sociology. NCP to Dean J. M. Page, 17 July 1915, NCP file, Office of the University Registrar, University of Virginia, Charlottesville.

Powell's high school teacher, S. M. Dinkins, told Dean Page that Noble "has not attended college" but "has had regular employment in the government service of a nature to improve his mind and develop him." Dinkins to Page, 16 July 1915, NCP file, Office of the University Registrar, University of Virginia.

97. NCP to Philip Noble Cilley, 10 November 1911, LHPM Papers (photocopy in author's possession).

98. NCP to the Cilleys, 28 October 1912, LCF Collection. Dr. Cilley died on 17 November 1912.

99. "Alabamian Elected Dean of Washington Cathedral," *Montgomery Advertiser,* 21 February 1937; "Rev. Dr. Powell Is Nominated for Coadjutor," *Baltimore Sun,* 15 January 1937. Whether Powell carried out this work after his period of employment as secretary to Dr. Hinds or as a part of that employment is not clear.

100. Roberta McGavock recalled in 1993 that "[Dr. Cilley] gave [Noble] money to study to be a doctor. So he didn't leave the Baptist church till after Bappa's death." In fact, Dr. Cilley was quite old, infirm, and deaf when Noble joined the Episcopal church and would die the following year at age ninety-one.

101. Interview with LHPM. The theologically conservative Robert M. Hunter was an exponent of the old-time Baptist religion; he opposed Darwinism, backed required Bible reading in public schools, and worried about the effect machines and industry would have on traditional southern culture. A supporter of white (Protestant) supremacy, in the 1930s he would score Franklin D. Roosevelt for being too friendly toward blacks. Flynt, *Alabama Baptists,* 236, 244, 331, 342, 345–46, 356–58, 394–95. A fragment of a Powell family letter (provenance, date, and addressee all unknown) contains a newspaper clipping describing an automobile accident that injured Hunter. The letter's author comments, presumably in jest, that "The Catholics are taking up a collection to buy a medal to present to the fellow who did it!"

102. In a slightly different context, Noble might have mentioned the name of Jefferson Davis as well. Raised a Baptist, Davis became an Episcopalian during the Civil War. See Wilson, "Baptized in Blood," 69.

103. NCP to the Reverend Robert M. Hunter (Flomaton, Ala.), 26 November 1912, Philip N. Powell Papers, Baltimore, Md. (hereafter PNP Papers).

104. Telephone interview with Barbara Brandon Schnorrenberg.

105. Andrew Doyle, "Foolish and Useless Sport: The Southern Evangelical Crusade against Intercollegiate Football," *Journal of Sport History* 24 (Spring 1997): 317–40.

106. NCP to Mary Irving Whitman Powell, 25 November 1912, LHPM Papers (photocopy in author's possession).

107. See Ayers, *Promise of the New South*, 313–15; Doyle, "Foolish and Useless Sport," 335–37.

108. NCP to Beckwith, 16 April 1913, photocopy in the author's possession.

109. LHPM notebook.

110. Ibid.

111. William S. Stafford, "Anglican Spirituality: A Many-Sided Tradition," *Cathedral Age,* Summer 1995, 6–8.

112. *Southern Student Conference,* pamphlet, 1914, LCF Collection.

113. According to Adrian Hastings, as the leader of the YMCA and the Student Volunteer Movement, Mott "represented very well the main American religious approach in these years . . . practical, optimistic, intellectually a bit naive." After quoting a contemporary who admired Mott's ability to make the obvious sound impressive, Hastings remarks: "It is the obviousness rather than the impressiveness of what he said which now remains with us." Adrian Hastings, *A History of English Christianity, 1920–1990* (Philadelphia: Trinity Press International, 1991), 219.

Bland and fairly unsophisticated, Mott nonetheless played a crucial role in placing church unity on the worldwide Christian agenda. Overcoming the divisions and discord among religious bodies—Roman Catholics and Eastern Orthodox as well as Protestants—would seem like an obvious vocation for Christians at the end of the twentieth century largely because of the groundbreaking work accomplished by Mott and his colleagues throughout the first half of the century. As the church historian Martin E. Marty has commented, "What seems commonplace today was a radical breach with the past by Mott." Martin E. Marty, *Pilgrims in Their Own Land: Five Hundred Years of Religion in America* (New York: Penguin Books, 1984), 345.

Carrying on a vigorous effort among American undergraduates was apparently not so obvious a good as to prevent mainstream Protestants from losing sight of its importance in the 1970s. Mott would have termed that neglect by a later generation of church leaders a failure to secure vital fortifications behind their own lines. See Marty, *Pilgrims in Their Own Land,* 345.

114. Elisabeth Ellicott Poe, typescript draft of newspaper article on NCP, Washington National Cathedral Archives, Washington, D.C. (hereafter WNC Archives).

115. Personnel index card, NCP file, Office of the University Registrar, University of Virginia.

116. *University of Virginia Catalogue, 1915–1917,* 151.

117. Dinkins explained that "[Noble] took under me the full high school course as required by the State of Alabama. This is a public school, but we have authority to teach the high school course, though we are not allowed to issue diplomas. In point of scholarship, Mr. Powell was entitled to a diploma from a high school." Dinkins to Page, 16 July 1915, NCP file, Office of the University Registrar, University of Virginia.

118. Dinkins to Page, 16 July 1915, NCP file, Office of the University Registrar, University of Virginia.

119. LHPM notebook.

120. NCP to Page, 24 July 1915, NCP file, Office of the University Registrar, University of Virginia.

121. Page to NCP, 27 July 1915, NCP file, Office of the Universty Registrar, University of Virginia. The rules governing the Skinner scholarship stipulated that it was to be held by white males intending to enter the Episcopal ministry (eventually these terms were considerably broadened). Later in the century the awarding of the scholarship was overseen by the rector of St. Paul's Memorial Church, the Episcopal parish at the University of Virginia.

122. Thomas Perkins Abernethy, *Historical Sketch of the University of Virginia* (Richmond, Va.: Dietz Press, 1948), 47.

123. Philip Alexander Bruce, *History of the University of Virginia, 1819–1919*, vol. 5 (New York: Macmillan, 1922), 249–50.

124. The book, still in the bookcase at Mockingbird Place in 1993, is carefully underlined and bears the inscription "Noble C. Powell, University of Virginia, 1916."

125. NCP transcript, 1915–1917, NCP file, Office of the University Registrar, University of Virginia.

126. John E. Booty, *Mission and Ministry: A History of Virginia Theological Seminary* (Harrisburg, Pa.: Morehouse Publishing, 1995), 180. Tucker was the first Rhodes Scholar from the University of Virginia. Paula S. Kettlewell, *A History of St. Paul's Memorial Church, Charlottesville, Virginia, 1910–1990* (Charlottesville, Va.: n.p., 1990), 10.

127. Kettlewell, *History of St. Paul's Memorial Church*, 8, 10.

128. NCP to family in Lowndesboro (no date), LCF Collection.

129. Booty, *Mission and Ministry*, 170.

130. George Julius Cleaveland, a former registrar of the Episcopal diocese of Virginia (and a fellow member with Noble Powell of the Virginia Seminary class of 1920), qtd. in David L. Holmes, "Restoration Ideology among Early Episcopal Evangelicals," in *The American Quest for the Primitive Church*, ed. Richard T. Hughes (Urbana: University of Illinois Press, 1988), 159.

131. Booty, *Mission and Ministry*, 162, 164, 197; James Thayer Addison, *The Episcopal Church in the United States, 1789–1931* (New York: Charles Scribner's Sons, 1951), 335; William A. R. Goodwin, "The Subsequent History of the Seminary," and "The Alumni Association," in *History of the Theological Seminary in Virginia and Its Historical Background: Centennial Edition*, 2 vols., ed. William A. R. Goodwin (New York: E. S. Gorham, 1923), 1:304, 2:167.

132. Walter Russell Bowie, *Learning to Live* (Nashville: Abingdon Press, 1969), 62–63, qtd. in Booty, *Mission and Ministry*, 193. Bowie, a native of Richmond, Virginia, was rector of Grace Church, New York City, and a leading advocate of the social gospel and theological liberalism. From 1939 to 1950 he served as professor of pastoral theology at Union Theological Seminary, New York, and from 1950 to 1955 as professor of homiletics at Virginia Theological Seminary.

133. Booty, *Mission and Ministry*, 180–81, 229–32; Addison, *Episcopal Church in the United States*, 335. Bell developed his views on evolution and the divine activity in creation in his first major work, *Sharing in Creation* (1925). Bell also supported the modern historical study of the life of Jesus.

134. Booty, *Mission and Ministry*, 229.

135. William A. R. Goodwin, "Rev. Dr. Samuel A. Wallis," in *History of the Theological*

Seminary in Virginia and Its Historical Background, vol. 1, ed. William A. R. Goodwin (New York: E. S. Gorham, 1923), 665.

136. Booty, *Mission and Ministry,* 137, 139, 180, 377.

137. Roland J. Moncure (class of 1923), "Student Life of Today," in *History of the Theological Seminary in Virginia and Its Historical Background,* vol. 1, ed. William A. R. Goodwin (New York: E. S. Gorham, 1923), 534.

138. Booty, *Mission and Ministry,* 165.

139. Ibid., 197; Goodwin, "Subsequent History of the Seminary," 304.

140. Booty, *Mission and Ministry,* 197.

141. The specific requirements for the B.D. degree (first authorized in 1898) varied over the years; see ibid., 171, 194, 196. The requirements that applied to Powell appear to have been the following: completion of the full course of study with an average of at least 85 and with no senior grade below 75, preparation of a thesis on a subject specified by the faculty, demonstration of an ability to do original work in theology, and ordination as a priest. The seminary awarded Powell the B.D. in 1921. His thesis considered "Some Elements in the Practical Religious Value of the Book of Revelation." Only fourteen pages, it reads more like a sermon than a scholarly essay; in it Powell stresses faith in the future and trust in the providence of God as the true sources of abundant life. Noble C. Powell Senior Essay, 1920, vertical file, Maryland Diocesan Archives, Baltimore.

142. Record of Class Averages on Examinations of Students, Theological Seminary in Virginia, Beginning with the Class of 1899 entering the Seminary in 1896, pp. 46–47, Seminary Archives, Bishop Payne Library, Virginia Theological Seminary, Alexandria.

143. Carl E. Grammer, "The Social Life of 'The Hill,'" in *History of the Theological Seminary in Virginia and Its Historical Background,* vol. 1, ed. William A. R. Goodwin (New York: E. S. Gorham, 1923), 387.

144. William A. R. Goodwin, "The Matrons of the Seminary," in *History of the Theological Seminary in Virginia and Its Historical Background,* vol. 1, ed. William A. R. Goodwin (New York: E. S. Gorham, 1923), 404.

145. Beckwith to NCP, 23 February 1920, Noble Powell Correspondence, Old Clergy Files, BPL.

146. See Samuel A. Wallis, "Seminary Mission Stations," in *History of the Theological Seminary in Virginia and Its Historical Background,* vol. 1, ed. William A. R. Goodwin (New York: E. S. Gorham, 1923), 417–21.

147. Wilson, "Religion of the Lost Cause," 235. Francis Bland Tucker, a classmate of Powell's at Virginia Theological Seminary and later the rector of St. John's Church, in Georgetown, Washington, D.C., told a newspaper interviewer in 1937 that "'[Powell] was the [seminary] student chosen to act as chaplain to the pupils of the Episcopal High School. This had sometimes been a rather routine job, but he made it something of deep personal interest, winning the affection . . . and admiration of the boys by his friendship, which was not put on but a real interest in each boy. Many of these boys afterwards went to the University of Virginia and formed a strong nucleus for his work there.'" Tucker also recalled that, as president of the student body of the seminary his senior year, Powell provided counsel that was "'wise'" and "'mature,'" although he could also "'always be counted on to be at the bottom of every student prank played and at the center of all the fun.'" Qtd. in Elisabeth Ellicott Poe, typescript draft of newspaper article on NCP, WNC Archives.

148. S. Cooper Dawson Jr. (Alexandria, Va.), telephone interview with the author, 2 October 1992.

149. John W. Avirett II (Baltimore, Md.), telephone interview with the author, 20 January 1992.

150. Richard Pardee Williams Jr., *The High School: A History of the Episcopal High School in Virginia at Alexandria* (Boston: Vincent-Curtis, 1964), 125.

151. NCP to "my dearest ones at home," October 1917, LHPM Papers (photocopy in author's possession).

152. William M. Dame, "Reminiscences," in *History of the Theological Seminary in Virginia and Its Historical Background,* vol. 1, ed. William A. R. Goodwin (New York: E. S. Gorham, 1923), 455.

153. Beverley D. Tucker Jr. to Beckwith, 3 May 1920, Noble Powell Correspondence, Old Clergy Files, BPL. Tucker became professor of liturgics and pastoral theology at the seminary, serving until 1923, when he left to succeed Walter Russell Bowie as rector of St. Paul's Church, Richmond, Virginia. Tucker was replaced in his seminary post by his older brother, the redoubtable churchman Henry St. George Tucker (VTS class of 1899), who would continue at the seminary until he became bishop coadjutor of Virginia in 1926.

154. Tucker to Beckwith, 3 May 1920, Noble Powell Correspondence, Old Clergy Files, BPL.

155. Beckwith to Tucker, 5 May 1920, Noble Powell Correspondence, Old Clergy Files, BPL.

Chapter 2: Parson, 1920–31

1. Beckwith to Tucker, 5 May 1920, Old Clergy Files, BPL. Powell had told Beckwith, "I am going to put in my best work here [at the seminary] this year and then will be ready to go to work with you wherever you want me to do so." NCP to Beckwith, 1 October 1919, Old Clergy Files, BPL.

2. Telephone interview with Barbara Brandon Schnorrenberg.

3. Beckwith to William Cabell Brown, 17 May 1920, Old Clergy Files, BPL. Brown served as bishop of Virginia from 1919 to 1927.

4. NCP to Beckwith, 7 May 1920, and Beckwith to NCP, 12 May 1920, Old Clergy Files, BPL.

5. NCP to Beckwith, 19 May 1920, Old Clergy Files, BPL.

6. Berryman Green to Beckwith, 15 May 1920, Old Clergy Files, BPL.

7. Beckwith to NCP, 28 May 1920, Old Clergy Files, BPL.

8. NCP to Beckwith, 3 June 1920, Old Clergy Files, BPL. The man that Powell dealt with directly regarding the post in Charlottesville was the senior warden of St. Paul's Memorial Church, Dr. Harry T. Marshall. Marshall, whose field was pathology and bacteriology, was a prominent member of the faculty of the university's medical school. After twenty years' service on the Virginia faculty, he died of pneumonia in 1929 in Paris. He was widely regarded and beloved as a gentleman of compassion and sensitivity. Virginius Dabney, *Mr. Jefferson's University: A History* (Charlottesville: University Press of Virginia, 1981), 125.

9. Kettlewell, *History of St. Paul's Memorial Church,* 3.

10. Allison Stokes, "Denominational Ministry on University Campuses," in *Beyond Establishment: Protestant Identity in a Post-Protestant Age,* ed. Jackson W. Carroll and Wade Clark Roof (Louisville, Ky.: Westminster/John Knox Press, 1993), 174–75. During Powell's years in Charlottesville, the national Episcopal church began to take its work on behalf of college students far more seriously. The denomination benefited from the arrival in

1926 of an aggressive new secretary for college work, the Reverend C. Leslie Glenn; and two years later church leaders read with interest the results of a new study revealing that Episcopal students were three-and-a-half times more numerous on college and university campuses than were Episcopalians in the U.S. population at large (5.5 percent of enrolled students were Episcopalians versus only 1.6 percent of the general population). The national church began a deliberate effort to encourage parishes that lay near college campuses to look after the Episcopal students there, and by 1930 it was placing twenty men and women a year in full- and part-time campus-ministry posts around the country. In 1940 the national church established a separate division of college work, which soon had its counterpart in most dioceses. Directors of these diocesan departments assigned clergy to work with students on nearby campuses of higher education. Raymond W. Albright, *A History of the Protestant Episcopal Church* (New York: Macmillan, 1964), 363; George E. DeMille, *The Episcopal Church since 1900* (New York: Morehouse-Gorham, 1955), 122–23; Addison, *Episcopal Church in the United States,* 334.

11. Kettlewell, *History of St. Paul's Memorial Church,* 4–6; *College Topics,* 5 May 1922, 5; *Journal of the 115th Annual Council of the Protestant Episcopal Church in the Diocese of Virginia, Held in the Church of the Holy Trinity, Richmond, Va., on the 18th, 19th, and 20th of May, 1910* (Richmond: William Ellis Jones Book and Job Printer, 1910), 96. This wooden structure, though modest, was not unattractive. Alumni of the university recalled that it had a beautiful sanctuary. See also *College Topics,* 29 November 1919, 5.

12. Kettlewell, *History of St. Paul's Memorial Church,* 6, 8; *Journal of the 116th Annual Council of the Protestant Episcopal Church in the Diocese of Virginia, Held in Christ Church, Winchester, Va., 17th, 18th, and 19th of May, 1911* (Richmond: Whittet and Shepperson, 1911), 101.

13. Kettlewell, *History of St. Paul's Memorial Church,* 8. The work of the Brotherhood of St. Andrew continued in essentially the same form under Parson Powell. See "Brotherhood Continues to Do Valuable Work," *College Topics,* 26 September 1928, 3.

14. Kettlewell, *History of St. Paul's Memorial Church,* 9–10.

15. Beverley D. Tucker Jr., "Religious Ministrations in State Universities by Denominational Agencies," *The Centennial of the University of Virginia, 1819–1921* (New York: n.p., 1922), 141–43; Dabney, *Mr. Jefferson's University,* 67.

16. *College Topics,* 1 February 1920, 1; the actual number at this time was 920.

17. Madison Hall had housed the YMCA since the building's construction in 1905. The YMCA, which was established at the University of Virginia in 1858, was an extremely active social and religious center. Before Newcomb Hall—the present student-activities center—was built in the 1950s, the YMCA in Madison Hall functioned as the student center and official clearinghouse for information on student life. Abernethy, *Historical Sketch of the University of Virginia,* 43; Amy Edgar and Bill Sublette, "In Matters of Religion," *University of Virginia Alumni News,* May 1993, 27.

18. See, for example, *College Topics,* 19 October 1920, 3; 11 January 1924, 1; 15 January 1924, 1.

19. Kettlewell, *History of St. Paul's Memorial Church,* 10. By the time he left, the church had 271 communicant members. *Journal of the 136th Annual Council of the Protestant Episcopal Church in the Diocese of Virginia, Held in St. Paul's Memorial Church, University, on the 20th and 21st of May, 1931* (Richmond: n.p., 1931), 200.

20. Virginia Yerby McNeill, "Mountaineers' Parson Makes Active Bishop," *Baltimore Sun,* 19 November 1944.

21. Kettlewell, *History of St. Paul's Memorial Church,* 11; *Journal of the 126th Annual*

Council of the Protestant Episcopal Church in the Diocese of Virginia, Held in Christ Church, Charlottesville, Va., on the 18th, 19th, and 20th of May, 1921 (Richmond: n.p., 1921), 167–68. See also *College Topics,* 29 November 1919, 5.

22. John Stewart Bryan, Murray McGuire, Lewis Williams, Randolph Williams, Rosewell Page, and Beverley D. Tucker made up the membership of the Richmond Committee.

23. Kettlewell, *History of St. Paul's Memorial Church,* 11–12; John Page Williams (B.A., 1931), telephone interview with the author, 23 July 1992.

24. Kettlewell, *History of St. Paul's Memorial Church,* 12–13; *College Topics,* 5 May 1922, 5; *Journal of the 140th Annual Council of the Protestant Episcopal Church in the Diocese of Virginia, Held in St. George's Church, Fredericksburg, on the 15th and 16th of May, 1935* (Richmond: n.p., 1935), 149. The report on St. Paul's in this diocesan journal indicates that the nave would accommodate 630 and the chapel 75; parochial reports issued during the Powell years state that the church could seat 800.

25. *College Topics,* 19 September 1927, 1. Bishop Murray celebrated the Holy Communion; Beverley D. Tucker Jr. preached. At the cornerstone-laying service, representing the university and reading President Alderman's remarks was John Calvin Metcalf, an English professor and dean of graduate studies who was renowned for the quality of his lectures on Shakespeare as well as for the quality of his life. Metcalf was a committed Christian who taught a Bible class every Sunday morning in Madison Hall that drew 150 to 200 students. Tucker was the principal speaker at the service. Representatives of the student bodies of Episcopal High School, Woodberry Forest, Virginia Episcopal School, and Virginia Theological Seminary were also present. *College Topics,* 14 April 1926, 1; Joseph L. Vaughan, *Rotunda Tales: Stories from the University of Virginia, 1920–1960* (Charlottesville: University of Virginia Alumni Association, 1991), 123–24.

26. Kettlewell, *History of St. Paul's Memorial Church,* 13, 15.

27. Ibid., 15; *College Topics,* 25 September 1924, 3. Tui Kinsolving later became rector of Trinity Church, Pittsburgh, and then bishop of Arizona. He was named after his uncle, Arthur Barksdale Kinsolving, the longtime rector of Old St. Paul's Parish, Baltimore. Tui received his nickname when his father, Lucien Kinsolving, was a bishop in Brazil. The Portugese nurse would call the one-year-old Arthur "Arturo"; and Arthur's three-year-old brother, Charlie, unable to say "Arturo," would call him "Tui" instead. Herbert Kinsolving, telephone interview with the author, 22 May 1992. After the birth of Arthur Lee Kinsolving, who became known as "Little Tui," Arthur B. Kinsolving II was called "Big Tui." Les Kinsolving, telephone interview with the author, 22 May 1992. Powell's assistant had served as vice president of the St. Paul's Club in 1917. *Corks and Curls* (University of Virginia yearbook), 1917.

28. Owen Chadwick, review of *John Henry Newman: A Biography,* by Ian Ker, *Journal of Ecclesiastical History* 41 (April 1990): 317.

29. Qtd. in Adrian Hastings, *Robert Runcie* (Philadelphia: Trinity Press International, 1991), 20.

30. See David Baily Harned, *Patience* (Cambridge, Mass.: Cowley Publications, 1997), 156.

31. Vaughan, *Rotunda Tales,* 143.

32. The office of dean of the university was a forerunner of the later office of vice president for student affairs. Vincent Shea, audiotaped interview by Raymond Bice, 18 November 1991 (in author's possession). A student at the University of Virginia in the mid 1930s, Shea was vice president for business and finance at the university as well as a member of the department of government and foreign affairs.

33. Vaughan, *Rotunda Tales,* 143. Powell told members of the St. Paul's Club that he and Tui Kinsolving were there to serve the students and to help solve their problems. *College Topics,* 29 September 1924, 3.

34. McNeill, "Mountaineers' Parson Makes Active Bishop."

35. B. F. D. Runk, audiotaped interview by Raymond Bice, 4 November 1991 (in author's possession). Runk was a member of the biology faculty from 1930 to 1976 and served as dean of the university from 1959 to 1968. A revered figure who was known as "Mr. University," he received the university's highest honor, the Thomas Jefferson Award; for twelve years until his retirement he led academic processions as university marshal. In 1980 the Board of Visitors created the Runk Professorship in biology in his honor. Upon Runk's death in 1994 it was revealed that he was a member of the Seven Society. See Dabney, *Mr. Jefferson's University,* 332, 456.

36. Vaughan, *Rotunda Tales,* 202. See also "'Greasy' Neale Signed to Coach Varsity Sports Here," *College Topics,* 16 January 1923, 1. John Page Williams said that "'Greasy' Neale . . . used to fear Virginia would make a gentleman of him." John Page Williams, letter to the author, 14 November 1991. On the gentlemanly behavior exhibited by Virginia players and fans of the 1920s, see Dabney, *Mr. Jefferson's University,* 114. This was also the era of the beloved track and basketball coach Henry (Pop) Lannigan.

37. "Seven Society Makes Present of New Pew to St. Paul's Church," *College Topics,* 16 April 1928, 1; interview with B. F. D. Runk.

38. Stettinius, a mediocre student, never graduated, having failed to earn enough credits for a degree. He was president of the YMCA chapter at Virginia and founded a student self-help bureau to locate jobs for needy students. From November 1944 to June 1945 he served as secretary of state and was present with Roosevelt at Yalta. He was rector of the University of Virginia from 1946 to 1947. Vaughan, *Rotunda Tales,* 196–97; Dabney, *Mr. Jefferson's University,* 254; Richard L. Walker, *E. R. Stettinius, Jr.,* vol. 14 of *The American Secretaries of State and Their Diplomacy,* ed. Robert H. Ferrell (New York: Cooper Square Publishers, 1965), 4. For a recent assessment of Stettinius's character and career, see Jack L. Hammersmith, "In Defense of Yalta: Edward R. Stettinius's *Roosevelt and the Russians,*" *Virginia Magazine of History and Biography* 100 (July 1992): 429–54. One of his contemporaries remembered that "Ed Stettinius was known at the University as a rich man's son." Thomas Pinckney, letter to the author, 16 February 1992. The senior Stettinius was a partner in the J. P. Morgan and Co. banking house and served as assistant secretary of war during World War I.

39. NCP to Edward R. Stettinius Jr., 30 April 1928, Letters to Stettinius, Special Collections Department, Alderman Library, University of Virginia, Charlottesville.

40. Rustin, who was born in Omaha, Nebraska, on 6 March 1901, was the daughter of Frederick and Grace Frances (How) Rustin of Massachusetts. She was educated at Miss Porter's School in Farmington, Connecticut. Noble and Mary's son Thomas remembered that his mother's father had died around 1908. Thomas Hooker Powell, interview with the author, Baltimore, Maryland, 25 August 1992.

41. McNeill, "Mountaineers' Parson Makes Active Bishop."

42. Laura Gilliam, interview with the author, Washington, D.C., 23 May 1993.

43. Letters (one is dated 11 March 1924; the other is from March or April 1924) from his mother to NCP, vertical file, Maryland Diocesan Archives, Baltimore.

44. [Josephine Powell] to NCP, 28 February 1924, vertical file, Maryland Diocesan Archives, Baltimore.

45. Interview with Laura Gilliam.

46. W. Gerow Christian, telephone interview with the author, 28 January 1992. See also William Gerow Christian, *My Story: The Parson Remembers,* ed. Elizabeth Becker (N.p.: Virginia Publishing Group, 1996), 39. The wedding was "informal" and the wedding party "small." Thomas Pinckney (B.A., 1925), letter to the author, 5 February 1992. Pinckney recalled that he and Langbourne Williams (B.A., 1924) served as groomsmen.

47. Thomas G. Faulkner (B.A., 1930), telephone interview with the author, 1 February 1992.

48. Of the 1,858 students enrolled in 1924, for example, 1,502 were members of some church, and an additional 317 expressed a preference for one of the fourteen leading denominations. Of these 1,819, 517 identified themselves as belonging to or preferring the Episcopal church. The next largest group was Methodists, with 384, followed by Presbyterians, 280, Baptists, 278, Jews, 112, Roman Catholics, 91, and Disciples of Christ, 63. "Episcopal Church Most Popular at University," *College Topics,* 25 March 1924, 7. Similarly, of the 2,378 students enrolled in 1929, 685 men and 21 women identified themselves as Episcopalians. *College Topics,* 2 October 1929, 1.

49. Woodberry Forest, for example, was not officially Episcopal but had strong relations with the Episcopal church; for many years the school employed an Episcopal priest as its chaplain. Telephone interview with John Page Williams. Williams, a Rhodes scholar, was associated with church schools throughout his long career as an Episcopal priest.

One Woodberry Forest alumnus, Richards D. Maxwell Jr. (B.A., 1933), recalled years later the time that he and his roommate had attempted to elude the local clergy—and thus not have to attend church—by giving "Mormon" as their religious affiliation on one of the many forms they had to complete on first matriculating. Sandy Gilliam, to whom Maxwell told this story circa 1984, reported what happened: "A few days later, Parson barged into their room without knocking and pushed them out of the door to St. Paul's. They were bound to be Episcopalians—as, of course, they were—he said; besides, if they had really been Mormons, they would have put down 'Latter-Day Saints.' They attended St. Paul's faithfully for the rest of their time here [at the university]." Alexander G. (Sandy) Gilliam Jr., letter to the author, 4 February 1992. Gilliam (B.A., 1955) was the assistant to the president of the University of Virginia; his family knew the Powells well for many years. His mother was a friend of Mary Rustin's before she married the parson, his parents were married by Noble Powell in 1931, and he was baptized by Powell at Emmanuel Church, Baltimore, in 1933.

50. The total number increased to seventeen hundred by January 1923. In 1924–25 there were still only 1,219 undergraduate students at the university. On the important efforts of President Edwin A. Alderman (1861–1931) to raise standards at the university not many years before Powell's arrival, see Michael Dennis, "Reforming the 'Academical Village': Edwin A. Alderman and the University of Virginia, 1904–1915," *Virginia Magazine of History and Biography* 105 (Winter 1997): 53–86.

51. It is significant, however, that Powell functioned as chaplain *to* rather than *of* the university. A university chaplain would have been employed by the university to provide ministry to the entire community. See Stokes, "Denominational Ministry on University Campuses," 177.

52. Julian Green, *Love in America,* trans. Euan Cameron (New York: Marion Boyars, 1994), 18. See Thomas Crampton, "Look Away, Look Away: For Parisian Writer Julian Green, the South Is Still Deep in the Heart," *University of Virginia Alumni News,* November/December 1993, 75–79.

53. Green, *Love in America,* 19.

54. Ibid., 20.

55. Ibid., 20–21.

56. Ibid., 130–31.

57. Ibid., 54.

58. Ibid., 55. See also William L. Marbury, *In the Catbird Seat* (Baltimore: Maryland Historical Society, 1988), 58–61.

59. See Green, *Love in America,* 172–78.

60. Edward Alvey Jr. (B.A., 1923; M.A., 1928; Ph.D. 1931), telephone interview with the author, 23 January 1992; Robert N. Page (B.A., 1927), telephone interview with the author, 11 February 1992.

61. Interview with Laura Gilliam. Miss Betty Cocke and Miss Betty Booker ran well-known rooming houses on University Avenue near St. Paul's Church. See Dabney, *Mr. Jefferson's University,* 88–89.

62. Green, *Love in America,* 30, 32; see also 181. Virginia students would obtain whiskey from bootleggers at such places as Shifflett's Hollow, where they would fill three-gallon kegs with the contraband. Richard Henry Lee (no degree, 1930), telephone interview with the author, 3 June 1992; C. Alfonso Smith (no degree, 1931), telephone interview with the author, 18 August 1992. (Smith was one of the many Virginia students who found the university "easy to get into and tough to graduate from." For confirmation of this assessment, see Dabney, *Mr. Jefferson's University,* 78; Dabney also discusses students' associations with bootleggers [92].) William Christian recalled that "in my days at U.Va., 'mountain corn' (there were other less delicate names) was the poor students' source of dissipation. And the revenuers . . . were very busy in Greene County" (*My Story,* 63). Another alumnus remembered that "we'd always try to get a gallon or two, put it in a charred keg with apples, and keep it for six months. That white lightning was awful hot. [You'd have to take] a drink of water, drink of liquor, drink of water. . . ." Telephone interview with S. Cooper Dawson Jr.

Noble Powell, while not a teetotaler, was "a moderation man" who could be critical of students' drinking habits. Benjamin M. Baker (B.A., 1922; M.D., 1926), telephone interview with the author, 20 January 1992. (On the career of the highly accomplished Ben Baker, see Christian, *My Story,* 42.) Cooper Dawson recalled that Parson "was agin' it [acquiring and consuming the bootlegged whiskey]; he didn't approve of it at all." Telephone interview with S. Cooper Dawson Jr.

Statewide prohibition took effect in Virginia in October 1916; under this law, every householder could still obtain one quart of liquor from outside the state each month. After nationwide prohibition took effect in 1920, this one-quart allowance was eliminated; and, as the historian Virginius Dabney has noted, "the moonshiners and bootleggers moved in at once. Thousands of otherwise law-abiding citizens began violating the law." Virginius Dabney, *Virginia: The New Dominion* (Charlottesville: University Press of Virginia, 1983), 463.

63. Green, *Love in America,* 34.

64. Ibid., 52, 73, 156. See also Dabney, *Mr. Jefferson's University,* 90.

65. Green, *Love in America,* 80. Albert W. Francis (B.A., 1928) had similar recollections of the rowdy behavior of Virginia students at the Jefferson. Telephone interview with the author, 25 August 1993. In 1922 students could have gone to the Jefferson to see Mary Pickford starring in *Through the Back Door. College Topics,* 28 March 1922, 8.

66. *College Topics,* 27 October 1922, 4. See Christian, *My Story,* 43–45.

67. Dabney, *Mr. Jefferson's University,* 86.

68. Green, *Love in America,* 83, 125, 161.

69. Ibid., 161; see also Dabney, *Mr. Jefferson's University,* 87.

70. *College Topics,* 5 November 1920, 8. In the student literary magazine of the mid 1920s, blacks are referred to as "niggers" and "darkies."

71. *College Topics,* 25 March 1921, 2.

72. *College Topics,* 22 January 1925, 4.

73. The Anglo-Saxon Club, led by the famed composer and concert pianist John Powell, successfully sponsored segregationist legislation in the Virginia General Assembly during the 1920s. See Dabney, *Mr. Jefferson's University,* 66, and *Virginia,* 483. Also see *Inside the Klavern: The Secret History of the Ku Klux Klan of the 1920s,* ed. David A. Horowitz (Carbondale: Southern Illinois University Press, 1999); Martin E. Marty, *The Noise of Conflict, 1919–1941,* vol. 2 of *Modern American Religion* (Chicago: University of Chicago Press, 1991), chap. 3, "The '100 Percent Americans' Attack." On the elitist attitudes of University of Virginia students, see Gregory Michael Dorr, "Assuring America's Place in the Sun: Ivey Foreman Lewis and the Teaching of Eugenics at the University of Virginia, 1915–1953," *Journal of Southern History* 66 (May 2000): 281–84.

74. Ayers, *Promise of the New South,* 315. During the 1920s, however, Virginia students were often highly individualistic and apathetic about participating in any activities, including supporting the athletic teams. See Dabney, *Mr. Jefferson's University,* 98, 115.

75. Vaughan, *Rotunda Tales,* 143. Lewis also served as dean of the university and dean of the College of Arts and Sciences (1934–53).

76. Dorr, "Assuring America's Place in the Sun," 257–96 (quotation on 272).

77. Vaughan, *Rotunda Tales,* 168.

78. Ibid., 129.

79. Ibid., 44, 126–27; interview with Laura Gilliam; *Journal of the 126th Annual Council of the Protestant Episcopal Church in the Diocese of Virginia,* 167. As a young man Abbot had earned money by singing French, Italian, and English folk songs on the vaudeville stage; Betty Booker had sung opera at London's Covent Garden. Marbury, *In the Catbird Seat,* 60.

80. Vaughan, *Rotunda Tales,* 118; telephone interview with John Page Williams; Green, *Love in America,* 28.

81. McNeill, "Mountaineers' Parson Makes Active Bishop"; "Rev. Dr. Powell Is Nominated for Coadjutor," *Baltimore Sun,* 15 January 1937.

82. Addison, *Episcopal Church in the United States,* 342; Robert Prichard, *The Bat and the Bishop* (Harrisburg, Pa.: Morehouse, 1989), 113; Dexter Ralph Davison Jr., "Frederick W. Neve: Mountain Mission Education in Virginia, 1888–1948" (Ph.D. diss., University of Virginia, 1982), 4–5. For a contemporary account, see Frank Whittington Creighton, *Our Heritage: The Church's Responsibility in the Home Field* (New York: National Council of the Episcopal Church, 1933), chap. 5, "Mountain People."

83. Prichard, *Bat and the Bishop,* 113–14; D. Ralph Davison Jr., "Frederick W. Neve, Archdeacon of the Blue Ridge: Mountain Mission Education," *Journal of Thought* 18 (Fall 1983): 91–103, and "Frederick W. Neve: Mountain Mission Education in Virginia," chaps. 1–9, 11–12; Elizabeth Copeland Norfleet, *Blue Ridge School: Samaritans of the Mountains* (Orange, Va.: Green Publishers, 1982), 1–61; *The Order of the Thousandfold* (Cincinnati: Forward Movement Publications, 1988), 3–4. One result of all this activity was that by the early

1930s, in rural Greene County northwest of Charlottesville, one out of every fifteen residents was an Episcopalian. Davison, "Frederick W. Neve: Mountain Mission Education in Virginia," 341. See also Christian, *My Story,* 59–63.

84. NCP to Neve, 12 February 1940, Frederick W. Neve Papers (no. 10505), Special Collections Department, Alderman Library, University of Virginia, Charlottesville.

85. NCP to Frederick W. Neve, 18 October 1948, Frederick W. Neve Papers, Special Collections Department, Alderman Library, University of Virginia, Charlottesville. In the 1920s Powell sat on the advisory board of the archdeaconry; another member was the distinguished southern educator James Hardy Dillard (1856–1940). Davison, "Frederick W. Neve: Mountain Mission Education in Virginia," 345.

86. Davison, "Frederick W. Neve: Mountain Mission Education in Virginia," 27. For example, William Cabell Brown and Lucien Lee Kinsolving were members of a team of American missionaries from Virginia Seminary who went to Brazil in 1890 and 1891. Kinsolving became the first bishop of the Brazilian church in 1898. Robert Prichard, *A History of the Episcopal Church* (Harrisburg, Pa.: Morehouse Publishing, 1991), 195; Goodwin, "Alumni Association," 178, 180.

87. NCP to Neve, 22 October 1941, Frederick W. Neve Papers, Special Collections Department, Alderman Library, University of Virginia, Charlottesville.

88. Davison, "Frederick W. Neve: Mountain Mission Education in Virginia," 31.

89. The Bishop Payne Divinity School, begun in 1878 and incorporated in 1884, was established as the Episcopal seminary where black deacons and priests would be trained; it was a branch of the Virginia Theological Seminary. Holmes, *Brief History of the Episcopal Church,* 84–85; Prichard, *History of the Episcopal Church,* 181. Brydon later published a study of *The Episcopal Church among the Negroes of Virginia* (1937).

90. *The Southern Churchman,* 11 October 1919, 10. The colored work fund was supported mainly by the special offerings of parishes and by the contributions of individuals; it never amounted to a large sum of money. I am grateful to Julia E. Randle, an archivist at the Bishop Payne Library, Virginia Theological Seminary, for locating this article and for providing other information about the early years of Trinity Parish.

91. Prichard, *History of the Episcopal Church,* 181, 215.

92. Austin Farrer, "Walking Sacraments," in *Austin Farrer: The Essential Sermons,* ed. Leslie Houlden (Cambridge, Mass.: Cowley Publications, 1991), 102–3.

93. Gabriel Marcel, *The Philosophy of Existentialism* (Secaucus, N.J.: Citadel Press, 1973), 39–40. Powell was ordained to the priesthood on 9 January 1921 by Bishop William Cabell Brown in St. Paul's Memorial Church. Six months earlier Bishop Brown had made him a deacon in Emmanuel Chapel, Virginia Theological Seminary.

94. McNeill, "Mountaineers' Parson Makes Active Bishop." Powell told a newspaper reporter in 1937, "'I had no Sunday night service at St. Paul's Church but was at home to the students of the University who wished to talk about religion and religious things. Sunday night after Sunday night my study was crowded with the students. The conversation was general and showed a real desire to understand religion, its place and meaning in their lives. It was not an unusual experience that after the greater number of the students had left to have a few men remain until 2 and even 3 in the morning of Monday to talk over religion in still greater detail.'" Qtd. in Elisabeth Ellicott Poe, typescript draft of newspaper article on NCP, WNC Archives.

95. Vaughan, *Rotunda Tales,* 143.

96. Statistics found in annual council journals of the diocese of Virginia.

97. James B. Platt Jr., telephone interview with the author, 18 May 1992. Platt was a member of the football squad, which Noble Powell supported enthusiastically.

98. Howe, *Making the American Self,* 121, 133.

99. William Blackstone, *Commentaries on the Laws of England,* vol. 1 (1765; reprint, New York: Oceana, 1966), 372. See L. William Countryman, *The Language of Ordination: Ministry in an Ecumenical Context* (Philadelphia: Trinity Press International, 1992), 31.

100. C. Edward Hilgenberg (B.A., 1932), telephone interview with the author, 9 June 1994; Marshall P. Graham (no degree, 1932), telephone interview with the author, 9 June 1994; telephone interview with Clifford L. Stanley (B.A., 1924; M.A., 1925); Maurice D. Ashbury (B.A., 1927), interview with the author, Frederick, Md., 21 January 1992; telephone interview with W. Gerow Christian; Thomas Pinckney (B.A., 1925), telephone interview with the author, 1 February 1992; Christian, *My Story,* 39; *College Topics,* 9 October 1923, 1.

Powell introduced Studdert-Kennedy to a crowd that filled Madison Hall. "Dr. Studdert-Kennedy is an apostle of truth," the parson said, "whether he learned it in the hell of Flanders field or before that. He is . . . a man who has seen with his own eyes the necessity for universal brotherhood." "Dr. Studdert-Kennedy Speaks to Large Crowd," *College Topics,* 8 February 1924, 7.

For an introduction to the thought and style of Geoffrey Studdert-Kennedy (1883–1929), see G. A. Studdert-Kennedy, *The Best of G. A. Studdert-Kennedy* (New York: Harper and Brothers, 1948); Horton Davies, *Varieties of English Preaching, 1900–1960* (Englewood Cliffs, N.J.: Prentice-Hall, 1963), 93–95, 97–101; Charles Sherlock, "Geoffrey A. Studdert-Kennedy," in *The SPCK Handbook of Christian Theologians* (London: Society for Promoting Christian Knowledge, 1998), 207–8. Studdert-Kennedy received his nickname from his habit of distributing Woodbine cigarettes to soldiers at the front.

Gerald Studdert-Kennedy points out that Geoffrey Studdert-Kennedy favored "cautious, ameliorative social change and the preservation of structures and processes that were vulnerable to challenge in the disturbed and tense conditions of the early 1920s." An advocate of a conservative form of Christian Socialism, the former World War I chaplain opposed Karl Marx, seeing him as "the enemy of individual personality and the prophet of teutonic social regimentation." Gerald Studdert-Kennedy, "'Woodbine Willie': Religion and Politics after the Great War," *History Today* 36 (December 1986): 40–45 (quotation on 42).

101. Thomas Pinckney, letter to the author, 5 February 1992; telephone interview with Thomas G. Faulkner Jr. (Faulkner [1908–97] served for thirty years as rector of St. George's Episcopal Church, Fredericksburg, Virginia); Hugh D. McCormick (B.A., 1927), telephone interview with the author, 11 February 1992.

Noble Powell was the only man ever elected to membership in the Varsity Club of the University of Virginia who had never played on a Virginia athletic team. According to Joseph Vaughan, "That 'V' symbolized how all of us felt about him. He wore a letter that he had earned because of his affection and sustained interest in the problems at Virginia" (*Rotunda Tales,* 143).

In 1921 Powell accompanied three students, including Thomas Pinckney, to Europe. They visited England, Scotland, France, Switzerland, and Italy. Thomas Pinckney, letter to the author, 5 February 1992. It was undoubtedly on this trip that Powell met Studdert-Kennedy and received a promise from him to visit St. Paul's in Charlottesville. See *College Topics,* 5 February 1924, 1.

Shortly after their return from Europe, Powell took Pinckney and a student named

Charlie Gleaves, from Roanoke, with him to New York City, where he and the students spoke at St. Thomas's Church, Fifth Avenue, about "the need and opportunity for a more suitable church" in Charlottesville (Pinckney, letter). See also *College Topics,* 9 November 1923, 8, which describes the activities of the St. Paul's Club in the campaign to raise funds for the new church building. Pinckney, who was president of the club in 1923, was involved in the effort to solicit donations from alumni and friends of the university, as was Langbourne M. Williams. During his last year at the university Pinckney served as president of the YMCA.

At a meeting at St. James's Episcopal Church in Richmond in March 1925, Powell, together with Pinckney, B. D. Tucker Jr., Bishop William Cabell Brown, and John Stewart Bryan (the chairman of the campaign committee), set forth the case for a new church building, contrasting the "pitiful" state of the equipment for dealing with the spiritual side of human life with the fine facilities at the university for training the mental and physical sides. *College Topics,* 1 April 1925, 3.

102. Telephone interview with Richard Henry Lee.

103. Telephone interview with Clifford L. Stanley. One alumnus recalled "class differences" at the University of Virginia that had "nothing to do with academic classes." Graduates of such places as Virginia Episcopal School (Lynchburg) and Episcopal High School (Alexandria) made up "the leading vanguard" at Virginia; but in the early twenties, when Noble Powell began his rectorate, veterans of the First World War were at the university and also stood out as a distinct group. The Delta Upsilon fraternity was started at this time; it included "a large number of war people" and was "more plebian" in its makeup. William W. Moss Jr. (no degree, 1921), telephone interview with the author, 20 January 1992.

Parson Powell's sociable nature is revealed in the list of organizations he belonged to while in Charlottesville. He was a Royal Arch Mason as well as a member of the Knights of Pythias, the Theta Chi fraternity, the Raven Society, and the Colonnade Club (the faculty club at the university). *Virginia: Rebirth of the Old Dominion,* vol. 5, ed. Philip Alexander Bruce (Chicago: Lewis Publishing Company, 1929), 381.

104. Phillips Brooks, *Lectures on Preaching* (New York: E. P. Dutton, 1877), 5. In February 1924 Beverley D. Tucker Jr., the rector of St. Paul's Church, Richmond, spoke on the value of personality in Christianity. It is a chief way, in addition to the printed word and the church, of imparting truth from one generation to another, he told his audience in the university chapel. "Dr. Tucker Speaks at Second Supper Service," *College Topics,* 5 February 1924, 7. See Warren I. Susman, "'Personality' and the Making of Twentieth-Century Culture," in *New Directions in American Intellectual History,* ed. John Higham and Paul K. Conkin (Baltimore: Johns Hopkins University Press, 1979), 212–26.

105. Telephone interview with Clifford L. Stanley; Norwood Orrick (J.D., 1932), telephone interview with the author, 18 May 1992.

106. Telephone interview with Clifford L. Stanley.

107. Lambert Davis (B.A., 1925), telephone interview with the author, 30 January 1992.

108. Telephone interview with W. Gerow Christian. The student was Langbourne M. Williams (B.A., 1924). The former president and chairman of the Freeport Sulphur Company, Williams assisted with the implementation of the Marshall Plan after the Second World War and later was elected chairman of the National Industrial Conference Board. A director of B. F. Goodrich and Texaco, he also served on the governing boards of Tulane University and the University of Virginia.

109. Robert D. Kemp (no degree, 1927), telephone interview with the author, 10 Febru-

ary 1992; telephone interview with Robert N. Page. Of course the students always wore coats and ties as well. Dabney, *Mr. Jefferson's University*, 84.

110. Interview with Maurice D. Ashbury.

111. Telephone interview with Edward Alvey Jr. Powell preached at the university chapel in September 1928 as part of a service conducted by students under the auspices of the YMCA in Madison Hall. In his sermon he said students would encounter "liberal views" in college. They should not cease to believe but should instead allow their beliefs to grow. Men, he cautioned, should not get too close to the truth; they might lose their sense of proportion and believe that a mere detail is the entire truth. As you enter this new year, he told the students, let your faith grow, but keep everything in perspective. *College Topics*, 24 September 1928.

112. Thomas T. Dunn (B.S., 1925), telephone interview with the author, 30 January 1992.

113. Telephone interview with John Page Williams.

114. Telephone interview with Clifford L. Stanley, who, between 1921 and 1925, enjoyed a regular acquaintance with Parson Powell. Stanley sang in the church choir, served under Powell in the nearby country missions, and often attended the Sunday evening gatherings in the rector's apartment. "So I heard much of what he said on such occasions, and what was said to him, and around him." Clifford L. Stanley, letter to the author, 4 November 1991.

115. Vaughan, *Rotunda Tales*, 156; James Orrick (B.A., 1922), telephone interview with the author, 28 January 1992. Orrick attended St. Paul's Memorial Church regularly, serving as usher, a St. Andrew's Brotherhood member, and a teacher of a Bible class for children.

116. Telephone interview with John Page Williams, who went on to say that, while Powell was never "an outstanding preacher," he was nonetheless "perfectly acceptable" and always a "popular speaker." Ben Baker said that Powell "was not an outstanding preacher, but he was an outstanding clergyman." Telephone interview with Benjamin M. Baker. Virginius Dabney recalled that Powell's "sermons were good but not brilliant." Virginius Dabney, letter to the author, 14 November 1991.

117. Telephone interview with S. Cooper Dawson Jr. (B.S., 1932).

118. Virginius Dabney, letter to the author, 14 November 1991. Dabney devotes an admiring paragraph to Parson Powell in *Mr. Jefferson's University*, 125. Dabney graduated from Episcopal High School in 1917 and taught there in 1921 and 1922. A leading southern moderate, Dabney (1901–95), the longtime editor-in-chief (1936–69) of the *Richmond Times-Dispatch*, won the Pulitzer Prize for "distinguished editorial writing." He called for a federal antilynching law, the desegregation of public transportation, and the repeal of the poll tax. He defended the right of workers to organize unions and advocated aid to distressed sharecroppers. In the 1950s and 1960s his views became more conservative and cautious, as he opposed protest and conflict in favor of gradual reform. John T. Kneebone, "Virginius Dabney," *Encyclopedia of Southern Culture*, ed. Charles Reagan Wilson and William Ferris (Chapel Hill: University of North Carolina Press, 1989), 951–52; John Egerton, *Speak Now against the Day: The Generation before the Civil Rights Movement in the South* (New York: Alfred A. Knopf, 1994), 137–39, 254–56, 314–15. Julian Green provides vivid descriptions of Virginius Dabney (as a student) and his father, the University of Virginia history professor Richard Heath Dabney, in *Love in America*, 170–72; for another perspective on the senior Dabney, see Vaughan, *Rotunda Tales*, 58–63.

119. George Bean (B.A., 1939), telephone interview with the author, 9 May 1992. Bean

grew up in Charlottesville and attended St. Paul's, where his father was senior warden in the late 1920s. He mentioned that during the Civil War the Union army slashed an old portrait in the Doswell home, and the Misses Doswell refused to have it repaired. The Doswell sisters lived two doors down from the church, on Chancellor Street.

120. Stephen Sykes, "An Anglican Theology of Evangelism," *Theology* 94 (November/December 1991): 410. See also James C. Fenhagen's brief but useful pamphlet *The Anglican Way* (Cincinnati: Forward Movement Publications, 1981).

121. NCP to [family in Lowndesboro], [1930], LCF Collection.

122. Earl C. Abell et al. to NCP, 29 October 1930, PNP Papers. In the midst of receiving various honors in his last year at the university, Noble wrote to his mother and thanked her for all she had given him. He told "Mamma" that "there is a richness of life far transcending all the money in the world and that is a real humanity and the love of Christ in our hearts. We [Noble and his sisters] have had that always. You have given it to us. And I would rather be able to look back upon a life which has scattered these riches far and wide as best it could, than one which counted its other riches in piles. You have made me rich, and I am trying to be God's Steward with the riches you have given me. So on your birthday, I want to send on to you what others have given to you through me—all sorts of honors: Phi Beta Kappa, Raven Society, Rectorship of a large and increasingly influential church, a doctor's degree, many friendships, and the opportunity to serve my fellow man. Thank you for them. I am trying as best I can to be a true representative of your's [*sic*]." NCP to Mary Irving Whitman Powell, n.d., LHPM Papers.

123. For additional articles, see *College Topics,* 23 January 1931, 1, 4.

124. "Noble Powell Bids University Good-By," *College Topics,* 26 January 1931, 1.

125. See "Dr. T. K. Nelson Speaks on Behalf of Seminary," *College Topics,* 12 February 1924, 5.

126. *College Topics,* 3 November 1930, 1. Powell came in fourth of five candidates for bishop coadjutor, with only a handful of votes from clerical and lay delegates. Tucker defeated the second-place finisher, F. D. Goodwin, by better than a three-to-one margin. *Journal of the 131st Annual Council of the Protestant Episcopal Church in the Diocese of Virginia, Held in St. James Church, Leesburg, on the 19th and 20th of May, 1926* (Richmond: n.p., 1926), 45.

127. *College Topics,* 25 March 1924, 6. One of the best sketches of Tucker's life and career is Virginius Dabney, "Henry St. George Tucker: Beloved Virginian," *Virginia and the Virginia Record* 77 (April 1955): 4–7, 19–24. Also valuable is the pamphlet by A. Pierce Middleton, *Henry St. George Tucker: Missionary and Bishop* (New York: The National Council [of the Episcopal Church], 1960). See also David Hein, "Henry St. George Tucker," in *American National Biography,* vol. 21, ed. John A. Garraty and Mark C. Carnes (New York: Oxford University Press, 1999), 895–96. The Reverend W. Gerow Christian called Tucker "the greatest Christian man I have ever known" (*My Story,* 71).

128. The parish probably bought the rectory in 1929. It was located on Chancellor Street across from the parish house and was later used as a guest house by the university hospital. Telephone interview with George Bean.

129. *Journal of the 136th Annual Council of the Protestant Episcopal Church in the Diocese of Virginia,* 200.

130. Kettlewell, *History of St. Paul's Memorial Church,* 16–17.

131. Telephone interview with George Bean.

132. Molly Laird Gould, telephone interview with the author, 22 May 1992; Helen Het-

lage, telephone interview with the author, 22 May 1992, who confirmed the recollections of her sister, Molly Gould. William Laird did not begin his tenure at St. Paul's until 1932, following the interim ministry of W. Gerow Christian, *locum tenens* between September 1931 and June 1932.

133. Theodore H. Evans to NCP, 3 November 1949, Powell Papers, "Schools—U.Va." file, Maryland Diocesan Archives, Baltimore. As a result of the fund-raising campaign led by Evans in the late 1940s, the St. Paul's debt was finally paid off; the church was consecrated in December 1950, almost twenty years after Noble Powell's departure. Jean Bowie Evans, letter to the author, 23 January 1998. Powell had known Theodore Evans (1898–1990) reasonably well even before the latter became rector of St. Paul's (1947–61). Powell probably met him when Evans was at Virginia Seminary and certainly got to know him when Evans was rector of St. John's Church in nearby Waynesboro, Virginia, from 1925 to 1927. Powell exchanged letters with Evans during the years that Phil Powell was an undergraduate at the university. From 1964 to 1967, just after Bishop Powell retired, Evans served as an assistant at the Church of the Redeemer in Baltimore. "The diocese [of Virginia] has always felt clergy should be provided a rectory." E. Holcombe Palmer, telephone interview with the author, 20 May 1992.

134. Dabney, *Mr. Jefferson's University*, 78, 84, 88. Alderman died in 1931; Noble Powell was invited back from Baltimore to participate in his funeral.

135. *College Topics*, 13 January 1925, 1; 15 April 1927, 1; 26 March 1928, 1; 14 December 1929, 1.

136. The historian Robert T. Handy has called the transformation of American Protestantism that occurred in the 1920s and 1930s "the second disestablishment," the first having taken place in the years following the American Revolution. See Robert T. Handy, *A Christian America: Protestant Hopes and Historical Realities,* 2d ed. (New York: Oxford University Press, 1984), chap. 7.

137. NCP, "Modernism," an address to the Albemarle (Va.) Convocation, in "Addresses, Meditations, Sermons" box, Maryland Diocesan Archives, Baltimore. See Dorr, "Assuring America's Place in the Sun," 269–71, 275–76.

138. See Ferenc Morton Szasz, *The Divided Mind of Protestant America, 1880–1930* (Tuscaloosa: University of Alabama Press, 1982).

139. See Robert Prichard's discussion of "The Debate over the Creeds" in *History of the Episcopal Church,* 206–11; also see Holmes, *Brief History of the Episcopal Church,* 121–22; Robert Wuthnow, *The Restructuring of American Religion: Society and Faith since World War II* (Princeton, N.J.: Princeton University Press, 1988), 134–36.

140. George M. Marsden, *Religion and American Culture* (San Diego: Harcourt, Brace, Jovanovich, 1990), 195–97. See also Winthrop S. Hudson and John Corrigan, *Religion in America,* 5th ed. (New York: Macmillan, 1992), 346–48.

141. Bruce Barton, *The Man Nobody Knows: A Discovery of the Real Jesus* (Indianapolis: Bobbs-Merrill, 1925); Marsden, *Religion and American Culture,* 197–98. See also Handy, *Christian America,* 173; Rolf Lundén, *Business and Religion in the American 1920s* (Westport, Conn.: Greenwood Press, 1988), 102–5; Marty, *Noise of Conflict,* 45–47.

142. Marsden, *Religion and American Culture,* 197.

143. John F. Piper Jr., "The American Churches in World War I," *Journal of the American Academy of Religion* 38 (June 1970): 149; Hudson and Corrigan, *Religion in America,* 354–59. See also Robert T. Handy, "The American Religious Depression, 1925–1935," *Church History* 29 (March 1960): 3–16, reprinted in *Religion in American History: A Reader,* ed.

Jon Butler and Harry S. Stout (New York: Oxford University Press, 1998), 371–83. Handy points to signs of a religious depression during these years: falling church attendance in rural and urban areas, declining enthusiasm for mission work, fewer converts and new members, and a prevailing mood of disillusionment. But he interprets this period as an important time of transition for the mainstream churches, leading to a healthier, more culturally detached, more incisive and relevant American Protestantism.

144. Charles Fiske, *The Confessions of a Puzzled Parson* (1928; reprint, Freeport, N.Y.: Books for Libraries Press, 1968), 14.

145. The house also had a cooking stove and gas lanterns. Interview with Thomas Hooker Powell, 25 August 1992; Carl F. Bessent, "Emmanuel Church in the Depression Period," paper presented at Emmanuel Church, Baltimore, 15 October 1995, 3; Ralph Hewitt (Powell's neighbor), interview with the author, Love, Va., 18 September 1992. Hewitt recalled that the property initially comprised over 150 acres, but the Blue Ridge Parkway "took about half of that" around 1940. "Mr. Powell never did like that parkway. He always walked with a long stick—a stick up over his head—[and he'd say] 'I wish I could wave this stick and put back every rock and tree just the way it was [before the parkway was built].'" In 1938 Powell wrote to his family in Lowndesboro complaining about having to give up a large portion of his property on account of one of "Mr. Roosevelt's fine schemes." He said, "I just wish I had money enough to fight this to the Supreme Court before R. gets another crack at appointing henchmen to it who will vote whatever way he tells them to." NCP to "My dearest ones at home," [1938], LCF Collection (photocopy in author's possession).

Ralph Hewitt also recalled the time he obtained a mortgage to buy some land and NCP told him, "I ain't rich but you buy any land you check with me before you go to the bank. If I got it I'll lend it at no interest, no interest at all. You check with me." Hewitt said Powell was "a pretty good carpenter" and "a wonderful good man; I thought a lot of him." "He'd come in on [our] front porch, and he and my daddy used to talk for hours and hours." Mary Powell, according to Hewitt and others, used to stay for a few days, then go to Florida or New York or abroad for her vacation. "[Noble Powell] was crazy about that place," Hewitt said, his wife less so.

146. NCP to Scott B. Berkeley (mayor of Goldsboro, N.C.), 28 February 1949, Powell Papers, "Schools—U.Va.," Maryland Diocesan Archives, Baltimore. In the 1930s the Powell family usually spent July in Rye Beach, New Hampshire, where Powell was rector of St. Andrew's-by-the-Sea, a small church that opened for only one month each year. The family—the father and his two sons at least—would then go to Devil's Knob in August. There, he said, he let Philip and Tommy "run wild" for a month. *Baltimore Evening Sun*, 20 December 1934.

147. It is doubtful that Powell actually read *I'll Take My Stand* in the 1930s; the book sold only two thousand copies before going out of print in 1941. It received more attention when it was reissued over twenty years later, by which time some of its contributors had become well known. Egerton, *Speak Now against the Day*, 68. Certainly Powell would not have agreed with all of the Agrarians' thinking. Egerton devotes several pages of his history to this southern manifesto, rightly criticizing it for its reactionary and racist stances, its defense of an elite culture of privilege (what John Crowe Ransom called the "squirearchy"), and its blindness to the actual problems of those who were struggling to survive as farmers in the impoverished South (64–69).

148. Philip N. Powell, interview with the author, Baltimore, Maryland, 30 September

1997. Noble Powell would have first met Chamberlain in the fall of 1920, when Bernard was president of the YMCA in Madison Hall. *College Topics,* 24 September 1920.

The highly successful Rural Electrification Administration, an agency of the U.S. Department of Agriculture, made long-term, self-liquidating loans to state and local governments, farmers' cooperatives, and nonprofit organizations. Noble and Mary Powell won their case in the Augusta County Circuit Court, in Staunton, Virginia, in a jury trial held on 2 August 1951. The following month, Judge Floridus S. Crosby denied the defendant's motion to set aside the jury's verdict and ordered the electric cooperative to pay the Powells $1,350 in damages plus the plaintiffs' costs. Notice of Motion for Judgment (photocopy), *Noble C. Powell and Mary Rustin Powell v. Shenandoah Valley Electric Cooperative,* 22 September 1951, Circuit Court of Augusta County. An official with the Shenandoah Valley Electric Cooperative said on 19 February 1998 that he had not known of any case in which a person had received service who had not first joined the electric cooperative. He also mentioned that in the early days of the program, customers identified the project with the REA so completely that they made out their checks to the REA—and that in fact some of the electric cooperative's older customers still do so.

Chapter 3: Big-City Rector and Dean, 1931–41

1. Carl F. Bessent, *Emmanuel Day: Celebrating 140 Years* (Baltimore: Emmanuel Episcopal Church, 1994).

2. Ibid. Birckhead became an assistant at St. George's in 1902, minister-in-charge in 1905, and rector in 1906.

3. Ibid. See Williams, *America's Religions,* 250–51; John Dillenberger, *A Theology of Artistic Sensibilities: The Visual Arts and the Church* (New York: Crossroad, 1986), 213.

4. Bessent, *Emmanuel Day.* Cardinal Gibbons, one of the nation's most popular Catholic leaders, was also a close friend of William Paret and John Gardner Murray, Episcopal bishops of Maryland. Thomas W. Spalding, *The Premier See: A History of the Archdiocese of Baltimore, 1789–1994* (Baltimore: Johns Hopkins University Press, 1995), 311. For a brief introduction to Gibbons's thought and career, see John Cogley, *Catholic America* (Garden City, N.Y.: Image-Doubleday, 1974), 64, 174–77; for a complete account, see the studies by the Catholic historian John Tracy Ellis.

5. Bessent, *Emmanuel Day.*

6. NCP, 1937, qtd. in Bessent, *Emmanuel Day.*

7. Edward T. Helfenstein to NCP, 29 September 1930, PNP Papers.

8. Jack Malpas, telephone interview with the author, 23 January 1993. Malpas was a member of Emmanuel Church in the 1930s when Powell was there and assistant minister at Emmanuel in the 1940s when Powell was bishop; he later served as rector of St. Bartholomew's Church in Baltimore.

9. Henry D. Harlan to NCP, 3 November 1930, PNP Papers; Dielman-Hayward File, Maryland Historical Society, Baltimore; NCP, "Bishop's Address," *Journal of the 160th Annual Convention of the Protestant Episcopal Church in the Diocese of Maryland, Held in the Cathedral of the Incarnation, Baltimore, January 26, 1944* (Baltimore: The Convention, 1944), 59–60 (hereafter *Journal*).

10. Dielman-Hayward File, Maryland Historical Society, Baltimore. Possibly it was Fisher who first suggested Powell's name as a successor to Birckhead, upon the recommendation of a member of the parish, David C. Trimble, a student at Virginia Theological Semi-

nary who had visited Parson Powell at St. Paul's, Charlottesville, in 1925. "I often reminded Noble that I was the one who brought him to Maryland in the first place!" David C. Trimble (Hagerstown, Md.), letter to the author, 21 March 1992. Unquestionably, though, before his call Powell was known to several other members of the congregation as well.

It is relevant to point out, while we are considering this group of influential individuals, that a study conducted in 1931, the year that Powell took over at Emmanuel, found that of the sixteen thousand religiously affiliated biographees in *Who's Who in America,* seven thousand were Episcopalians or Presbyterians. C. Luther Fry, qtd. in Marty, *Noise of Conflict,* 48.

11. Dielman-Hayward File, Maryland Historical Society. See Allen C. Guelzo, *For the Union of Evangelical Christendom: The Irony of the Reformed Episcopalians* (University Park: Pennsylvania State University Press, 1994), 144–45, 218, 262–67, 274, 299.

12. Apparently Birckhead did have a taste for elaborate vestments, however; parishioners remembered the beautiful copes he wore for special services. Bessent, *Emmanuel Day.*

13. Dielman-Hayward File, Maryland Historical Society; Sherry H. Olson, *Baltimore: The Building of an American City,* rev. ed. (Baltimore: Johns Hopkins University Press, 1997), 303–4, 325. Olson notes that in the 1930s Guilford had only one Jewish homeowner—and the milkman, the breadman, and the paper boy all refused to deliver to him (325).

In politics Powell was a moderate-to-conservative Democrat. A critic in the 1930s of FDR and the New Deal, in the bipartisan fifties he was one of the many who liked Ike. One of Powell's friends and camping buddies in the late twenties and early thirties was Harry Byrd of Virginia (1887–1966), a conservative Democrat, lifelong Episcopalian, and avid hiker and hunter. Powell would have been one of those companions of Byrd's who noticed that wherever Byrd, a devout Christian, found himself at the end of the day, he would kneel down and say his prayers. Like Powell, Byrd was no religious bigot but counted many Jews and Roman Catholics among his friends. Moreover, Byrd believed that Christianity, a religion of personal freedom, undergirded American institutions. Ronald L. Heinemann, *Harry Byrd of Virginia* (Charlottesville: University Press of Virginia, 1996), 290–91; Thomas Hooker Powell, telephone interview with the author, 4 February 1998.

On Byrd's later career, see J. Harvie Wilkinson III, *Harry Byrd and the Changing Face of Virginia Politics, 1945–1966* (Charlottesville: University Press of Virginia, 1968). Wilkinson points out that Byrd, well known for his pay-as-you-go philosophy and for massive resistance in the fifties, was not always so conservative. His years as governor (1926–30)—when he made lynching a state offense, won approval for voting and tax reforms, and promoted conservation and rural electrification—could be termed progressive, although his consolidation of the state government had a conservative effect (6–7).

14. In the 1890s and early 1900s record numbers of Alabama Baptist males, including preachers seeking middle-class respectability, joined the Masons. See Flynt, *Alabama Baptists,* 169.

15. *Baltimore Evening Sun,* 20 December 1934; *Baltimore Sun,* 29 May 1941; "Episcopal Bishop Dies," *Baltimore Sun,* 30 November 1968. These *Baltimore Sun* articles—some lacking titles—are from the newspaper clippings in the vertical file on Noble Powell in the Maryland Room of the Enoch Pratt Free Library (Central Branch), Baltimore. See also James Waldo Fawcett, "Dr. Noble C. Powell Elected Dean of Washington Cathedral," *Washington Evening Star,* 6 February 1937.

The Eclectic Club was an early exercise in fostering ecumenical relations among Baltimore clergy; founded in 1871, the small, select group met eight times a year. The Maryland Home for Friendless Colored Children, located west of Baltimore City, between Catonsville and Ellicott City (near Neepier's Station), was formed as a corporation in 1899 by the Reverend George F. Bragg Jr. and taken over by the diocesan convention in 1920. Located on thirty-two acres, the home—which included classrooms, chapel, gym, and dormitory—accommodated about thirty boys. Neither a corrective institution nor an orphanage, the home existed for boys whose parents could not care for them. *Inventory of the Church Archives of Maryland: Protestant Episcopal: Diocese of Maryland* (Baltimore: Maryland Historical Records Survey Project, 1940), 294–95. The home closed in 1949, and proceeds from its sale were used to establish a scholarship fund for African-American youth.

Martin Marty writes of the lay and ordained leaders of "original-stock Protestantism" who "held common memberships in uncommon clubs" and participated in a "serene culture" whose calm center was threatened in the twenties and thirties by rising challenges and sources of conflict (*Noise of Conflict*, 48; see chap. 2, "Religious America's Search for Steadiness").

16. Powell backed a proposal that came before the general convention of 1934 to add four women to the National Council, the body—predecessor of the Executive Council—that assisted the presiding bishop in administering the national church between the triennial meetings of the general convention. "Noble Cilley Powell," *National Cyclopedia of American Biography* 54:75. Women had been specifically excluded from the National Council since its establishment in 1919, when the national church was reorganized. The proposal passed, and four women, nominated by the Woman's Auxiliary and elected by the general convention, took their seats on the National Council in January 1935. Pamela W. Darling, *New Wine: The Story of Women Transforming Leadership and Power in the Episcopal Church* (Cambridge, Mass.: Cowley Publications, 1994), 44–48, 63–64, 71–72. Women could not actually serve as deputies to the general convention until 1970. See Mary Sudman Donovan, *A Different Call: Women's Ministries in the Episcopal Church, 1850–1920* (Wilton, Conn.: Morehouse-Barlow, 1986), 173.

17. H. Richard Niebuhr, Wilhelm Pauck, and Francis P. Miller, *The Church against the World* (Chicago: Willett, Clark and Co., 1935); see Marty, *Noise of Conflict*, 310–20. William R. Hutchison, "Preface: From Protestant to Pluralist America," in *Between the Times: The Travail of the Protestant Establishment in America, 1900–1960*, ed. William R. Hutchison (Cambridge: Cambridge University Press, 1989), viii.

18. Edwin S. Gaustad, "The Pulpit and the Pews," in *Between the Times: The Travail of the Protestant Establishment in America, 1900–1960*, ed. William R. Hutchison (Cambridge: Cambridge University Press, 1989), 21.

19. Carl F. Bessent, "Emmanuel Day: Emmanuel Church in the Depression Period," paper presented at Emmanuel Episcopal Church, Baltimore, 15 October 1995. Martin Marty comments that in the liturgical churches—such as the Roman Catholic, Episcopal, and Lutheran—worship provided little indication of the church's response to the Depression: "The visitor could worship without recognizing from the service that America was in a depression period" (*Noise of Conflict*, 254).

20. Huntington Williams Jr., telephone interview with the author, 19 May 1992.

21. Olson, *Baltimore*, 333. The Depression brought about a significant expansion of the role of the national government in cities. Olson notes that prior to the crash, the federal government's presence in Baltimore had been largely confined (outside of wartime) to the post office, the immigration center at Locust Point, and the custom house (339). In

his baccalaureate sermon for the graduates of Johns Hopkins University in 1931, Powell complained that "more and more government is ironing out individual lives." Sermon, Emmanuel Church, 7 June 1931, PNP Papers.

In the Episcopal church nationwide, combined parish receipts fell from $44.7 million in 1927 to $30.6 million in 1934, and severe cutbacks were made in such areas as foreign missions and work among the deaf. Seminary graduates had trouble finding positions, and those that did find jobs encountered difficulty supporting themselves on their meager wages. Prichard, *History of the Episcopal Church,* 205, 218–19; Holmes, *Brief History of the Episcopal Church,* 150–51.

In general the Depression undermined Americans' confidence in the saving power of business. Their belief "in the redemptive power of the American way of life faltered, the 'religion of business' lost votaries in droves, [and] faith in automatic progress evaporated." At the same time, many Americans experienced a "revival of spirit" and gained "a new sense of solidarity." Sydney E. Ahlstrom, *A Religious History of the American People,* vol. 2 (Garden City, N.Y.: Image-Doubleday, 1975), 410. After 1929 churches no longer looked to the business paradigm with uncritical approval. Rolf Lundén, *Business and Religion in the American 1920s* (Westport, Conn.: Greenwood Press, 1988), 182.

22. Bessent, "Emmanuel Day."

23. Holmes, *Brief History of the Episcopal Church,* 151; Robert Moats Miller, *American Protestantism and Social Issues, 1919–1939* (Chapel Hill: University of North Carolina Press, 1958), 82–84, 124, 238–41.

24. Olson, *Baltimore,* 344.

25. Rev. Charles W. (Buck) Carnan (1908–96), telephone interview with the author, 20 May 1992. As a young man Carnan served as an acolyte and crucifer at Emmanuel. Inspired and guided by Powell, he went on to earn degrees from the University of Virginia (1936) and Virginia Theological Seminary (1939) before being ordained. Charles W. Carnan, letter to the author, 2 June 1992; NCP to Charles W. Carnan, 6 June 1932 (in author's possession).

26. Marty, *Noise of Conflict,* 17, 43, 47.

27. Samuel Johnson, *The Rambler,* ed. W. J. Bate and Albrecht B. Strauss (New Haven: Yale University Press, 1969), 13.

28. NCP, "Dr. Green: Teacher, Counsellor, Friend," typed address given by NCP at Virginia Theological Seminary, June 1931, in box of Powell addresses, Maryland Diocesan Archives, Baltimore. See Gaustad, "Pulpit and the Pews," 30.

29. *The Pelican* (Emmanuel Church newsletter), 29 December 1935.

30. Noble P. Wong (b. 1931), letter to the author, 4 November 1991.

31. NCP, "On Leaving Emmanuel Church, Baltimore," 7 February 1937, vertical file, Maryland Diocesan Archives, Baltimore.

32. *The Pelican,* 6 June 1937.

33. Mary wrote to her mother-in-law on 16 October 1937: "There will never be a place like Emmanuel in my heart I know. We were pretty lucky to have been there for those happy years but perhaps if we'd stayed longer we would have taken it for granted. Who knows? I don't really think so for we both loved and appreciated it all the time we were there." LHPM Papers (photocopy in author's possession).

The man who followed Noble Powell at Emmanuel gained quick acceptance in his new post. Theodore Parker Ferris (1908–72), formerly the assistant to Walter Russell Bowie at Grace Church, New York City, would go on to win renown as one of America's finest and most admired preachers. He served as Emmanuel's rector until October 1942, when he left to take charge of Trinity Church, Boston, home of Phillips Brooks's long and influential ministry in the last decades of the previous century. Ferris's appeal was not rooted in the power of his prophetic utterance, for he scanted the role of prophet, believing that the church should fight against the sin and sorrows of individuals rather than wage war against corrupt social structures. Thus, while he lent his support to the establishment of such agencies as the Big Brother Association, the Massachusetts Half-Way House, and the Low-Cost Housing Corporation, he believed that the more the church became involved in the political sphere, the less influence it would have in the moral and spiritual realm. The church, he believed, lost its unique position and power when it confused the just society, however desirable, with God's kingdom. John Harold Sullivan, "Theodore Parker Ferris: The Man, His Method and Message" (D.Min. thesis, School of Theology at Claremont, 1976), 60–62; Don S. Armentrout, "Theodore Parker Ferris," in *American National Biography,* vol. 7, ed. John A. Garraty and Mark C. Carnes (New York: Oxford University Press, 1999), 856–57. See Wuthnow, *Restructuring of American Religion,* 65.

34. Holmes, *Brief History of the Episcopal Church,* 92; see also chap. 4, "Church Life and Worship."

35. Prichard, *History of the Episcopal Church,* 192–93.

36. Ibid., 193.

37. Kit Konolige and Frederica Konolige, *The Power of Their Glory: America's Ruling Class: The Episcopalians* (New York: Wyden Books, 1978), 37; Peter W. Williams, *Houses of God: Region, Religion, and Architecture in the United States* (Urbana: University of Illinois Press, 1997), 74. Roosevelt was a member of the Dutch Reformed church, but he regularly attended services of the Episcopal church, the denomination of his wife and children.

38. Konolige and Konolige, *Power of Their Glory,* 38. The Konoliges also speak, somewhat breathlessly, of the Washington Cathedral as the "crowning glory of the power of the semiofficial church of America" (7), constructed in the days "when building an Episcopal cathedral to the skies showed the limitless aspirations and confidence of the Episcocratic elite" (300). The church historian Peter W. Williams has written that the Cathedral "overlooks the entire city, symbolic of its conceivers' aspirations to build a spiritual *axis mundi* for the nation's capital and, implicitly, the nation itself" (*Houses of God,* 74).

39. Konolige and Konolige, *Power of Their Glory,* 359.

40. *Step by Step and Stone by Stone: The History of Washington National Cathedral* (Washington, D.C.: Washington National Cathedral, 1990), 3.

41. NCP, fragment on "Christian Unity," PNP Papers.

42. "Dr. Powell's Statement," 19 November 1936, WNC Archives.

43. NCP, memorandum to Canon A. P. Stokes, 4 April 1938, WNC Archives.

44. NCP to Josephine McLeod (University of Virginia Hospital), 11 March 1937, Emmanuel Church Archives, Baltimore.

45. NCP to "my dearest ones at home," [1937], LCF Collection.

46. NCP, Report of the Cathedral Foundation, *Journal of the 46th Annual Convention of the Protestant Episcopal Church in the Diocese of Washington, Held in St. Stephen's and Incarnation Parish, Washington, Wednesday and Thursday, May 7–8, 1941* (Washington, D.C.: The Convention, 1941), 177.

47. NCP to Canon William Bradner, 29 July 1939, WNC Archives.

48. *A Guide to the Washington Cathedral* (Washington, D.C.: National Cathedral Association, 1945), 39.

49. "Seating of the Presiding Bishop," *Cathedral Age,* Winter 1941, 3–6. James Freeman, bishop of Washington, said that "'it seems eminently proper that there should be at the disposal of the Presiding Bishop a Cathedral Church in a great metropolitan center from whose pulpit from time to time he could make pronouncements of signal importance, not only to the Church of which he is the chief officer, but to the nation at large'" (6). Powell believed that making the Washington Cathedral the official seat of the presiding bishop would give "us much more responsibility than we have had before. While the legal status is unchanged, yet the general situation is considerably changed. There are many problems attendant to this, but I believe we can work them out all right." NCP to Leonard Hodgson, 6 November 1940, WNC Archives.

50. Hein, "Henry St. George Tucker," 895–96; "For Aid to Britain," *Cathedral Age,* Summer 1941, 19.

51. NCP to Mrs. Macneil of Barra, 18 July 1940, WNC Archives.

52. NCP to Leonard Hodgson, 5 September 1940, WNC Archives; Hodgson to NCP, 18 October 1940, WNC Archives. Hodgson (1889–1969) taught at General Theological Seminary in New York City from 1925 to 1931 and came to know Powell then. A graduate of Hertford College, Oxford, Hodgson was Regius professor of moral and pastoral theology and canon of Christ Church, Oxford, during the war years. He wrote several books that examined the problems of this difficult era: *Democracy and Dictatorship in the Light of Christian Faith* (1935), *This War and the Christian* (1939), and *The Christian Idea of Liberty* (1941). Hodgson's background in the international ecumenical movement—particularly as the general secretary of Faith and Order—would have appealed to Powell.

53. NCP to Gerald O. Hill (Bristol, England), 12 September 1940, WNC Archives.

54. NCP to Leonard Hodgson, 6 November 1940, WNC Archives.

55. Certainly he had people around him who reminded him of the potential importance of his position in relation to world events: "Because of the world situation," Canon Stokes told Powell in 1939, "there should be strong men in positions of leadership, which gives an added importance to the Deanship of the Cathedral at the Nation's Capital. We may have very critical times ahead where the voices of the Bishop of Washington and the Dean of its Cathedral will be of vital significance not only to America but to the world." Anson Phelps Stokes to NCP, 14 April 1939, WNC Archives.

56. Konolige and Konolige, *Power of Their Glory,* 313. See George Wharton Pepper, *Philadelphia Lawyer: An Autobiography* (Philadelphia: J. B. Lippincott, 1944). From 1922 to 1927 Pepper served as a U.S. senator from Pennsylvania. In 1948 he published an *Analytical Index to the Book of Common Prayer.* See also his article "Washington Cathedral: What It Is and What It Stands For," *Cathedral Age,* Spring 1941. For over fifty years Pepper was a vestryman and warden of Philadelphia's fashionable St. Mark's Church, Rittenhouse Square; and for more than fifty summers he went to Northeast Harbor on Maine's Mount Desert Island, a beautiful resort favored by the Pulitzers, Fords, and Rockefellers—as well as by prominent leaders of the Episcopal church, including bishops (William Doane of Albany and William Lawrence of Massachusetts), headmasters (Endicott Peabody of Groton and S. S. Drury of St. Paul's, Concord), and much of the lay aristocracy of Philadelphia, New York, and Boston. E. Digby Baltzell, *Philadelphia Gentlemen: The Making of a National Upper Class* (Glencoe, Ill.: Free Press, 1958), 169, 220–22, 227, 249, 253.

57. John R. Mott, "World Possibilities of the Cathedral," *Cathedral Age,* Spring 1937, 61–62. Mott addressed the annual meeting of the National Cathedral Association on 6 May 1937, the same day that Noble Powell was installed as dean.

58. James E. Freeman, "Fifteen Years: An Unfolding Vision," *Cathedral Age*, Autumn 1938, 10–11. "[W]orld authorities such as John R. Mott and William Adams Brown," Canon Stokes pointed out to Powell, "feel that with our tradition and commitments here we have through the Cathedral and the College [of Preachers] a unique opportunity to advance the cause [of Christian unity]. To this the Bishop and you are fully committed. . . . You feel with me that there is no greater call for the Church than to make a contribution towards Christ's idea of one fold and one shepherd." Stokes to NCP, 14 April 1939, WNC Archives.

59. Eleanor Roosevelt, "My Day," 18 April 1938.

60. "All agree . . . that your preaching has been greatly strengthened during the Washington stay, due, doubtless, largely to the stimulating influence of the work at the College of Preachers—both what you have heard there and your work in criticizing and training others." Anson Phelps Stokes to NCP, 14 April 1939, WNC Archives.

61. "Dr. Powell's Statement," 19 November 1936, WNC Archives. See Noble C. Powell, *The Post-Ordination Training of the Clergy: The Twenty-fifth Annual Hale Memorial Sermon* (Evanston, Ill.: Seabury-Western Theological Seminary, 1939), and "Post-Ordination Training in the Episcopal Church," *Anglican Theological Review* 24 (July 1942): 210–16.

Cochran, a carpet manufacturer and philanthropist, donated nearly 1.5 million dollars to build and endow the College of Preachers. His benefaction owed something to his friendship with the bishop of Washington and something to his belief that Episcopal preaching was not as good as it could be. Henry Bradford Washburn, *Philip Mercer Rhinelander* (New York: Morehouse-Gorham, 1950), 173–74.

One of Powell's important achievements was effecting a closer working relationship between the cathedral and the College of Preachers. See Anson Phelps Stokes to NCP, 14 April 1939, WNC Archives.

62. Donald Coggan, the retired archbishop of Canterbury, recalled meeting Powell at the College of Preachers in the early forties. He remembered him as "a very gracious and 'happy-looking' man." Lord Donald Coggan, letter to the author, 23 October 1991.

63. See *Theodore Otto Wedel: An Anthology*, ed. William S. Lea (Cincinnati: Forward Movement Publications, 1972).

64. "Rev. Dr. Powell Is Nominated for Coadjutor," *Baltimore Sun*, 15 January 1937.

65. NCP to Warren Kearny [secretary of the Standing Committee of the diocese of Louisiana], 10 May 1939, PNP Papers; "Dean Powell Is Elected Bishop of Louisiana," *Washington Evening Star*, 13 April 1939. This article mentions that Powell was "regarded as a mentor of the younger generation in the Episcopal Church throughout the United States." "To be bishop of Louisiana has many strong appeals," Powell acknowledged at the time. "I am a Southerner, my traditions are Southern, and the church in the South has a tremendous opportunity. My interests chiefly are missions and student work, though all of church work is a thrill." *New Orleans Times-Picayune*, 25 April 1939 (in PNP Papers).

66. Richard T. Feller and Marshall W. Fishwick, *For Thy Great Glory*, 2d ed. (Culpeper, Va.: Community Press, 1979), 29; *Cathedral Age*, Winter 1936–37, 44–50; "Dean Change," *Time*, 22 February 1937, 34, 36, 38; *Newsweek*, 20 February 1937, 20; Van Rensselaer Gibson, *Grand Man of God: James Edward Freeman* (Yonkers, N.Y.: n.p., 1944), 9. In November 1942, when the Reverend Sam Shoemaker was being considered for the deanship of the National Cathedral, Bishop Freeman invited him to lunch and impressed upon him the difference between English and American cathedrals. In the former, Freeman observed, the bishop has his throne but no say about how the cathedral is run; in the United States

the cathedral is the bishop's church and the dean serves as the bishop's vicar. Helen Smith Shoemaker, *I Stand By the Door: The Life of Sam Shoemaker* (New York: Harper and Row, 1967), 97.

67. "Dean Powell Again Refuses Bishopric," *Baltimore Evening Sun,* 9 October 1939.

68. Hodding Carter and Betty Werlein Carter, *So Great a Good: A History of the Episcopal Church in Louisiana and of Christ Church Cathedral, 1805–1955* (Sewanee, Tenn.: University Press, 1955), 332. A later bishop of Louisiana, Girault McArthur Jones (diocesan from 1949 to 1969), confirmed this interpretation: the convention was divided, Powell was "elected on a distant ballot," and he "may not have felt the call was there strongly enough." Girault McArthur Jones, telephone interview with the author, 23 April 1992. In 1939 Jones was rector of St. Andrew's Church in New Orleans.

69. The Maryland diocese comprised nearly fifty thousand Episcopalians, Louisiana only thirteen thousand. On 28 May 1941 the annual convention of the Episcopal diocese of Maryland elected Powell bishop coadjutor on the second ballot. Already on the first ballot, Powell had received the requisite number of lay votes and had run well ahead of his closest rival, Don Frank Fenn, in the voting by clergy. *Journal,* 1941, 69, 71. For several years various churchmen had assured Powell that he would be a leading candidate for the Maryland post and probably for others as well. Stokes, for example, in attempting at the time of the first Louisiana election to persuade the dean to remain at the cathedral, said to Powell that "the time may well come when you may wish to accept the Bishopric of Maryland, or of Virginia, or of Washington, or of a similar Diocese, which will undoubtedly be offered to you." Anson Phelps Stokes to NCP, 14 April 1939, WNC Archives. Bishop Freeman told Powell that he "had long felt that it was inevitable that Maryland would call you [to be bishop]." James E. Freeman to NCP, 2 June 1941, WNC Archives.

Chapter 4: Bishop, 1941–63

1. "He [NCP] was the last bishop of the old church, the church which relied on personal knowledge and its own tradition, rather than on structures borrowed from business or the social sciences. [I met with him about going into the priesthood, and] he allowed me to apply to Virginia Seminary and provided funds for me to go. I contrast that with the involved system we use now, and I am not convinced anything could improve on Bishop Powell." Thomas Nelson Rightmyer, letter to the author, 20 April 1992.

2. James Nuechterlein, "Getting the Fifties Right," *First Things,* May 1995, 11. With regard to racial justice, however, "All political virtues have their corresponding vices, and the judicious moderation of the decade was offset by its absence of passion," that is, by an unwillingness to follow up on the *Brown* decision with significant civil rights legislation (12).

3. Robert S. Ellwood, *The Fifties Spiritual Marketplace: American Religion in a Decade of Conflict* (New Brunswick, N.J.: Rutgers University Press, 1997), 5–6.

4. The number of people who claimed to have worshiped in the previous seven days jumped from 37 percent in 1940 and 39 percent in 1950 to 46 percent in 1954 and 49 percent in 1958. These numbers are probably somewhat inflated, however, because of the tendency of polling respondents to exaggerate the extent of their actual attendance. Martin E. Marty, *Under God, Indivisible, 1941–1960,* vol. 3 of *Modern American Religion* (Chicago: University of Chicago Press, 1996), 279; Ellwood, *Fifties Spiritual Marketplace,* 1.

5. Ellwood, *Fifties Spiritual Marketplace,* 5.

6. See Marty, *Under God,* 295–96; Wuthnow, *Restructuring of American Religion,* 66, 143–44; James T. Patterson, *Grand Expectations: The United States, 1945–1974* (New York: Oxford University Press, 1996), 329.

7. Ellwood, *Fifties Spiritual Marketplace,* 6, 9–10. Ellwood writes that "Protestant churches, influenced by neoorthodoxy, could be reasonably demanding theologically, and even the stereotypical suburban superchurch with all its spiritual/social activities could be demanding in terms of time and participation" (9); "religion was presented in fundamentally consumer-friendly, nonthreatening ways, though with sufficient demands on people's time, energy, and life-style to make faith appear serious" (24). One well-known Baltimore priest, Bennett Sims, rector of the Church of the Redeemer from 1951 to 1964 and later bishop of Atlanta, recalled little that was challenging about religion in the 1950s. He cited "the easy popularity of post–World War II 'churchianity,'" a form of cultural piety that "lacked depth and breadth of discipleship, starting with me." Bennett J. Sims, *Servanthood: Leadership for the Third Millennium* (Cambridge, Mass.: Cowley, 1997), 55.

8. William L. O'Neill, *American High: The Years of Confidence, 1945–1960* (New York: Free Press, 1986). See Wuthnow, *Restructuring of American Religion,* chap. 3, "A Vision of Promise and Peril."

9. Prichard, *History of the Episcopal Church,* 229–30; Holmes, *Brief History of the Episcopal Church,* 157.

10. During Powell's episcopate the general population of the counties making up the diocese of Maryland increased by roughly 50 percent.

11. "Busy Prelate Steps Down," *Baltimore Sun,* 27 October 1963.

12. Powell's admirable sense of tradition and history contributed to his timely and valuable support of the diocesan archives and to his sponsorship of a history of the colonial church in Maryland: Nelson Rightmyer's *Maryland's Established Church* (Baltimore: Church Historical Society for the Diocese of Maryland, 1956), which is dedicated to Bishop Powell. The "man and his era" went together like a "hand in a glove." Powell was a "southern gentleman, tall, soft-spoken, with a beautiful accent; he looked like a bishop. He had a straight back, a gracious smile, and could tell wonderful, funny stories. People would feel so good. And no one was attacking him." Rt. Rev. David K. Leighton, telephone interview with the author, 4 November 1992.

13. Telephone interview with Rt. Rev. David K. Leighton.

14. NCP, "Fifteenth Anniversary," *Maryland Churchman,* October 1956, 3. In the twentieth century the diocese of Maryland, which was organized in 1783, no longer comprised all the counties of the state. Excluded were the counties of the Eastern Shore, which made up the diocese of Easton (created in 1868), and four Maryland counties near Washington, D.C. (Prince George's, Montgomery, Charles, and St. Mary's), which were part of the diocese of Washington (created in 1895).

15. Whittingham (diocesan from 1840 to 1879) and Powell were both devoted to institutions that Whittingham had helped to establish, the College of St. James (later St. James School), near Hagerstown, and the Church Home and Infirmary (later Church Home and Hospital), in Baltimore. Both inherited a diocese that had long been in a weakened condition and labored tirelessly to rebuild it; both were conservative in matters of ritual, disliking ceremonial innovations Anglo-Catholics borrowed from the Roman Catholic church; both consistently required strict obedience to the canons and the prayer book. Whittingham, however, was an uncompromising opponent of Rome, whereas Powell was not. Both cared deeply about the church's commitment to foreign

and domestic missions; both responded to a society struggling with issues related to the basic rights of African Americans. Powell's ecumenism was adumbrated by Whittingham's overtures to the Greek Orthodox church, the Orthodox church in Russia, and the Old Catholics. Both men were strong, assertive leaders who loved the church and demanded everything of themselves on its behalf.

16. Philip J. Jensen, "The Rt. Rev. Edward Trail Helfenstein," *Maryland Churchman,* January 1948, 5.

17. At the 1955 general convention Fenn tried to have the Church's Teaching series and a related Seabury series (a curriculum program) declared heretical. Michael Lawrence Mickler, "James A. Pike: Bishop and Iconoclast" (Ph.D. diss., Graduate Theological Union, 1989), 274.

18. "St. James Parish to Celebrate Its 125th Anniversary," *Maryland Churchman,* May 1949, 5–6. See Frederick V. Mills Sr., "George Freeman Bragg, Jr.," in *American National Biography,* vol. 3, ed. John A. Garraty and Mark C. Carnes (New York: Oxford University Press, 1999), 398–99; Shattuck, *Episcopalians and Race,* 21.

19. Edward T. Helfenstein, "Bishop Helfenstein's Address," *Journal,* 1941, 82. Helfenstein delivered his address on 28 May 1941.

20. John Maury Allin, telephone interview with the author, 18 May 1992.

21. George H. Callcott, *Maryland and America, 1940–1980* (Baltimore: Johns Hopkins University Press, 1985), 39–46, 60, 98–99. "Within four years, from 1939 to 1943, the population of Middle River grew from almost nothing to 125,000 people, the second largest population center in Maryland" (40).

22. NCP, "Bishop's Address," *Journal,* 1945, 81; see also Wuthnow, *Restructuring of American Religion,* 47. Powell returned to this theme seven years later. Human beings, he said, have looked to knowledge, power, and economic well-being as saviors. But our knowledge "placed us on the brink of destruction," and power and money do not necessarily enrich our lives. Nor is the answer to be found in new leaders: "We do not need leaders, we need a Saviour. There is a great difference between a leader and a saviour. A leader accepts the best his people have envisioned and seeks to realize that. A saviour questions the validity of all those objectives, and in the light of the truth he has in his soul from God, he seeks to show God's way, not man's. This is what Jesus does." NCP, "Easter 1952," *Maryland Churchman,* April 1952, 2. An optimist, Powell nevertheless was always closer to neo-orthodoxy in his theological outlook than to the older Protestant liberalism.

23. NCP, "Bishop's Address," *Journal,* 1947, 98–99. "An unwarranted tendency to place faith in science for absolute answers to every human problem has characterized most Western thinking throughout the twentieth century. The disease of scientism reached its most acute phase, however, in American popular culture in the 1950s. During this brief era, scientism expressed itself most potently in a confidence in the power of psychology and in a fascination with atomic energy. As an ideology in competition with other worldviews, scientism posed challenges to religious thinking that far outstripped the abilities of most individuals to critically evaluate what they believed, the consistency of their beliefs, and the reasons for their beliefs." James Hudnut-Beumler, *Looking for God in the Suburbs: The Religion of the American Dream and Its Critics, 1945–1965* (New Brunswick, N.J.: Rutgers University Press, 1994), 8–9.

24. Ellwood, *Fifties Spiritual Marketplace,* 14–17.

25. Edward Carpenter, *Archbishop Fisher: His Life and Times* (Norwich: Canterbury Press, 1991), 447–51.

26. Craig E. Taylor, "Canterbury Archbishop Speaks Here," *Baltimore Sun,* 19 September 1946.

27. The Thirty, convened by Noble Powell, met in January 1947 at Kenyon College and continued to meet annually for several years. One of the original members, Edward R. Welles, who was dean of St. Paul's Cathedral, Buffalo, New York, and later (1950–73) bishop of Western Missouri, recalled that The Thirty "helped to unify some of the younger leadership of the Episcopal Church, across churchmanship and geographical barriers." Among the members were Stephen Bayne, Horace Donegan, John Heuss, John Seville Higgins, Alden Kelley, Arthur Lichtenberger, Urban Holmes, Clifford Morehouse, John Krumm, James Pike, and DeWolfe Perry. Welles noted that "When a priest became a bishop he was dropped from 'The Thirty.'" This happened so often "that 'The Thirty' ceased to function; its work of reconciliation was probably done." Edward Randolph Welles II, *The Happy Disciple: An Autobiography* (Manset, Maine: n.p., 1975), 76–77.

Higgins (1904–92), rector in the forties of a parish in Minneapolis and later (1955–72) bishop of Rhode Island, said that Powell was "the instigator" of The Thirty, which "started at the interval between Tucker and Sherrill [and sought] to . . . produce some reasonable answers" to the following questions: What is the mission of the church? How can the parish be effective in the community? How can the church function better through the diocese, the province, and the National Council? How should we train leadership? How can we deal with the problem of churchmanship? Higgins remembered that the group issued its findings to the national church in 1951.

Higgins also recalled that Bishop Powell arrived at the Kenyon meeting rather badly shaken after a particularly stormy flight from Maryland to Ohio in a DC-3. J. S. Higgins, letter to the author, 14 March 1992, and telephone interview with the author, 2 May 1992.

28. J. S. Higgins, letter to the author, 14 March 1992.

29. Powell was well known and respected around the country, but he was never a serious contender for presiding bishop. The person who assumed the office in 1947, Henry Knox Sherrill, bishop of Massachusetts, had a strong reputation and possessed an impressive resume: Yale graduate, World War I chaplain, rector of Trinity Church, Boston, diocesan since 1930 (Powell was considered too "young" in office), chairman during World War II of the church's Commission on Army and Navy Chaplains, member of the National Council, vice chairman of the House of Bishops, accomplished organizer and fundraiser. "Bishop Sherrill Unanimously Made Presiding Bishop," *Maryland Churchman,* October 1946, 5–6; Don S. Armentrout, "Henry Knox Sherrill," in *American National Biography,* vol. 19, ed. John A. Garraty and Mark C. Carnes (New York: Oxford University Press, 1999), 823–24.

In 1950 Bishop Sherrill was elected the first president of the newly established National Council of the Churches of Christ in the U.S.A. Robert Ellwood describes the *Time* story that profiled Sherrill, who appeared on the cover of the 26 March 1951 issue: "The story presents this dignified, snowy-haired prelate as a stable, unruffled churchman with a kindly manner and a knack for administration who had risen to the top via tours of duty in the most proper of Bostonian parishes. . . . Bishop Sherrill was a great and large-hearted man by no means limited by his personal background. In the darkest hours of McCarthyist hysteria and the Korean War, his clear vision and steady hand were undoubtedly what his church and the cooperative churches needed. Yet he somehow also personifies the mainline Protestantism of his day, both at its best, and as it was ultimately connected to a class and geographical base" (*Fifties Spiritual Marketplace,* 44).

30. Harry W. Shipps, "Reflections on the Proposed Concordat of Agreement between the Episcopal Church and the Evangelical Lutheran Church of America," *Ecumenical Trends,* April 1996, 8; Holmes, *Brief History of the Episcopal Church,* 54–55; John Macquarrie, *Principles of Christian Theology* (New York: Scribner's, 1966), 391. See also Paul Moore, *Presences: A Bishop's Life in the City* (New York: Farrar, Straus and Giroux, 1997), 251.

31. NCP, "From the Bishop's Annual Address," *Maryland Churchman,* February 1950, 1.

32. Powell "was instrumental in keeping St. James School going. After the Depression and World War II, he kept it afloat. He had a great interest in the school and was inspiring to me and the boys." Rev. John E. Owens Jr., chaplain (1948–50) and headmaster (1955–84) of St. James School, telephone interview with the author, 26 August 1993. Like Bishop Whittingham, Noble Powell saw St. James School as "a center for the training of young men and boys in Christian character." NCP, "Bishop's Address," *Journal,* 1944, 64. See David Hein, "The High Church Origins of the American Boarding School," *Journal of Ecclesiastical History* 42 (October 1991): 577–95.

33. NCP, "Bishop's Column," *Maryland Churchman,* June 1957, 5. See "Bishop Powell at Buckeystown Consecrates Diocesan Center," *Baltimore Sun,* 17 May 1952; William H. Fallowfield, *Claggett Center: A Personal Review and Guide* (N.p., 1980).

34. Qtd. by Rev. William D. White, telephone interview with the author, 25 July 1992. St. James School and Claggett Diocesan Center have prominent buildings named in honor of Bishop Powell.

35. Ellwood, *Fifties Spiritual Marketplace,* 2.

36. The original intention was that the congregations so assisted would eventually return with interest all monies lent to them from this fund.

37. *Maryland Churchman,* March 1958, 3. In 1955, thirty-five years after the laying of its cornerstone, Bishop Powell consecrated the Cathedral of the Incarnation and installed its first dean. Plans for the design of the cathedral had changed considerably over the years—the structure was originally intended to be much larger. Architects who worked on the project included Henry Vaughan, Bertram G. Goodhue, and Philip Frohman. The edifice, which was known for many years as the "pro-cathedral," was completed in 1932. In 1955 the diocesan convention officially designated the building as the cathedral of the diocese, and the newly elected cathedral chapter approved Bishop Powell's nomination of John N. Peabody as dean. Many more years would pass, however, before the diocesan headquarters were moved to the cathedral grounds.

38. Henry Lee Doll, "Bishop's Address," *Journal,* 1965, 94. Bishop Leighton recalled that "we were about $100,000 short [of our goal]. One other thing was to have been done, besides building about nine churches. A diocesan center was to be built, but that was thirty years getting done. About $115,000 went for our share toward the building of the 815 skyscraper in New York [the Episcopal Church Center]; our part was the panelling and furnishing of the presiding bishop's office on the top floor. The reason we got to do that—an honor—was because John Gardner Murray was the first elected presiding bishop of our church and the seventh bishop of Maryland. The money for the PB's office meant that Bishop Powell suffered the loss of the diocesan center. He wanted it very much. The parking was getting bad [around Diocesan House], and downtown was deteriorating even in the late fifties." Leighton was the eleventh bishop of Maryland. Telephone interview with Rt. Rev. David K. Leighton.

39. Rt. Rev. John E. Hines, telephone interview with the author, 18 May 1992; David Hein, "The Episcopal Church and the Ecumenical Movement, 1937–1997: Presbyterians, Luth-

erans, and the Future," *Anglican and Episcopal History* 66 (March 1997): 4–13; NCP, "Bishop's Address," *Journal*, 1947, 97 (quotation).

40. Mark A. Noll, *A History of Christianity in the United States and Canada* (Grand Rapids, Mich.: Eerdmans, 1992), 537.

41. Quoted in Henry Lee Doll, "Bishop's Address," *Journal*, 1969, 104. None of the sharp and pervasive anti-Catholicism that Powell must have known in his youth in Alabama seems to have had any impact—except as a negative example—on his later attitudes and conduct. See Flynt, *Alabama Baptists*, 199–200, 232, 301–2, 354–58.

42. Jane Libby, interview with the author, Ellicott City, Md., 6 May 1992.

43. Msgr. Thomas A. Whelan, interview with Randy Beehler, 17 August 1979, Maryland Historical Society, Baltimore. Whelan hosted the luncheon on 8 October 1963.

44. NCP, "Bishop's Address," *Journal*, 1963, 113.

45. "Episcopal Bishop Dies," *Baltimore Sun*, 30 November 1968.

46. NCP to Archbishop Lawrence Shehan, 15 January 1963, NCP folder, Shehan Papers, Archives of the Archdiocese of Baltimore.

47. NCP to Archbishop Lawrence Shehan, 13 September 1963, Powell Papers, Maryland Diocesan Archives, Baltimore.

48. "Busy Prelate Steps Down," *Baltimore Sun*, 27 October 1963.

49. "Bishop Noble Powell Is Dead at 77; Rites Monday," *Baltimore Evening Sun*, 29 November 1968.

50. "Episcopal Bishop Dies," *Baltimore Sun*, 30 November 1968.

51. *The Catholic Review*, 6 November 1964, 2.

52. "Bishop Powell," *Baltimore Sun*, 28 October 1963. The Reverend Donzel C. Wilden, executive director of the Maryland Council of Churches, praised Powell for the "strong support he gave to the ecumenical life of the community and throughout the state. He will long be remembered for his contribution toward better understanding and cooperation between the Roman Catholic and Protestant communities." "Bishop Doll to Officiate at Powell Rites Monday," *Baltimore News-American*, 30 November 1968. Powell also enjoyed warm friendships with local Jewish leaders, including Rabbi Abraham Shusterman of Har Sinai Temple. Rabbi Abraham Shusterman, telephone interview with the author, 7 June 1994.

53. NCP, "Bishop Powell's Address," *Journal*, 1942, 65. In 1943 the general convention of the Episcopal church passed the first of many resolutions on race relations and integration.

54. "Episcopal Bishop Flays Racism and Nationalism," *Mobile Register*, 13 February 1951.

55. Rev. Robert M. Powell, telephone interview with the author, 5 August 1992.

56. Rt. Rev. Cedric E. Mills, telephone interview with the author, 8 February 1992.

57. Rev. Charles W. Fox Jr., telephone interview with the author, 6 August 1992.

58. "Unrest Is Laid to Agitators' 'Cruel' Calls," *Baltimore Sun*, 4 October 1954.

59. "Integration at Southern Stirs Unrest," *Baltimore Sun*, 2 October 1954; " 'No Disorder,' Baltimore Police Pledge" and "No Retreat on Democracy in Baltimore Schools," *Baltimore Afro-American*, 9 October 1954.

60. "19 Groups O.K. School Board Firmness on Desegregation," *Baltimore Sun*, 3 October 1954. See also "Washington-Baltimore Clergy Act on Segregation," *The Witness*, 21 October 1954.

61. See Callcott, *Maryland and America*, 151–52, 244; Elinor Pancoast et al., *The Report*

of a Study on Desegregation in the Baltimore City Schools (Baltimore: Maryland Commission on Interracial Problems and Relations and the Baltimore Commission on Human Relations, 1956); Olson, *Baltimore,* 369–70. For the larger historical context of the *Brown* decision, see Patterson, *Grand Expectations,* 389–98.

62. Edward Berkowitz, "Baltimore's Public Schools in a Time of Transition," *Maryland Historical Magazine* 92 (Winter 1997): 415.

63. "Bishop Powell," *Baltimore Evening Sun,* 28 October 1963. For a perceptive essay on the effects of the *Brown* decision on the development of the civil rights movement, see Michael J. Klarman, "How *Brown* Changed Race Relations: The Backlash Thesis," *Journal of American History* 81 (June 1994): 81–118. See also Shattuck, *Episcopalians and Race,* chap. 3, "The Impact of the *Brown* Decision."

64. NCP, "Bishop's Address," *Journal,* 1956, 97; see also NCP, "Bishop's Address," *Journal,* 1957, 86–87.

65. NCP, "Bishop's Address," *Journal,* 1958, 83.

66. Lenora Heilig Nast, "The Clergy and the Interfaith Movement, 1945–1980," in *Baltimore: A Living Renaissance,* ed. Lenora Heilig Nast, Laurence N. Krause, and R. C. Monk (Baltimore: Historic Baltimore, 1982), 90–92; Chester L. Wickwire, "Integrating Gwynn Oak," *Baltimore Evening Sun,* 16 July 1993. Wickwire was chaplain of Johns Hopkins University and one of those arrested at the demonstration. Gwynn Oak Park was finally opened to all races on 28 August 1963. Spiro T. Agnew, the Baltimore County executive, played a major role in the events surrounding the Gwynn Oak controversy; see Jules Witcover, *White Knight: The Rise of Spiro Agnew* (New York: Random House, 1972), 75–85.

67. Wickwire, "Integrating Gwynn Oak."

68. "Dr. Blake among 283 Held in Racial Rally in Maryland," *New York Times,* 5 July 1963; Rev. Chester Wickwire, telephone interview with the author, 7 June 1994.

69. R. Douglas Brackinridge, *Eugene Carson Blake: Prophet with Portfolio* (New York: Seabury, 1978); Paul A. Crow, "Eugene Carson Blake: Apostle of Christian Unity," *Ecumenical Review* 38 (April 1986): 228–36; Michael B. Friedland, *Lift Up Your Voice Like a Trumpet: White Clergy and the Civil Rights and Antiwar Movements, 1954–1973* (Chapel Hill: University of North Carolina Press, 1998), 82–85. On 1 March 1963 Archbishop Lawrence J. Shehan declared in a pastoral letter that "'We [Catholics] have a special obligation to place ourselves in the forefront of movements to remove the injustices and discriminations which remain.'" Qtd. in Callcott, *Maryland and America,* 155.

70. Qtd. in Brackenridge, *Eugene Carson Blake,* 94. See Eugene Carson Blake, "Law and Order and Christian Duty," in *The Pulpit Speaks on Race,* ed. Alfred T. Davis (New York: Abingdon Press, 1965), 107–18. Harvey G. Cox later identified Blake as "a hero of the New Breed" of activist clergy who were directly engaged in the struggle to change social structures and help the poor and exploited. Harvey G. Cox, "The 'New Breed' in American Churches: Sources of Social Activism in American Religion," *Daedalus* 96 (Winter 1967): 139.

71. Brackenridge, *Eugene Carson Blake,* 95; Callcott, *Maryland and America,* 155; "Clergymen Lead Fight in Baltimore," *Baltimore Afro-American,* 13 July 1963.

72. Qtd. in "News Flash," *The Living Church,* 14 July 1963, 1. See also "Dr. Blake Among 283 Held in Racial Rally in Maryland," *New York Times,* 5 July 1963. Monsignor Healy telephoned the archbishop from the park to tell him people were about to be arrested; what should he do? "Do whatever the others are doing," Shehan replied. Healy and Father Jo-

seph M. Connolly were among those arrested under the Maryland Trespass Act. Many Maryland Catholics were upset by their archbishop's apparent approval of the conduct of these "rabble-rousing" clergy. Spalding, *Premier See,* 435.

73. Brackenridge, *Eugene Carson Blake,* 95.

74. Taylor Branch, *Pillar of Fire: America in the King Years, 1963–65* (New York: Simon and Schuster, 1998), 124, 221.

75. Brackenridge, *Eugene Carson Blake,* 95–96. See Trueblood Mattingly, "Gwynn Oak," *America,* 10 August 1963, 136–37. An editorial in the *Christian Century* noted the ecumenical overtones of the demonstration: "all churchmen should stand a little taller because of what they did. Such action by Presbyterian and Episcopal leaders adds a wholesome social dimension to the prospects of church union, and the cooperation of Catholics, Jews and Protestants in such a cause adds vitality to the ecumenical purpose." "Blake and Corrigan Lead Bias Protest," *Christian Century,* 17 July 1963, 902. See also Shattuck, *Episcopalians and Race,* 130–31.

76. "Studies have shown," Harvey Cox noted in 1967, "that ministers who do not serve a local parish, and hence are somewhat more insulated from direct lay control, are much more likely to demonstrate and become involved in direct action than are pastors of local churches." Cox, "'New Breed' in American Churches," 142.

77. NCP, "Bishop's Address," *Journal,* 1960, 100. Samuel S. Hill has discussed four types of religiopolitical activism that have been common in southern history. Samuel S. Hill, "Religion and Politics in the South," in *Religion in the South,* ed. Charles Reagan Wilson (Jackson: University of Press of Mississippi, 1985), 143–46.

78. Rev. Frederick J. Hanna, interview with the author, Baltimore, Md., 3 October 1992.

79. See Wuthnow, *Restructuring of American Religion,* 65–67; Sullivan, "Theodore Parker Ferris," 61–63.

80. David Milobsky, "Power from the Pulpit: Baltimore's African-American Clergy, 1950–1970," *Maryland Historical Magazine* 89 (Fall 1994): 281–82; David Chalmers, *And the Crooked Places Made Straight: The Struggle for Social Change in the 1960s* (Baltimore: Johns Hopkins University Press, 1991), 29.

81. NCP, Journal, vol. K, 21 July 1961–24 November 1963, Maryland Diocesan Archives, Baltimore. See Marbury, *In the Catbird Seat,* 335–36. Marbury was chancellor of the diocese between 1962 and 1971. Bishop Powell's entry indicates that he consulted with the Reverend Robert Powell, *inter alios,* and that Father Powell was among those who advised "strongly against it." It is not completely clear whether "it" refers to Corrigan's coming into the diocese or to Bishop Powell's attendance at the protest. The Reverend Robert Powell reported to me (on 5 August 1992 and again on 7 July 1998) that he advised Bishop Powell to participate in the Gwynn Oak demonstration: "I said he had to take a personal stand, [and I told him] I would be by your side."

Besides Marbury and Powell, the bishop sought the counsel of three members of the Standing Committee: Walter G. J. Hards, rector of St. David's, Roland Park; and Page Dame and Harrison Garrett, both laymen.

Presiding Bishop Arthur Lichtenberger was strong on civil rights; his May 1963 Whitsuntide message had encouraged Episcopalians to work on behalf of racial justice. Christianity, he believed, ought to be concerned with the transformation of society. Gardiner H. Shattuck Jr., "A Worldly Gospel: Episcopalians and the Civil Rights Movement," paper presented at the Conference on Faith and History, Messiah College, 7 October 1994, 12–13.

82. Rt. Rev. Bennett J. Sims, telephone interview with the author, 7 May 1992.

83. Elizabeth Waters Corrigan, telephone interview with the author, 27 April 1992.

84. David H. Pardoe, telephone interview with the author, 8 August 1992.

85. Rev. Charles A. Bryan, telephone interview with the author, 11 July 1992. Corrigan probably felt that his participation in the protest at Gwynn Oak was not tantamount to performing official episcopal acts, or he might have believed that the presiding bishop's permission sufficed as authorization. Otherwise, Bryan has a point. The 1961 constitution of the Episcopal church (art. II, sec. 3) states that "A Bishop shall confine the exercise of his office to his own Diocese or Missionary District, unless he shall have been requested to perform episcopal acts in another Diocese or Missionary District by the Ecclesiastical Authority thereof [i.e. the diocesan], or unless he shall have been authorized and appointed by the House of Bishops, or by the Presiding Bishop by its direction, to act temporarily in case of need within any territory not yet organized into Dioceses or Missionary Districts of this Church."

86. Telephone interview with Rev. Charles W. Fox Jr.

87. Sims, *Servanthood*, 3–5. The two buses that left Baltimore from the Church of the Redeemer carried approximately fifty Episcopalians and over thirty Methodists, Lutherans, and others. Among those who marched in Washington on 28 August 1963 were the archbishop of Baltimore, his auxiliary, fifty-five priests, and hundreds of local lay Catholics. Spalding, *Premier See*, 435. Bishop Doll's wife recalled that he blessed the Maryland contingent as they boarded the buses. Delia G. Doll, interview with the author, Baltimore, Md., 25 September 1993. See Shattuck, *Episcopalians and Race*, 131–33.

88. Sims, *Servanthood*, 76. See Wuthnow, *Restructuring of American Religion*, 145–50; Patterson, *Grand Expectations*, 482–84. The inclusion of white moderates was one of the few concrete accomplishments of the March on Washington, which was criticized then and later as having been overly controlled by white officials in the Kennedy administration and subverted by the media. See Paula F. Pfeffer, *A. Philip Randolph: Pioneer of the Civil Rights Movement* (Baton Rouge: Louisiana State University Press, 1990), 244–79.

89. Sims, *Servanthood*, 76–77. In point of fact, on 24 October 1963 (in the last days of Bishop Powell's episcopate), Martin Luther King Jr. came to Morgan State College in Baltimore to speak to a special convocation of clergy about Christian witness and social transformation. Churches must stop "mouthing pious and sanctimonious trivialities," he said, and start standing up and challenging the status quo; they must "break the mores, if necessary." To those who advocated waiting, King declared that the "'be nice, pray, and in 200 years the problem will work itself out'" idea was a pious myth. The old order, he observed, is passing away; the new order is slowly and sometimes painfully taking its place. "Old Order Passing, King Tells 1,400," *Baltimore Afro-American*, 2 November 1963.

90. NCP to David H. Pardoe, 27 September 1963, photocopy in author's possession. Of course Powell was right that more than legislation was required to realize the goal of equal citizenship for all Americans. For thought-provoking comments on the dangers of undue reliance on legal remedies, see Ivan Hannaford, "The Idiocy of Race," *Wilson Quarterly*, Spring 1994, 11–12. But, as King pointed out in Baltimore on 24 October 1963, legislation had a foundational role to play. In urging Maryland religious leaders to "'stand up with determination and courage'" in support of a proposed Baltimore civil rights bill, King noted that while "'you can't legislate integration . . . you can legislate the conditions that keep integration from coming into being,'" and while "'you can't legislate the heart . . . you can restrain the heartless.'" "Dr. King Urges Support of Bill," *Baltimore Sun*, 25 October 1963.

91. See Chalmers, *And the Crooked Places Made Straight,* xv-xvi.

92. Telephone interview with Jack Malpas. Powell's response when people suggested he wasn't doing enough on civil rights was, a white priest recalled, "Boy, the first face I looked into was that of my black mammy." Interview with Rev. Frederick J. Hanna. See Litwack, *Trouble in Mind,* 237.

93. The constitution of the Episcopal church was amended in 1943 to make mandatory the resignation of a bishop upon attaining seventy-two years of age.

94. Upon Powell's death in 1968, Harry Lee Doll said of his predecessor as bishop of Maryland: "Bishop Powell was a jovial, outgoing, loving person who drew people to him. He was never content unless he did the work of two men. His vocation and avocation was work." "Episcopal Bishop Dies," *Baltimore Evening Sun,* 29 November 1968.

95. Rt. Rev. (John) Joseph Meakin Harte, retired bishop of Arizona, telephone interview with the author, 21 April 1992. Another bishop, Richard Emrich of Michigan (1948–73), said, "That was a very, very happy, united time." Richard Emrich, telephone interview with the author, 21 April 1992. On the intradenominational unity of the period 1945–60, see Wuthnow, *Restructuring of American Religion,* 138, 142.

David Leighton, bishop of Maryland from 1972 to 1985, recalled the years of Powell's episcopate as "a wonderful era of harmony, the golden era of being a bishop." Telephone interview with Rt. Rev. David K. Leighton.

96. "Busy Prelate Steps Down," *Baltimore Sun,* 27 October 1963.

97. Telephone interview with Rev. William D. White.

Chapter 5: Dénouement, 1963–93

1. Telephone interview with Rt. Rev. David K. Leighton.

2. Alice Tuten, telephone interview with the author, 7 August 1992.

3. Very Rev. Robert D. Schenkel Jr., telephone interview with the author, 6 January 1995. Powell's "retirement was a pathetic one," recalled Dr. E. Holcombe Palmer of the diocese of Virginia. Bishops then "assumed their role as bishop and were dedicated to that role"; they "were married to the church," to the exclusion of just about everything else. Telephone interview with E. Holcombe Palmer.

4. Rev. Horatio M. Richardson Jr., telephone interview with the author, 11 July 1992.

5. Philip N. Powell, telephone interview with the author, 6 January 2000.

6. NCP to James N. Purman, 19 October 1966, in author's possession.

7. Interview with Thomas Hooker Powell, 25 August 1992. The Reverend Charles Fox recalled the following: "I was one of the last priests to talk with him before he retired. He was bitter about having to retire. He didn't want to retire, [and then he] wilted right on out of here." Telephone interview with Rev. Charles W. Fox Jr.

8. Mary R. Powell to Ruth G. Hein, [December 1968], in author's possession; Rev. Charles L. Hein, telephone interview with the author, 6 June 1998.

9. Powell died on 28 November 1968. Dr. Thomas H. Powell noted that his father's "death was even less explicable than usual. There was no apparent cause. He had an excellent heart and no serious organ disease. I think, and this is just an educated guess, that he wanted to die and did so. He refused nourishment in a nice sort of way and let inanition take its course over a period of about 45 days." Thomas Hooker Powell, electronic-mail communication with the author, 23 June 1998.

10. NCP, "Bishop's Address," *Journal,* 1958, 76–77.

11. NCP, "Bishop's Address," *Journal,* 1959, 96. Stressing on another occasion the importance of parish calling, Powell adjured a seminarian, "If you want to see your people on Sunday, you had better be seeing them during the week." Rev. Frederic S. Burford III, letter to the author, June 1992. Powell "knew the clergy intimately. There was no big-business stuff, no bureaucracy. He kept the diocese simple. I've never met a man like him. Again and again, I'd run into signs of him. There were pictures of him on priests' walls in Arizona." Telephone interview with Rev. William D. White.

12. David S. Ketchum, of Pittsburgh, Pennsylvania, provided the following anecdote concerning Powell's approach to diocesan unity: "In 1958 when some of my colleagues and I were providing fund-raising counsel to the . . . Diocese of Maryland in a . . . capital campaign, we became aware of a spirited disagreement within the Diocese regarding the relative merits of 'high' and 'low' styles of worship. One night as we drove to a campaign meeting . . . I asked Bishop Powell where he stood on the issue. 'Mr. Ketchum,' he replied—with a twinkle in his eye and in his voice—'I personally favor the low church order of worship, but I don't care if some of our members want to crawl up the aisle on their hands and knees as long as they support the Diocese!'" David S. Ketchum, letter to the author, 25 August 1992.

According to David H. Pardoe, a former priest in Maryland, Don Frank Fenn, who was "a power in the diocese," was collecting sermons by the Reverend Alfred B. Starratt, the theologically liberal rector of Emmanuel Church, Baltimore, in order to bring about an ecclesiastical trial for heresy. Bishop Powell called Fenn into his office and told him "there will be no heresy trials in my diocese." Telephone interview with David H. Pardoe.

13. Qtd. in "Busy Prelate Steps Down," *Baltimore Sun,* 27 October 1963.

14. "Bishop Powell," *Baltimore Evening Sun,* 29 November 1968. Upon Powell's death, Bishop Doll said that his predecessor made the diocese "a unified family, and left as distinct a mark on the church as any bishop has ever done." "Episcopal Bishop Dies," *Baltimore Sun,* 29 November 1968.

15. "Fifteen Years," *Maryland Churchman,* October 1956, 3. Early in his years as a bishop, Powell wrote: "I conceive it to be the primary duty of a bishop to give most careful attention to those whom he admits as postulants and then, once admitted, to keep in close and intimate personal relationship with each man. . . . I have enjoyed no pleasanter contacts than those I have had with candidates before their ordination. It has not been possible thus far to spend several days with candidates in my home where we can, informally, talk and meditate and pray together, but it is my purpose to do this as soon as circumstances permit." NCP to Rev. Benjamin B. Lovett, 25 July 1942, Archives of the Episcopal Church, Austin, Tex.

One of the most difficult pastoral problems Powell faced with his clergy involved the case of the Reverend Julius Velasco, the gifted and dedicated but also disputatious and intractable rector of St. Peter's, Ellicott City (1927–29, 1931–45). A blunt-speaking, cape-and-biretta-wearing Anglo-Catholic, Father Velasco was a cause for concern that Powell inherited from Bishop Helfenstein. In 1950 Velasco brought a civil action against the diocese of Maryland for allegedly preventing his employment as an Episcopal priest; the courts ruled against him. See Richard F. Mitchell, *Standing on a Hill: The History of St. Peter's Church, 1842–1992* (N.p., 1993), chaps. 5 and 6.

16. Rt. Rev. Paul Moore, retired bishop of New York, telephone interview with the author, 20 May 1992.

17. James N. Purman, telephone interview with the author, 8 June 1994.

18. At the end of World War II there was a 20 percent shortage of clergy in the Episco-

pal church nationwide. Wuthnow, *Restructuring of American Religion,* 29. In 1964 Powell said, "I have ceased to pray for more men in the ministry. We don't know what to do with those we already have." NCP to Jack [?], 2 January 1964, in the author's possession.

19. Powell served as a trustee and vice president of the Church Pension Fund.

20. In 1958 the Reverend Charles W. Wood (b. 1910), rector of St. John's, Huntingdon, shot himself to death in the rectory. He had served as a member of the Executive Council and was chairman of the diocese's Department of Christian Social Relations as well as the first president of Valley House, a small institution in Baltimore for the rehabilitation of chronic and destitute alcoholics. Powell took himself to task for Wood's suffering and death, feeling that his perception of and response to Wood's problems, including his drinking, were less than they should have been.

James Purman remembered the time he went to see the bishop about some matter; at the conclusion of their business, "he asked me to be a witness [to a deposition]. It was an unpleasant task. He had to pronounce the sentence of deposition on a priest [who had engaged in seriously immoral conduct]. Bishop Powell was in terrible [emotional] pain. He went into the little chapel [at Diocesan House]. There was no nonsense. Bishop Claggett's mitre was in a glass case. When Bishop Powell pronounced the sentence of deposition, he was on the verge of tears. It was very solemn, very sad." Telephone interview with James N. Purman.

21. Telephone interview with Rev. William D. White. White said Powell's statement "expressed [the idea] that the time [we would spend] as deacons was valuable in itself."

22. NCP to the Reverend Charles L. Hein, 1 October 1954, in author's possession.

23. Telephone interview with James N. Purman.

24. Qtd. in "Busy Prelate Steps Down," *Baltimore Sun,* 27 October 1963.

25. A man who served under Powell spoke of the bishop's faculty for reading a situation (sometimes of great delicacy, involving temptations of the flesh and the heart) and helping the priest deal with it. Powell knew how to "put the right weight on it" and shore up the priest for future service. In the specific case of this individual, after Powell applied a mixture of admonition, vocation, hope, and prayer, the priest "felt totally restored—to the church, to my ministry, to my value. It established a special pastoral relationship. He had an uncanny ability to do that" (personal communication).

26. Rev. Philip B. Roulette, interview with the author, Glyndon, Md., 3 May 1994.

27. Telephone interview with Rev. Charles A. Bryan.

28. James C. Fenhagen, "The Bishop and the Diocese in a Time of Change: Reconnecting Function and Symbol in the Episcopal Church," *Anglican Theological Review* 77 (Winter 1995): 47–57. Fenhagen was dean of General Seminary from 1978 to 1992 and director of the Cornerstone Project of the Episcopal Church Foundation from 1992 to 1995. Begun in 1987, the Cornerstone Project was a ministry designed to strengthen the personal and professional lives of clergy.

29. Ibid., 53.

30. Fenhagen said that Bishop Powell on this occasion had simply "dropped in, and asked, 'How is it going?' We spent the afternoon together, and worked it out. It wouldn't have worked out otherwise. [He fulfilled the] pastoral role. He was very sensitive." Telephone interview with James C. Fenhagen, 27 June 1994.

Powell worked hard at nurturing these relationships. "One or two weeks after my arrival in the diocese," a former vicar reported, "the bishop came around. That was very characteristic—he'd stay maybe five minutes. He was so pastoral, so personal; that's not the way it's done today." Telephone interview with James N. Purman. See also Moore, *Presences*, 227.

31. This anecdote has several sources, including a telephone interview with Alice Tuten. Gresham Marmion, the retired bishop of Kentucky, related a story about Powell's sense of humor that involved Lady Astor, the first woman to sit in Parliament. At the time of the 1948 Lambeth Conference, she invited the American bishops to her residence for tea. When Powell and two of his cronies in the House of Bishops—probably Oliver Hart of Pennsylvania and Big Tui Kinsolving of Arizona—were asked to give the names of their ecclesiastical jurisdictions to be formally announced, they gave the names of little towns west of Charlottesville, which of course was territory thoroughly familiar to Lady Astor, who was from the area. When the three Americans were announced—as the Lord Bishop of Afton, the Lord Bishop of Ivy Depot, and the Lord Bishop of Crozet—Lady Astor "told them they could all go to blazes." Gresham Marmion, telephone interview with the author, 18 May 1992.

32. Qtd. in Harry Lee Doll, "Bishop's Address," *Journal*, 1969, 103.

33. "Fifteenth Anniversary," *Maryland Churchman*, October 1956, 14, 16. Bishop Powell, noted a former chancellor of the diocese, "detested the trappings of politics, the smoke-filled room, the logrolling, and the trade-offs that characterize an open political convention. He thought they played no part in the process of electing someone to the episcopate. . . . He thought that if the delegates prayed and meditated enough, they would, with God's help, reach the right decision." Arthur W. Machen Jr., letter to the author, 25 July 1992.

The newly elected suffragan bishop, Harry Lee Doll, later spoke of Powell's unprecedented request for silence throughout the election process: "Until the tellers returned we all thought that we would talk or go outside and smoke or do as we pleased. But by the power of his vision and wisdom and personality the Bishop did what I have never heard of being done before and I do not think anyone who was there had heard of being done. . . . He called [us] to our seats [and] reiterated the single, serious purpose of this Convention, to have God use us as He used the eleven Apostles in the choice of Matthais. Then he led us in a meditation on what God's business entailed until the tellers returned. . . . The process was repeated for all three ballots. It was a most solemn and serious and moving experience. . . . One was distinctly conscious of the presence of the Holy Spirit. The Bishop, himself under the guidance of the Holy Spirit, had led us to the place where we, too, could recognize His presence." Photocopy of typed sermon, 23 January 1955, Delia Doll Collection, Baltimore.

34. Max Weber, *The Theory of Social and Economic Organization*, trans. A. M. Henderson and Talcott Parsons (New York: Free Press, 1947), 324–86.

35. Since Powell's day this threefold foundation of bishops' authority has been undermined, both by conscious design and by accident of historical circumstances.

36. Rt. Rev. William Crittenden, telephone interview with the author, 7 April 1992.

37. Rt. Rev. Robert McConnell Hatch, telephone interview with the author, 21 April 1992. Hatch was suffragan bishop of Connecticut from 1951 to 1957 and bishop of western Massachusetts from 1957 to 1970.

38. Telephone interview with Girault McArthur Jones.

39. See NCP, "Discipline," *Maryland Churchman*, March 1946, 2. Powell stressed to ordinands and beginning clergy the importance of prayer and a regular spiritual life (and a prayer life that included their spouses, if they were married). He told a young priest, "I see [from the church's newsletter] that you are busy. Do not neglect your prayers. Other-

wise the hungry sheep will look up and not be fed." Telephone interview with James N. Purman. He told new priests that they should create Bible classes in their churches and teach the Bible. Telephone interview with Rev. William D. White.

Powell was also careful to emphasize with deacons and new rectors the more mundane details of daily life: cleanliness, good manners, and proper conduct toward boys and girls, men and women. Avoid gossip, he told them; never be condescending or patronizing. If you go into a liquor store to buy liquor, wear your clerical collar; people will know who you are anyway. In sum: don't forget that you represent the church in your community; remember the high ideals of your calling. NCP, "Meditations and Instructions for Deacons," in "Addresses, Meditations, Sermons" box, Powell Papers, Maryland Diocesan Archives, Baltimore; interview with Jane Libby.

40. Minute adopted by the Diocesan Council, qtd. in Harry Lee Doll, "Bishop's Address," *Journal*, 1969, 104.

41. Rt. Rev. William C. R. Sheridan, telephone interview with the author, 12 January 1993; Rt. Rev. Charles L. Longest, interview with the author, Baltimore, Md., 17 March 1994.

42. Rev. Richard L. Kunkel, interview with the author, Bethesda, Md., 19 August 1993.

43. Interview with Rt. Rev. Charles Longest; telephone interview with Rev. William D. White. Powell "didn't like the cope and mitre," White recalled; he "felt that pomp and ceremony contrasted with the simplicity of Christ. The church is called to servanthood; it should maintain that simplicity." White also reported that one Sunday at St. Andrew's Church, an Anglo-Catholic parish in Baltimore City, a "very scared" acolyte timidly swung the censer toward Bishop Powell, who successfully put the boy at ease by giving him a reassuring smile and saying, "I'll take a couple more, son."

A well-known story involving Bishop Powell features him telephoning an Anglo-Catholic clergyman of the diocese and asking for the rector (whose name was not "Smith"). "May I speak with Mr. Smith, please?" "*Father* Smith is not in," the secretary replied. "When will Mr. Smith be back?" "*Father* Smith will be back tomorrow." "Well," the bishop said, "kindly tell Father Smith that *Grandfather* Powell called."

44. Telephone interview with Rev. Charles A. Bryan.

45. Telephone interview with E. Holcombe Palmer.

46. Rev. William M. Plummer Jr., telephone interview with the author, 20 June 1994.

47. Welles, *Happy Disciple*, 91.

48. *Maryland Churchman*, October 1948, 5.

49. Very Rev. John N. Peabody, telephone interview with the author, 23 June 1994.

50. Telephone interview with Rt. Rev. Bennett J. Sims; Molly Finney (daughter of Philip N. Powell), telephone interview with the author, 4 January 2000; "The Woman's Auxiliary," *Maryland Churchman*, January 1954.

51. "Mrs. Powell belonged to the Valley lot." Rev. H. Martin P. Davidson, telephone interview with the author, 29 June 1994. Davidson was referring to the wealthy sections of northern Baltimore County.

52. Thomas Hooker Powell, telephone interview with the author, 12 January 2000.

53. Telephone interview with Thomas Hooker Powell, 12 January 2000.

54. Interview with Rt. Rev. Charles L. Longest.

55. In the 1970s the Episcopal church retained the idea that confirmation involved a strengthening by the Holy Spirit but rejected on theological and historical grounds the interpretation of confirmation as a completion of baptism. The sacrament of baptism was recognized as effecting full incorporation of the baptized into the body of Christ. Not until

the thirteenth century did bishops in the West start to require confirmation as a prerequisite to receiving Holy Communion. Since baptism was now seen—in the 1979 Book of Common Prayer—as constituting full initiation into the church, confirmation lost its standing as a gateway to the Lord's Supper; all baptized Christians were permitted to receive Holy Communion. See Marion J. Hatchett, *Commentary on the American Prayer Book* (New York: Seabury, 1980), 251–88; Linda L. Gaither, "Ecclesiology and Episcopacy in the Contemporary Context," *Sewanee Theological Review* 40 (Easter 1997): 200; John Macquarrie, *A Guide to the Sacraments* (New York: Continuum, 1997), chap. 8, "Confirmation."

The older view of confirmation is represented in James A. Pike and W. Norman Pittenger, *The Faith of the Church* (Greenwich, Conn.: Seabury, 1951), a volume in the Church's Teaching series. The authors present confirmation not only as a strengthening by God's Holy Spirit but also as an action in which "The work of Baptism is completed and initiation into Christian membership is brought to its fullness" (157).

For a history of these developments since World War II, see Michael Moriarty, *The Liturgical Revolution: Prayer Book Revision and Associated Parishes* (New York: Church Hymnal Corp., 1996), 167–77. Interestingly, when the founding members of Associated Parishes—which spearheaded the liturgical movement in the Episcopal church—first met in November 1946 in the common room of the College of Preachers, they spent the morning in a two-and-a-half-hour meditation led by Noble Powell (45).

See also "Confirmation," *Maryland Churchman*, Summer 1953, 18; John H. Westerhoff III, "Confirmation: An Episcopal Church Perspective," *Reformed Liturgy and Music* 24 (Fall 1990): 198–203; Geoffrey Lampe, *The Seal of the Spirit: A Study in the Doctrine of Baptism and Confirmation in the New Testament and the Fathers,* 2d ed. (London: Society for Promoting Christian Knowledge, 1976); Robert W. Prichard, *The Nature of Salvation: Theological Consensus in the Episcopal Church, 1801–73* (Urbana: University of Illinois Press, 1997), 72, 91–92, 116–17, 125–27; Simon Jones, "Integration or Separation? The Future of Confirmation within the Church of England," *Theology* 98 (July/August 1995): 282–89.

56. Catherine Bell, *Ritual: Perspectives and Dimensions* (New York: Oxford University Press, 1997), 95, 98, 100–101. I would not want to push this analogy too far: even prior to the 1970s confirmation lacked most of the essential components of the classic rite de passage, including ritual separation, liminality, and ordeal.

57. Before the service commenced, for example, an older acolyte might turn to a younger one and proudly and humbly say, "Last year Bishop Powell told me he liked how I carried the cross," that is, in a natural manner rather than with elbows stuck out at right angles to the body. Secular events were also enhanced by his presence. Every year, the Church of the Resurrection, a Baltimore mission, would hold a Christmas tree sale and Powell would go there to pick up trees for the Diocesan House and his own home. "He'd stay a little bit," the former vicar recalled. "They'd look forward to his coming and talk about it after he left. To be present with them—that's what Jesus did, and it's the greatest gift we can give another person." Telephone interview with James N. Purman.

58. "He was very biblical and a good storyteller; he really held your interest. He could speak to anyone, and everyone was moved. [Preaching] was one of his great gifts. It was a treat to listen to him." Telephone interview with James C. Fenhagen.

59. The phrase "knowledge carried to the heart" is from Allen Tate's "Ode to the Confederate Dead," in his *Collected Poems, 1919–1976* (New York: Farrar Straus Giroux, 1977), 22.

60. 2 Tim. 3:14–15.

61. The Yale theologian Paul Holmer has written cogently of the need for theology to be developed and displayed not primarily in syllogisms and arguments but in metaphors, parables, stories, informal conversation, and everyday speech. Theology requires imagination so that the hearer can be caught up in the drama of salvation and become familiar with the grammar of faith. Theology is carried to the hearts and minds of listeners through "the positive projection of real preaching [that] becomes theology in action." This kind of effort "works," according to Holmer, "as it envelops the hearer in the divine correction of disposition, of love, of orientation that is life-long." Paul Holmer, *The Grammar of Faith* (San Francisco: Harper and Row, 1978), 26, 27. See also Paul Holmer, *C. S. Lewis: The Shape of His Faith and Thought* (New York: Harper and Row, 1976), esp. 21, 24–25, 85, 102.

62. See Moore, *Presences,* 172–73.

63. NCP, letter to the author, 25 December 1964.

64. T. R. Glover, *The Jesus of History* (New York: Association Press, 1926), 72; Austin Farrer, *Lord I Believe: Suggestions for Turning the Creed into Prayer* (Cambridge, Mass.: Cowley, 1989), 60.

65. NCP, "Bishop's Address," *Journal,* 1960, 98–100. Powell appears to have been influenced by the work of the widely admired Methodist clergyman Leslie D. Weatherhead, whose preaching drew thousands to London's City Temple. In *The Transforming Friendship: A Book about Jesus and Ourselves* (New York: Abingdon Press, 1931), Weatherhead spoke of the way in which companionship with Christ made the disciples into new men: "those friends who . . . watched the change know the secret. They have been with Jesus. The friendship has done it" (45).

66. Cicero, *De Amicitia,* trans. W. A. Falconer (London: William Heinemann, 1938), 177.

67. William H. Whyte Jr., *The Organization Man* (Garden City, N.Y.: Doubleday Anchor Books, 1957), 418. See also Gaustad, "Pulpit and the Pews," 30.

68. NCP, "Missions" folder, "Addresses etc." box, Powell Papers, Maryland Diocesan Archives, Baltimore.

69. NCP, "Bishop's Address," *Journal,* 1961, 101–2.

70. NCP, "Bishop's Address," *Journal,* 1959, 95.

71. Roberta Bondi, "Prayer in Friendship with God," *Christian Century,* 29 January 1997, 99–101. See also Roberta Bondi, *To Pray and to Love: Conversations on Prayer with the Early Church* (Minneapolis: Fortress Press, 1991); C. S. Lewis, *The Four Loves* (San Diego: Harcourt Brace and Co., 1960); David Konstan, *Friendship in the Classical World* (Cambridge: Cambridge University Press, 1997); Carolinne White, *Christian Friendship in the Fourth Century* (Cambridge: Cambridge University Press, 1992); Jürgen Moltmann, "Open Friendship: Aristotelian and Christian Concepts of Friendship," in *The Changing Face of Friendship,* ed. Leroy S. Rouner (Notre Dame, Ind.: University of Notre Dame Press, 1994), 34–41; Paul J. Waddell, *Friendship and the Moral Life* (Notre Dame, Ind.: University of Notre Dame Press, 1989); Gilbert Meilaender, *Friendship: A Study in Theological Ethics* (Notre Dame, Ind.: University of Notre Dame Press, 1981); L. Gregory Jones, *Transformed Judgment: Toward a Trinitarian Account of the Moral Life* (Notre Dame, Ind.: University of Notre Dame Press, 1990), 75–119; Stanley Hauerwas and Charles Pinches, *Christians among the Virtues: Theological Conversations with Ancient and Modern Ethics* (Notre Dame, Ind.: University of Notre Dame Press, 1997); Ann Loades, "'I Have Called You Friends,'" *Theology* 99 (March/April 1996): 97; Stephen J. Pope, "'Equal Regard' versus 'Special Relations'? Reaffirming the Inclusiveness of Agape," *Journal of Religion* 77 (July 1997): 353–79; Rich-

ard J. Klonoski, "On Friendship as Our Ownmost Salvation," *The McNeese Review* 34 (1995–96): 91–102; Andrew Sullivan, *Love Undetectable: Notes on Friendship, Sex, and Survival* (New York: Alfred A. Knopf, 1998), 176–80, 186–89, 204–5, 209–16, 220–25, 240–51.

Powell would have given his hearty assent to Jürgen Moltmann's statement that "The *congregatio sanctorum,* the community of brethren is really the fellowship of friends who live in the friendship of Jesus and spread friendliness . . . by meeting the forsaken with affection and the despised with respect." Jürgen Moltmann, *The Church in the Power of the Spirit* (New York: Harper and Row, 1977), 316.

72. "Bishop Powell," *Baltimore Sun,* 1 December 1968. Another *Sun* editorial put it slightly differently: "There are lively senses in which [Powell] was clergyman at large to the community." "Bishop Powell," *Baltimore Sun,* 28 October 1963.

73. "The city [the Baltimore metropolitan area] was a much smaller town back then. Most power lay with the Episcopalians and the Roman Catholics." Richard Harwood Jr. (diocesan treasurer, 1963–71), interview with the author, 21 January 1995.

74. Will Scarlett, for example, who served as bishop of Missouri from 1930 to 1952, was revered by members of other denominations, including his state's blue-collar workers.

A priest who served under Powell in the diocese of Maryland recalled that "clergy of other denominations turned to him—Methodist, Presbyterian—he really was *the* bishop of Maryland." Telephone interview with Rev. William D. White.

75. Interview with Thomas Hooker Powell, 25 August 1992; Callcott, *Maryland and America,* 100.

76. Interview with Rev. Philip B. Roulette. Lane was the scion of Hagerstown's leading family. The historian George Callcott wrote that the Silver Star recipient returned home from World War I and inherited "the bank, the newspaper, and the law practice," and also found time to marry "Dorothy Byron, the daughter of the town's second most prominent family" (100). As Maryland attorney general in the 1930s, Lane, a Democrat, waged a courageous war against lynching. As governor from 1947 to 1951 he eschewed federal public service programs and what he called the "trend toward nationalization, compounding the American people into a common mass" (102), but he believed in an active role for government within each state. His program, which required adopting a new sales tax and raising existing taxes, included major outlays for education, roads, and hospitals. His most significant road project was the Chesapeake Bay Bridge, an impressive feat of engineering that linked the two halves of the state. Callcott, *Maryland and America,* 99–107. The Byrons, especially David Byron, were great supporters of the diocese and of St. James School in particular.

77. William R. Hutchison, "Protestantism as Establishment," in *Between the Times: The Travail of the Protestant Establishment in America, 1900–1960,* ed. William R. Hutchison (New York: Cambridge University Press, 1989), 6.

78. Gaustad, "Pulpit and the Pews," 22.

79. Calhoun Bond (member of the Executive Council of the diocese and vice chairman of the Episcopal Advance Fund), telephone interview with the author, 23 March 1994. Bishop Powell, Bond said, "had a great manner; he was very sincere, not haughty. People didn't like to say no to him; they had great respect for him as a person. He had a touch that reached all people."

80. Douglas C. Turnbull Jr., telephone interview with the author, 21 May 1992.

81. Rev. H. Kearney Jones, interview with the author, 3 May 1994.

82. Ellwood, *Fifties Spiritual Marketplace,* 232.

83. "They alone were regularly called on by . . . editors and broadcasters, or referred to by prime literary, intellectual, and academic leaders, when issues that brought theology and culture together were brought up." Martin E. Marty, "Recent Times," in *Makers of Christian Theology in America*, ed. Mark G. Toulouse and James O. Duke (Nashville: Abingdon Press, 1997), 524.

84. John M. Nelson III, letter to the author, May 1998. Nelson's father was president of the Nelson Company, which manufactured wood products.

85. H. Richard Niebuhr, *Christ and Culture* (New York: Harper and Row, 1951), chap. 4; Charles Scriven, *The Transformation of Culture: Christian Social Ethics after H. Richard Niebuhr* (Scottdale, Pa.: Herald Press, 1988), 18–20, 39, 45–47, 94–97.

86. NCP, *The Honor System: An Address to Entering Undergraduates* [Charlottesville: University of Virginia, 1963], PNP Papers.

87. Niebuhr points out that, according to those who affirm the "synthetic" relationship, Christ above culture, "there is in [Christ] something that neither arises out of culture nor contributes directly to it. He is discontinuous as well as continuous with social life and its culture. The latter, indeed, leads men to Christ, yet only in so preliminary a fashion that a great leap is necessary if men are to reach him, or, better, true culture is not possible unless beyond all human achievement, all human search for values, all human society, Christ enters into life from above with gifts which human aspiration has not envisioned and which human effort cannot attain unless he relates men to a supernatural society and a new value-center" (*Christ and Culture*, 42). Powell surely would have agreed with this statement.

88. Ibid., chap. 6.

89. H. Richard Niebuhr, "The Responsibility of the Church for Society," in *The Gospel, the Church and the World*, ed. Kenneth Scott Latourette (New York: Harper and Brothers, 1946), 129–32.

90. Niebuhr, *Christ and Culture*, 42–43. It is not surprising that an actual person, such as Noble Powell, should incorporate in his thought and practice more than one of Niebuhr's five types. "Each historical figure," Niebuhr points out when discussing his use of types, "will show characteristics that are more reminiscent of some other family than the one by whose name he has been called" (44).

91. James E. Griffiss, *The Anglican Vision* (Cambridge, Mass.: Cowley Publications, 1997), 9–10. See Hudnut-Beumler, *Looking for God in the Suburbs*, 65–71.

For vast numbers of Episcopalians and other Christians in this period the most widely read books were not by highbrow theologians but rather such works as Norman Vincent Peale's *The Power of Positive Thinking* (1952), Catherine Marshall's *A Man Called Peter* (1951), and Fulton Oursler's *The Greatest Story Ever Told* (1949), while at the box office such films as *Ben Hur* (1959) and *The Ten Commandments* (1956) were big draws. What the popular works had in common was that they were all easy to understand, they offered religion as a simple key to success and contentment, and they appealed to people's hunger for a sense of meaning and hope. In a direct and uncritical manner, they offered peace, power, and happiness to men and women trying to find their way in an exciting, opportunity-filled, but threatening new world. Ellwood, *Fifties Spiritual Marketplace*, 12–13.

92. Griffiss, *Anglican Vision*, 10, 12. Robert Wuthnow discusses the heightened individualism consistently represented in the mainline churches of the postwar era: Popular sermons advocated personal redemption and the moral formation of individual Christians rather than a social gospel, as churches focused on what they felt they did best—preach-

ing and teaching. The churches assumed that religious individuals would have a healthy influence on the values of the larger culture, and church leaders were confident—in these days before the pervasive influence of cultural relativism and the theory of the social construction of knowledge—that religious values were part of a universal truth that applied to society as well. Wuthnow, *Restructuring of American Religion*, 61, 64–66, 140.

93. "Bishop Powell," *Baltimore Afro-American*, 16 November 1963.

94. Gibson Winter, *The Surburban Captivity of the Churches: An Analysis of Protestant Responsibility in the Expanding Metropolis* (Garden City, N.Y.: Doubleday and Co., 1961), 165.

95. Ibid., 166, 177 (quotation). Similarly, the Lutheran Peter L. Berger criticized mainline Christianity as a "cultural religion" that merely ratified and sanctified the values of the general community. This vague religiosity made middle-class white churches into "communities of the respectable," in which success often meant little more than larger congregations, bigger budgets, and more programs. Peter L. Berger, *The Noise of Solemn Assemblies: Christian Commitment and the Religious Establishment in America* (Garden City, N.Y.: Doubleday, 1961), 39–41, 51, 89, 163. For commentary on the Winter and Berger volumes, see Hudnut-Beumler, *Looking for God in the Suburbs*, 131–66.

96. Hudnut-Beumler, *Looking for God in the Suburbs*, 177.

97. "[W]ith Kennedy's assassination that [earlier] sense of unity dissipated. The fault lines [exposed in the 1950s] fractured. . . . The confident invincibility of authority was revealed to be hollow; the vulnerability of institutions was exposed." Sam Portaro and Gary Peluso, *Inquiring and Discerning Hearts: Vocation and Ministry with Young Adults on Campus* (N.p.: Scholars Press, 1993), 48.

98. Doll began his addresses to the annual conventions, "To the family of God in this diocese," and he regularly spoke of the church as "a family." His relations with his own family (he and his wife had three daughters) were close and strong. Every year on Valentine's Day Bishop Doll sent cards to all the children of clergy families. Doll's retirement anticipated the early withdrawal from office of his friend John Hines, presiding bishop from 1965 to 1974.

99. Interview with Delia G. Doll.

100. Harry Lee Doll, "Address of the Bishop Coadjutor," *Journal*, 1961, 131.

101. Qtd. in "Bishop's Voice," *Baltimore Sun*, 6 May 1964. This quotation appeared in a *Sun* editorial praising Doll for speaking out against racist, hate-filled campaign literature that was being distributed in the days before the Democratic primary election.

102. Frank P. L. Somerville, "Harry L. Doll, Episcopal Bishop of Maryland during '60s Strife, Dies," *Baltimore Sun*, 28 August 1984. Other prominent clergy who testified, including Cardinal Shehan, received the same hostile treatment.

103. Shehan and Doll were the major forces behind the establishment in 1967 of the Ecumenical Institute of Theology at St. Mary's Seminary in Baltimore. The Ecumenical Institute comprised various graduate programs in theology and was open to members of all religious traditions.

104. The Reverend Chotard Doll was a candidate in 1986 for suffragan bishop of Washington. She led the field of six candidates on the first two ballots but eventually lost to Ronald Haines. Three years later Barbara C. Harris became suffragan bishop of Massachusetts.

105. Telephone interview with Rt. Rev. Bennett J. Sims.

106. Rev. Robert P. Patterson, telephone interview with the author, 20 June 1994.

107. Leonard I. Sweet, "The Modernization of Protestant Religion in America," in *Al-*

tered Landscapes: Christianity in America, 1935–1985, ed. David W. Lotz et al. (Grand Rapids, Mich.: Eerdmans, 1989), 26.

108. See Chalmers, *And the Crooked Places Made Straight,* 30–32; Ronald B. Flowers, *Religion in Strange Times: The 1960s and 1970s* (Macon, Ga.: Mercer University Press, 1984), 184–87; John L. Kater Jr., "Experiment in Freedom: The Episcopal Church and the Black Power Movement," *Historical Magazine of the Protestant Episcopal Church* 48 (March 1979): 69–81; Robert E. Hood, *Social Teachings in the Episcopal Church* (Harrisburg, Pa.: Morehouse Publishing, 1990), 122.

109. Qtd. in Gilbert A. Lewthwaite, "Bishop's Farewell Recalls His Time of Trial," *Baltimore Sun,* 13 October 1971. On Forman and the black manifesto, see Robert S. Ellwood, *The Sixties Spiritual Awakening: American Religion Moving from Modern to Postmodern* (New Brunswick, N.J.: Rutgers University Press, 1994), 275–77; Shattuck, *Episcopalians and Race,* 187–97.

110. Telephone interview with Rev. Robert P. Patterson. For a more complete account of Doll's life and career, see David Hein, "Harry Lee Doll (1903–1984): Bishop of the Episcopal Diocese of Maryland, 1963–1971," *The Maryland Historian* 27 (1996): 52–61. I am grateful to the editor of *The Maryland Historian* for permission to use several paragraphs from this article in the present work.

111. Prichard, *History of the Episcopal Church,* 249–50; Williams, *America's Religions,* 334–35; William Clark Roof and William McKinney, *American Mainline Religion: Its Changing Shape and Future* (New Brunswick, N.J.: Rutgers University Press, 1988), chap. 5.

112. Ahlstrom, *Religious History of the American People,* vol. 2, 600. See also John F. Wilson, *Public Religion in American Culture* (Philadelphia: Temple University Press, 1979), 16–18.

113. Hudnut-Beumler, *Looking for God in the Suburbs,* 200.

114. Ibid., 173–74; Roof and McKinney, *American Mainline Religion,* 13, 27; Leonard I. Sweet, "The 1960s: The Crises of Liberal Christianity and the Public Emergence of Evangelicalism," in *Evangelicalism and Modern America,* ed. George Marsden (Grand Rapids, Mich.: Eerdmans, 1984), 31–40.

115. Hudnut-Beumler, *Looking for God in the Suburbs,* 179–80; see Roof and McKinney, *American Mainline Religion,* 12–13.

116. Roof and McKinney, *American Mainline Religion,* 7; Peter L. Berger, "Religion in Post-Protestant America," *Commentary,* May 1986, 43. See Langdon Gilkey, "The Crisis of Christianity in North America," in *Morphologies of Faith: Essays in Religion and Culture in Honor of Nathan A. Scott Jr.,* ed. Mary Gerhart and Anthony C. Yu (Atlanta: Scholars Press, 1990), 32–36.

117. Wuthnow, *Restructuring of American Religion,* chap. 5. Ellwood has observed that in the tumultuous decade of the sixties, a confusion of religious brands made it hard for churches to hold onto consumer loyalty: In both Roman Catholicism and liberal Protestantism, the "new liturgies, guitars, speaking in tongues, [and] inflammatory political stances . . . shook confidence in standard brands and produced associations, even in the established outlets, unsettling to some consumers. At the same time, new vendors seemed to be moving into the market and confusing it. . . . Religion was no doubt of better quality in the Sixties than before from the suppliers' standpoint, but it was also less familiar . . . to the consumer" (*Fifties Spiritual Marketplace,* 16). See also Wade Clark Roof, "Southern Protestantism: New Challenges, New Possibilities," in *The Changing Shape of Protestant-*

ism in the South, ed. Marion D. Aldridge and Kevin Lewis (Macon, Ga.: Mercer University Press, 1996), 11–27; Phillip E. Hammond, *The Protestant Presence in Twentieth-Century America: Religion and Political Culture* (Albany: State University of New York Press, 1992), 19–21; Richard Cimino and Don Lattin, *Shopping for Faith: American Religion in the New Millennium* (San Francisco: Jossey-Bass, 1998).

118. Nancy T. Ammerman, "Denominations: Who and What Are We Studying?" in *Reimagining Denominationalism: Interpretive Essays,* ed. Robert Bruce Mullin and Russell E. Richey (New York: Oxford University Press, 1994), 124–25.

119. Williams, *America's Religions,* 335.

120. "What had once been called 'the secular city' turned out to be not all that secular once you looked beyond a certain educated elite. In recent years the prevalence of religion and rituals in modern societies worldwide has seemed not to be waning but growing." Tom F. Driver, *Liberating Rites: Understanding the Transformative Power of Ritual* (Boulder, Colo.: Westview Press, 1998), 231. See the special issue of the *New York Times Magazine,* "God Decentralized," 7 December 1997.

121. Bell, *Ritual,* 199.

122. Roof and McKinney, *American Mainline Religion,* 33. Cf. Daniel Joseph Singal's comment on the differences between Victorian and modernist in the matter of personal identity: "The Victorian expectation that a person be consistent and sincere rested on the assumption that character was defined largely by social role, which in turn was normally fixed by heredity, upbringing, and vocation. Accordingly, once an individual matured, any shift in his or her character was viewed with suspicion. By contrast, the Modernists, as Ronald Bush puts it, view human nature 'in a state of continuous becoming.' . . . As a result, one must constantly create and re-create an identity based upon one's ongoing experience in the world." Singal, "Towards a Definition of American Modernism," 15.

123. Roof and McKinney, *American Mainline Religion,* 31.

124. See Gaustad, "Pulpit and the Pews," 21–47; Thomas C. Reeves, *The Empty Church: The Suicide of Liberal Christianity* (New York: Free Press, 1996), 18, 24, 152, 198.

125. See Richard Kew and Roger White, *Toward 2015: A Church Odyssey* (Cambridge, Mass.: Cowley Publications, 1997), 50–51; John S. Ruef, "Not So Great Expectations: The Ordination Process Seems to Reward Mediocrity," *The Living Church,* 2 January 2000, 18.

126. Portaro and Peluso, *Inquiring and Discerning Hearts,* xiii, 63, 64, 86, 88, 181–83; see Hammond, *Protestant Presence in Twentieth-Century America,* 169–70.

127. Stokes, "Denominational Ministry on University Campuses," 184.

128. See Richard Kew and Roger J. White, *New Millennium, New Church: Trends Shaping the Episcopal Church for the 21st Century* (Cambridge, Mass.: Cowley Publications, 1992), 39; Audrey R. Chapman, *Faith, Power, and Politics: Political Ministry in Mainline Churches* (New York: Pilgrim Press, 1991), 27–29, 121–22.

129. In the 1980s, when the Episcopal church at large was experiencing no appreciable growth, Episcopal schools enjoyed a striking resurgence. Ann Gordon, the former executive director of the National Association of Episcopal Schools, referred to this phenomenon as "the second day-school movement," the first having occurred in the 1950s. Seventy-five percent of the students in these schools were non-Episcopalians. Ann Gordon, telephone interview with the author, 16 October 1996.

130. Telephone interview with Rt. Rev. David K. Leighton. See Robert Wuthnow, *The Crisis in the Churches* (New York: Oxford University Press, 1997), in which the author

discusses the financial and spiritual crises in middle-class churches and urges clergy to relate theology to the ordinary lives of their parishioners—to the workplace and the marketplace of everyday experience.

131. Roof and McKinney, *American Mainline Religion,* 149.

132. Ellwood, *Sixties Spiritual Awakening,* 26.

133. Richard W. Reifsnyder, "Changing Leadership Patterns in the Presbyterian Church in the United States during the Twentieth Century," "Transformations in Administrative Leadership in the United Presbyterian Church in the U.S.A., 1920–1983," and "Looking for Leadership: The Emerging Style of Leadership in the Presbyterian Church (U.S.A.), 1983–1990," in *The Pluralistic Vision: Presbyterians and Mainstream Protestant Education and Leadership,* ed. Milton J. Coalter, John M. Mulder, and Louis B. Weeks (Louisville, Ky.: Westminster/John Knox Press, 1992), 235–51, 252–75, 276–88.

134. See Alvin F. Kimel Jr., "Being Church: Theological Theses on Parish and Diocese," *Sewanee Theological Review* 38 (Christmas 1994): 61.

135. Marty, "Recent Times," 524.

136. Roof and McKinney, *American Mainline Religion,* 26, 37.

137. Ibid., 29.

138. See Francis Fukuyama, *The Great Disruption: Human Nature and the Reconstitution of Social Order* (New York: Free Press, 1999); William Leach, *Country of Exiles: The Destruction of Place in American Life* (New York: Pantheon Books, 1999).

139. Rev. Churchill J. Gibson Jr., telephone interview with the author, 27 May 1998.

140. See Michael Ramsey, *The Anglican Spirit,* ed. Dale Coleman (Cambridge, Mass.: Cowley Publications, 1991), 21–22, 104.

141. Robert Benne, "The Calling of the Church in Economic Life," in *The Two Cities of God: The Church's Responsibility for the Earthly City,* ed. Carl E. Braaten and Robert W. Jenson (Grand Rapids, Mich.: Eerdmans, 1997), 115.

142. Duncan Gray Jr., "In Defense of the Steeple," in *The Failure and the Hope: Essays of Southern Churchmen,* ed. Will D. Campbell and James Y. Holloway (Grand Rapids, Mich.: Eerdmans, 1972), 140–46.

143. Robert Runcie, *Christian Thinking: The Anglican Tradition of Thoughtful Holiness* (Tulsa, Okla.: University of Tulsa, 1991), 11.

Index

DAVID HEIN is a professor of religion and philosophy at Hood College, where he has also served as department chair and interim dean. His previous books include *Essays on Lincoln's Faith and Politics* (with Hans J. Morgenthau), *A Student's View of the College of St. James on the Eve of the Civil War,* and *Readings in Anglican Spirituality.*

STUDIES IN ANGLICAN HISTORY

Typeset in 10.5/13 Minion
with Minion display
Designed by Paula Newcomb
Composed by Celia Shapland
for the University of Illinois Press
Manufactured by Thomson-Shore, Inc.

University of Illinois Press
1325 South Oak Street
Champaign, IL 61820-6903
www.press.uillinois.edu